LANDSCAPEBODYDWELLING

Charles Simonds at Dumbarton Oaks

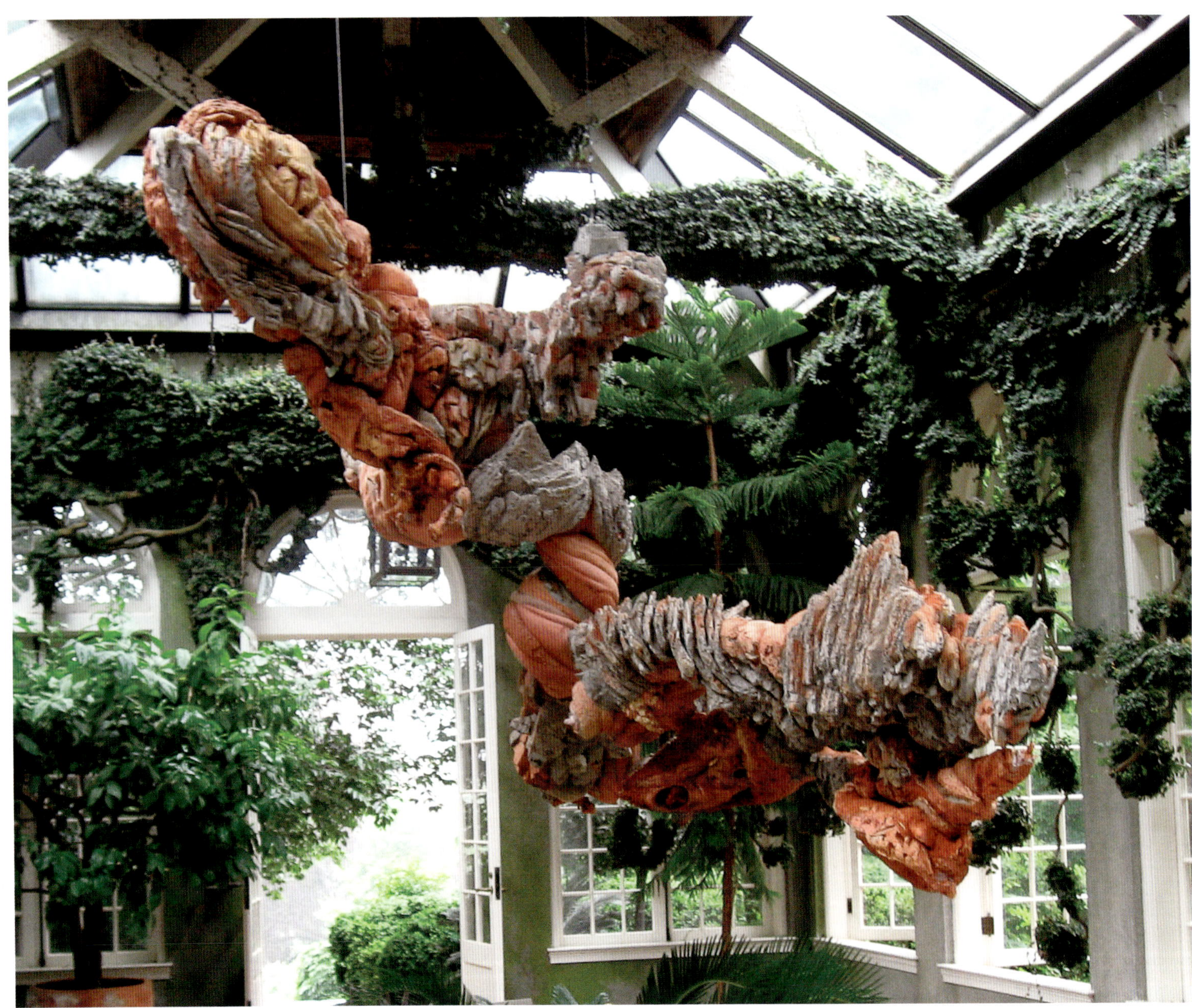

LANDSCAPE BODY DWELLING

Charles Simonds at Dumbarton Oaks

John Beardsley, editor

DUMBARTON OAKS CONTEMPORARY LANDSCAPE SERIES

DUMBARTON OAKS RESEARCH LIBRARY AND COLLECTION, WASHINGTON, D.C.

Library of Congress Cataloging-in-Publication Data
Simonds, Charles, 1945–
   Landscape body dwelling : Charles Simonds at Dumbarton Oaks /
   John Beardsley, editor.
      p. cm. — (Dumbarton Oaks contemporary landscape series ; 3
              —formerly Dumbarton Oaks contemporary landscape design series)
   Includes bibliographical references.
   ISBN 978-0-88402-371-5 (pbk. : alk. paper)
1. Simonds, Charles—Exhibitions.
I. Beardsley, John.   II. Dumbarton Oaks.
III. Title.   IV. Title: Charles Simonds at Dumbarton Oaks.
   NB237.S565A4   2011
                  730.92–dc22

Book and cover design: Kathleen Sparkes

Project editor: Sara Taylor

Cover photographs: Front: *Head* (*from I, Thou*), 1993, clay and plaster, collection of the artist. © Dumbarton Oaks Research Library and
   Collection. Back: *Uroboros*, 1973, resin, collection of the artist. Photograph courtesy of Charles Simonds.

Frontispiece: *Mental Earth*, 2003, metal, polyurethane, clay, and wood, collection of the artist.
   Photograph courtesy of Charles Simonds.

www.doaks.org/publications

CONTENTS

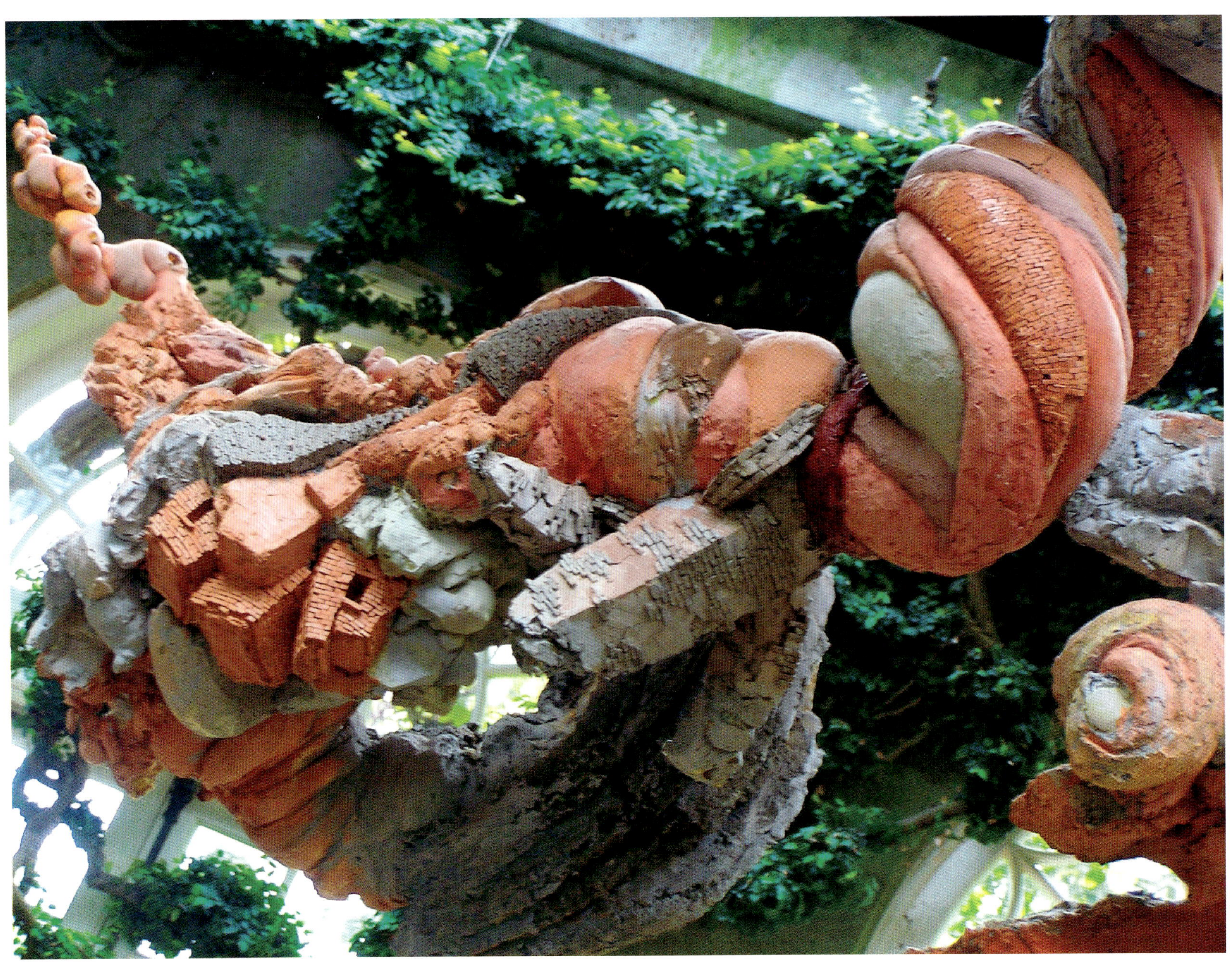

Charles Simonds The Dumbarton Oaks Project
John Beardsley

In the spring of 2009, Dumbarton Oaks inaugurated an occasional series of contemporary art installations intended to provide unexpected experiences and fresh interpretations of its remarkable gardens and collections. The first artist selected for the program was the American sculptor Charles Simonds, who is well known for clay sculptures that document the wanderings of a fantastical civilization of Little People whose landscapes, architectures, and rituals have been imagined by the artist since the early 1970s. Because ideas about landscape and nature are so pervasive in his art, Simonds was invited initially to intervene in the gardens. As he came to know Dumbarton Oaks, however, he found that he was also intrigued by correspondences among his sculptures and the Pre-Columbian and Byzantine collections; moreover, he found himself captivated by the institution's trove of rare garden books, a number of which contained images of the kind that have inspired his work over the years. The outcome was a project that spanned the whole institution. A wide range of his current sculptures—some architectural, some figural, and some evocative of landscape; most pre-existing but one made especially for the exhibition—was installed between May and October 2009 in various spaces at Dumbarton Oaks: in the Orangery (left) and several terraces in the garden, in the Byzantine and Pre-Columbian galleries in the museum, and in the space outside the Rare Book Room. For this last space, the artist also assembled a "cabinet of curiosities" and presented films and photographs that collectively comprised the beginnings of a creative autobiography. Simonds mined collections across the institution; he also collaborated with staff in most of its divisions. He worked with me to select sculptures for the installation and to identify a range of locations for them within Dumbarton Oaks; with Linda Lott, the librarian of the Rare Book Room, to identify materials for the cabinet of curiosities; with museum director Gudrun Bühl and her staff to position sculptures in the galleries; and with garden director Gail Griffin to install sculptures outdoors.

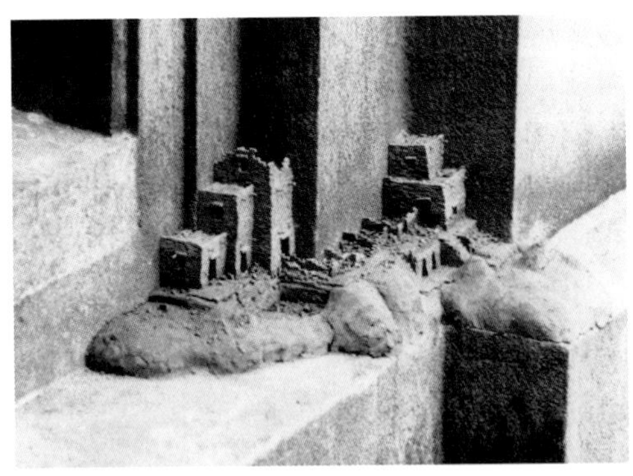

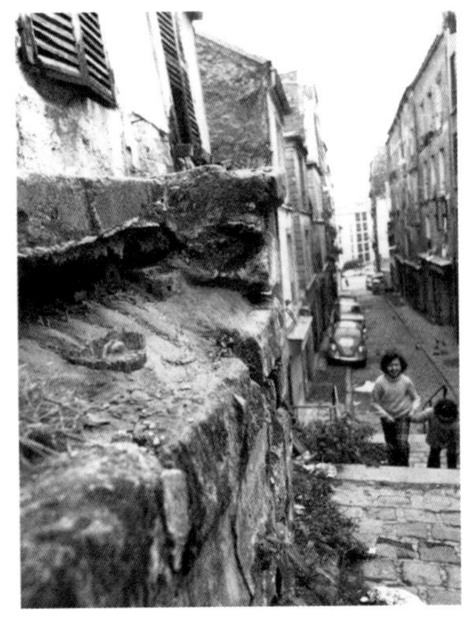

As detailed in essays by Ann Reynolds and Germano Celant in this volume, Simonds introduced his imaginary civilization on the streets of New York in the early 1970s, building their habitations on sidewalks and window ledges on the Lower East Side. He subsequently took them around the world to dozens of cities, including Dublin (top left), Paris (bottom left), Berlin, Genoa, and Shanghai, and was eventually invited to present them to museum audiences. While the Little People still make an appearance in his more recent work, this work displays an expanding range of concerns—especially an exploration of the analogies among the body, earth, and architecture (all of which are conceptualized as different forms of dwelling), and a comparison of these elements to plants. In particular, Simonds sees in the growth and decay of plants parallels to the growth and decay of the body, the rise and fall of buildings, and the formation and erosion of landscape. Thus, many of his sculptures combine human, vegetal, architectural, and geomorphic elements—a rich stew distinctly suited to the environment of Dumbarton Oaks.

Simonds's installation at Dumbarton Oaks was far from his first institutional project. He has been the focus of numerous exhibitions around the world, beginning with a solo exhibition at the Centre National d'Art Contemporain, Paris, in 1975 and an installation for the "Projects" gallery at the Museum of Modern Art, New York, in 1976. Subsequent solo exhibitions were held at the Museum of Contemporary Art, Chicago (1981); Guggenheim Museum, New York (1983); Architecture Museum, Basel (1985); Galerie Nationale du Jeu de Paume, Paris (1994); and Institut Valencià d'Art Modern, Valencia (2003). But the Dumbarton Oaks project was unprecedented in his work in several respects. It was his first exhibition to be dispersed around an institution and to reach across the internal boundaries of the institutional environment. It was uniquely calibrated to its place, as it used the collections to shed light on his work and conversely used his work to provide new views into the collections and gardens of Dumbarton Oaks. Other artists have done similar projects: in recent years, such interpretive installations have become a more frequent, if still somewhat unusual, way of shedding reciprocal light on artists and the institutions that collect and display their work. In 2006, for instance, the French-born sculptor Louise Bourgeois installed thirty-nine of her sculptures throughout the galleries of the Walters Art Museum in Baltimore, setting up dialogues between her work and similarly themed artifacts from the museum's collection. More analogous to Simonds's work at Dumbarton Oaks, however, might be Mark Dion's project, Travels of William Bartram Reconsidered, with Bartram's Garden in Philadelphia. Dion set out to retrace Bartram's 1773–77 botanical expedition to the Carolinas, Georgia, and North Florida; he sent back seeds, bark, leaves, soil, shells, shark's teeth, water samples, dead

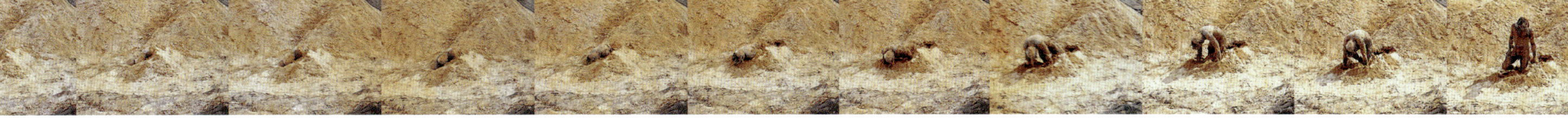

birds, and bugs that, together with paintings, drawings, postcards, and a host of cultural curiosities (including bottle caps, fish hooks, old tools, ceramic fragments, and alligator figurines), were assembled into an installation at the garden in the summer of 2008.[1]

Simonds's project for Dumbarton Oaks falls somewhere between those of Bourgeois and Dion. Like Bourgeois, he juxtaposed his work with museum artifacts in an act of reciprocity. Like Dion, he engaged the institution's particular assets to create an installation that reinforced shared themes from natural and cultural history. By dispersing his work throughout the institution, he intended to provoke speculation on a wide range of unexpected comparisons, including—but not only—between his sculpture and plant morphology, between the ritual practices of the Little People and those of the Byzantine and Pre-Columbian cultures, and between his architectures and those of the ancient Americas. At the same time, he underlined some of the more idiosyncratic attributes of the institution: the chronologically and geographically far-flung sources of its collections, their narrow but sharp focus, and the often overlooked presence in the garden of narrative and decorative elements—some of the latter with a decidedly grotesque character. In all, Simonds created a unique occasion in his life and in the life of Dumbarton Oaks to explore some hidden but essential trajectories of his work along with some of its more arcane autobiographical and cultural resonances, even as he underlined some of the more intriguing, even idiosyncratic attributes of the institution.

In the introductory gallery to the exhibition adjacent to the Rare Book Room hung a series of twenty-two color photographs entitled *Birth* (1970, above), in which the artist is seen to emerge naked from the muck of a New Jersey clay pit. Nearby played a sixteen-millimeter film with the same title that recorded the same event. In both the photo sequence and the film, Simonds affirmed his identity with the moist earth as the source and primary material of life while simultaneously signifying his genesis as an artist and the importance of clay to his work. Alternating on a continuous loop with *Birth* was another film, *Landscape/ Body/Dwelling* (1973, right), a record of a ritual the artist performed regularly in the 1970s, in which he smeared his body with clay to make a landscape, on which he then constructed the dwellings of the Little People. These rituals underscored his notion of the analogies

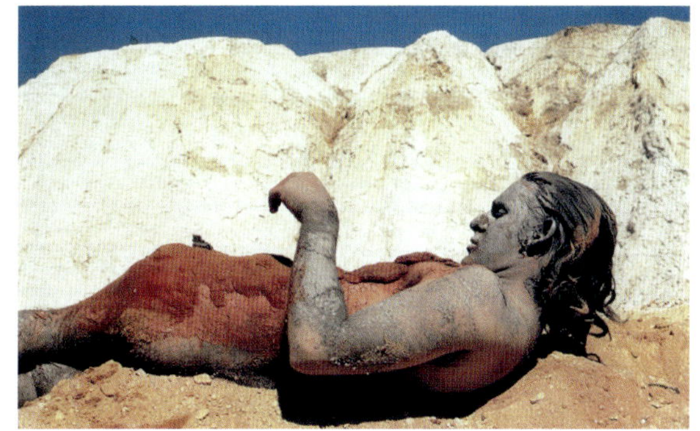

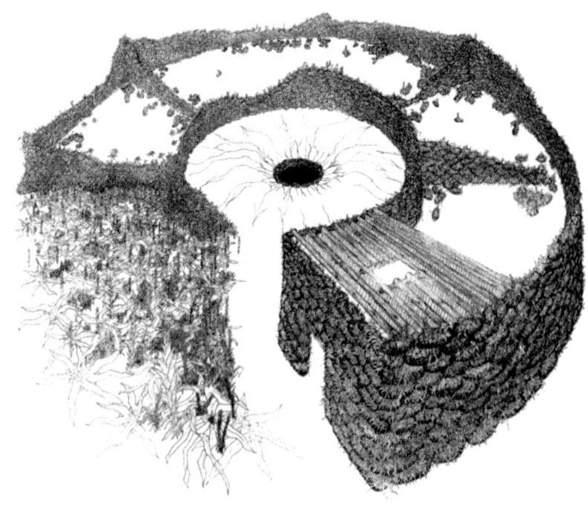

among the body, earth, and architecture—all animate, all human habitations, and all subject to cycles of growth, maturation, and decay. The connections between plants and architecture were underlined in the print of an installation entitled *Growth House* (1975, left). This is a depiction of a seasonally renewable dwelling, constructed at full scale on several occasions, with earthen bricks that have edible plant seeds in them. As the seeds sprout, growth transforms the built structure—the dwelling is converted from shelter to food and is harvested and eaten.

The principal components of the first part of the exhibition, however, were two cases that Simonds imagined as contemporary variations on the traditional cabinet of curiosities. They presented some of the many images and texts from which the artist has drawn inspiration, interspersed with autobiographical materials and several small sculptures (facing page). Simonds culled the archival material from sources including the Rare Book Room at Dumbarton Oaks, the C. G. Jung Institute and the Archive for Research in Archetypal Symbolism in New York, his family's papers, and his own collection; the material included both particular images and texts the artist used in the past and related materials uncovered more recently. Books, papers, and illustrations were paired with sculptures that began to suggest how the historical material has shaped his work; these, in turn, were complemented with photographs of larger sculptures that were installed around Dumbarton Oaks, with the aim of facilitating in the viewer a sense of the resonances among the historical materials, the autobiographical narratives, and the sculptures that composed the rest of the exhibition.

A complete portfolio of images of the case materials can be found elsewhere in this volume, together with the accompanying notes by Linda Lott. For the purposes of this essay, it is important only to establish their general character. The cases included some artifacts from the artist's earliest works on the Little People: a plaster cutting board on which he made the bricks for their dwellings, and a mixed-media collection of their tools, games, building materials, and ritual objects. Also exhibited were some manipulated postcards, including a selection of reproductions of Van Gogh landscapes that Simonds assembled end to end to suggest a narrative of birth, death, and resurrection. The cases included some early publications on the artist, including *Charles Simonds* (1975), the first book on his work, which features a cover photograph of Simonds enacting one of his *Landscape/Body/Dwelling* rituals; and *Three Peoples* (1975), his own narrative of the three groups, known by the geometric form assumed by their architecture (linear, circular, and spiral), in his imaginary civilization.

While these materials had a fairly straightforward archival character, they were surrounded by curiosities that evoked a number of themes not previously presented by the artist in any depth, which added remarkable detail to an understanding of his work and its links to natural and cultural history. The son of two Vienna-trained psychoanalysts, Simonds is attentive to a wide array of psychological notions, including traditional Freudian ideas of psychosexual development, his mother's challenge to those ideas, and his own discovery of the language of Jungian archetypes. More pertinent to the research and collections of Dumbarton Oaks, he finds inspiration in the conflation of plant and animal forms characteristic of the grotesque, in alchemical images of plants transmuted into animals, in archaic physiognomies that compare human and animal or human and plant morphology, and in myths of figures transformed into trees. Materials that evoked this wide range of intellectual and psychological inspirations were assembled in the cases. Included in one cabinet, for instance, were offprints of his mother's writings on castration anxiety in boys, which, contrary to orthodox Freudian theory, was traced to fears about the loss of the testes rather than the penis. Nearby was a small sculpture that resembled a scrotal sac or plant tubers; this conflation of body parts and plants was reinforced in the other cabinet, which featured a copy from the Dumbarton Oaks Library of Giambattista della Porta's *Phytognomonica* (1588), an early effort at plant classification based on concepts of resemblance. Porta (1535?–1615) was an Italian scholar, playwright, and polymath who lived in Naples during the scientific revolution; his book applied a belief common in the sixteenth century called the Doctrine of Signatures, which suggested that there were analogies between a plant's form and its properties—for instance, poisonous roots might resemble snakes. The book was opened to a plate comparing the orchid with like objects, such as the testicles of a small animal (indeed, the name for the Orchidaceae family derives from *Orchis,* a flower whose roots were believed to resemble testicles, which in Greek is ὄρχεις. Such zoophytes were also of interest to Claude Duret (d. 1611), a French judge with a fascination for mystical and mythological plants, whose *Histoire admirable des plantes et herbes esmerueillables & miraculeuses en nature* (1605), also from the Dumbarton Oaks Library, was opened to a page showing the mushroom "Phalle Hollandique" whole and in three parts.

Simonds's fascination with archaic analogies between the body and plants was reinforced in the cases by copies of a fourteenth-century print of Adam with a tree sprouting from his loins and a fifteenth-century print of Apollo and Daphne. But examples of human-botanical connections were drawn not only from European sources, as the cases also included photographs of Classic Maya ceramic figurines from Jaina, an island off the

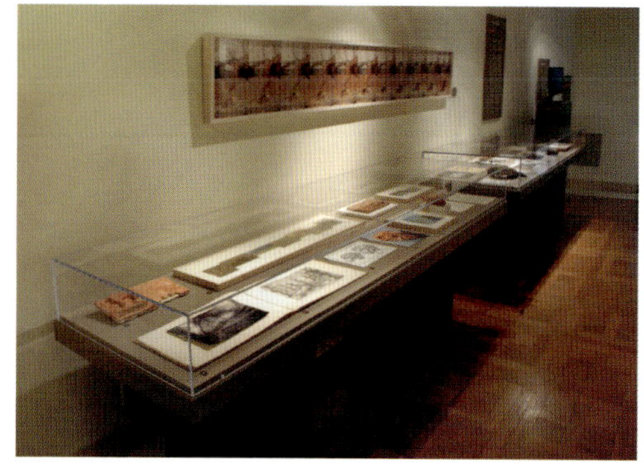

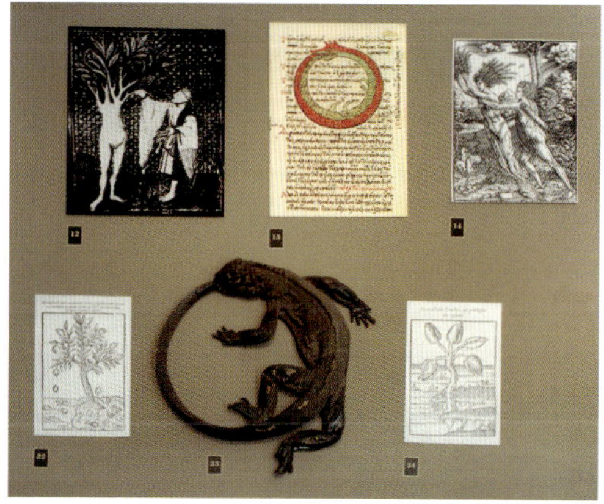

Yucatan coast that is believed to have served as a necropolis for Maya elites. The figurines were of a type unknown to the artist before this project; they showed figures emerging from flowers, much like one found in the Pre-Columbian Collection at Dumbarton Oaks. (More on the surprising affinities between Simonds's work and the Pre-Columbian Collection can be found in Joanne Pillsbury's essay in this volume.) The cases also featured materials that presented the analogies between human and animal physiognomy, including *The Man and the Ram* (left), an illustration from a copy of Ernst Kris's *Psychoanalytic Explorations in Art* (1952) that once belonged to the artist's mother. (Given his parents' profession, it is perhaps not surprising that Simonds reports that everything in their household was given a psycho-analytic spin—even art.) Kris presumably took the illustration from Porta's 1586 publication on human physiognomy. Although now largely dismissed as a pseudoscience (and this may help explain Simonds's interest in it), physiognomy, like the Doctrine of Signatures, sug-gested that there was a connection between outward form and internal characteristics—a man with goatlike features might have goatlike qualities, for instance.

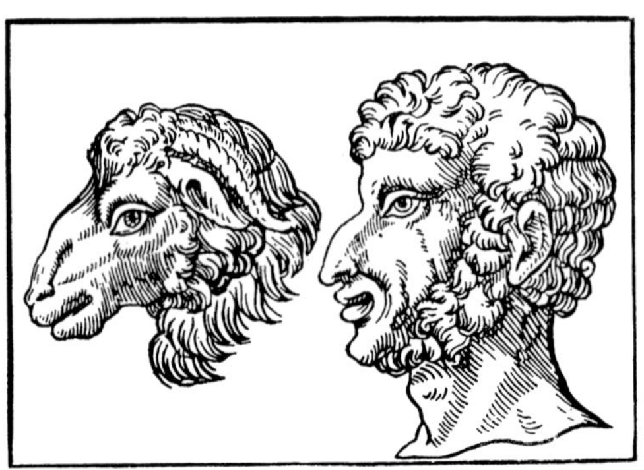

These ideas descend directly into Simonds's work: the exhibition included a clay slip- and sand-covered plaster *Head* (1991, page 33) suggestive of ideas about physiognomy. Part desiccated skull, part leering face, part rocky landscape, *Head* embodies a universe of allusions that only get stranger and more elusive the more they are pursued. Combining what appears to be a death mask with the parted lips of an aroused male goat, it suggests attention to the effects of aging on the body in general and on sexuality in particular. The cases helped establish a partial genealogy for the sculpture by juxtaposing a photograph of it with Porta's illustration in Kris's book, suggesting the rich imaginative possibilities of conflat-ing human and animal morphologies. Other specific comparisons were drawn in the cases: a photograph of the sculpture *Stugg* (1991, page 95), on view in the garden, was juxtaposed with images of Jaina figures similar to the one from the Pre-Columbian Collection; like the latter, *Stugg* features a torso and head emerging from what might be a seed pod or sprout.

From this introductory gallery, the visitor, armed with an exposure to some of the botanical, art historical, psychoanalytical, and mythological notions that converge in Simonds's work, could set off in search of the rest of the exhibition: the sculptures dispersed through the museum galleries and the gardens. Indoors were six sculptures, several related to the Little People. *Pyramid* (1972, page 38) was located in the museum courtyard, juxta-posed with Late Classic and Byzantine artifacts. It was an appropriately archaic form for the setting; it also evoked some of the artist's ancient history, as it was one of his first efforts to present the ritual places of the Little People. In an adjacent gallery hung the enigmatic *Y*

(2001, page 37). While it deploys the tiny clay bricks of the Little People, this sculpture is not an explicitly architectural piece. Instead, it suggests both a saguaro cactus and a headless body, with hips and rounded belly below outstretched arms. Here again is the fanciful combination of human and botanical elements, but seen in the context of the Byzantine Collection at Dumbarton Oaks, the sculpture took on different connotations (right). What was surprising was how much it conversed with some of the liturgical objects nearby. The shared cross motif was perhaps most evident (the artist has even described the sculpture as "a pregnant cross"), but the slight pink swellings that protrude from the sculpture also took on new associations. What might be read as buds in a botanical context here looked like sores, as if they were some sort of diabolical affliction.

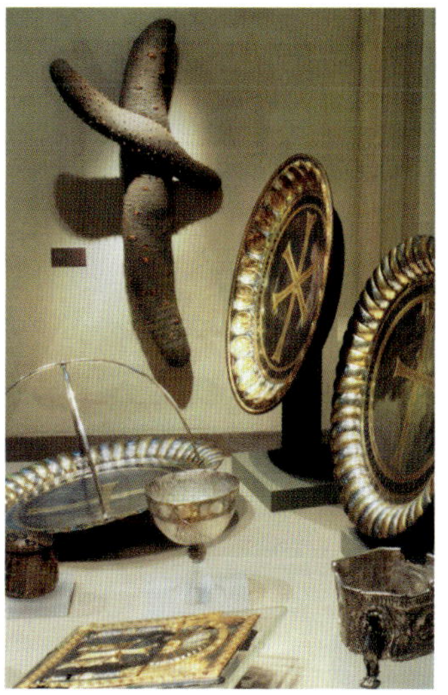

The Pre-Columbian galleries housed four more sculptures, one in each of the corner galleries of the square building designed by Philip Johnson in the early 1960s and composed of eight circular domed spaces around a central courtyard. *Head* was in Gallery One, juxtaposed with Aztec skull necklaces and carved stone masks. *Rock Flower* (1986, page 39) was in Gallery Three among Classic Maya artifacts (including Jaina figurines); it beautifully evoked the artist's idea of the correspondences among plants, earth, and architecture by featuring rock walls opening like the petals of a flower to reveal the bud of a building within. If this was an image of architecture blossoming, then *Wilted Towers* (1984, right) was an image of a building in decay: a collection of limp structures sprawling in the sand, an implausible combination of desiccated tubers, detumescent phalluses, and collapsing columns. In Gallery Seven was Simonds's most explicitly botanical creation: a porcelain *Tumbleweed* (1993, page 35) made at the Sèvres factory in Paris. Working with resident craftsmen, Simonds fabricated elongated strands of porcelain on string, which incinerated during firing; these were then assembled into an evocation of the matured and dried desert plants that blow about in western landscapes—and western movies. (Often called Russian Thistle, tumbleweed is an invasive Eurasian plant partial to disturbed ground; it can be one of several species of *Salsola* or other members of the family Amaranthaceae.) But unusual details—such as spiky flowers that are variations on the delicate blossoms that often adorn Sèvres creations—make this particular tumbleweed, already evocative of desolation, seem more like a crown of thorns. While thus suggestive of Christian iconography, *Tumbleweed* also evoked the Peruvian desert landscape that is the source of the Nazca, Moche, and Chimu objects that surrounded it at Dumbarton Oaks.

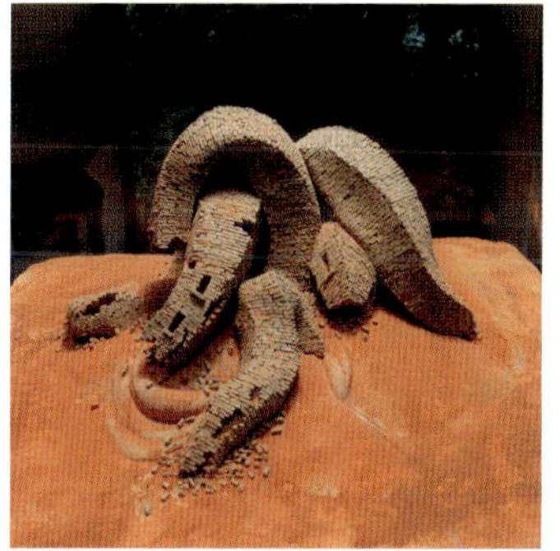

Outside in the gardens were other species of Simonds's sculptures. An enormous landscape, *Mental Earth* (2003), was suspended from the roof beams of the Orangery, an

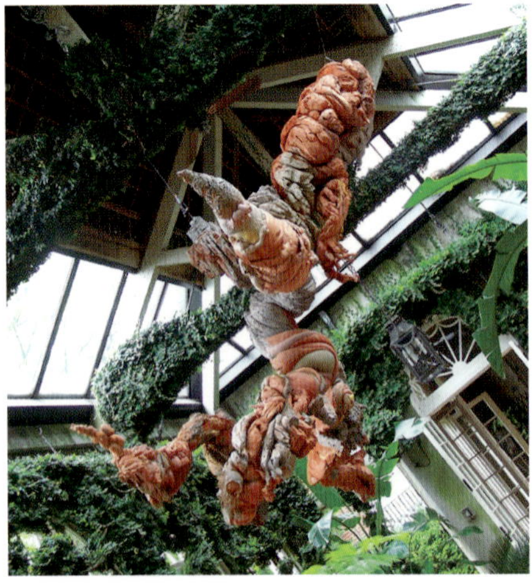

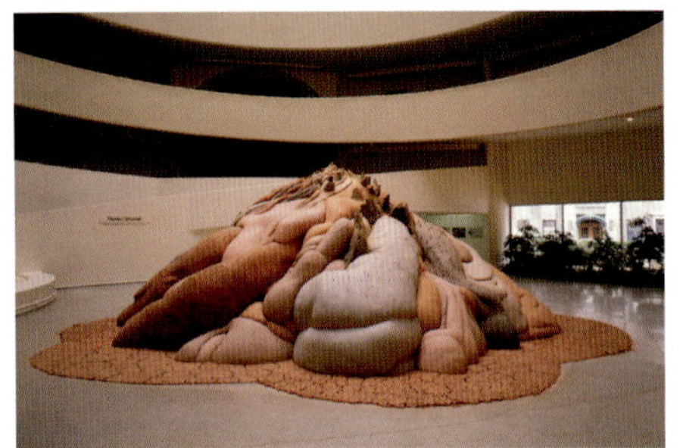

1810 brick conservatory open to the elements in the summer and enclosed to shelter tropical plants in the winter. A fantasy of a landscape freed from gravity, *Mental Earth* (top left) is representative of a number of very large pieces that the artist made from time to time over the years, including a vast spiral mountain created for the rotunda of the Guggenheim Museum in New York in 1983 (*Age*, bottom left). *Mental Earth* was made for his retrospective at the Institut Valencià d'Art Modern in 2003. Although conceived for another space, the piece could not have looked more suited to the Orangery. Its size was perfect for the place; its elongated elements, made of steel rods covered with extruded foam finished with clay, clay slip, and sand, seemed to fill the rectilinear space. But more than this, the sculpture's organic forms—its fleshy tubers, sprouting rocks, and spiraling or dangling towers—were oddly consonant with the 150-year-old ficus vine that ornaments the inside walls of the Orangery: the vine has been pruned over its long life into pendulous green globes. Hidden in the sculpture's surface was a vast dreamscape: cliffs and deserts, pathways and debris pits, buildings with faces, and even an eel's head.

From the Orangery, an axis extends east and down through several of the garden's principal spaces: the Beech, Urn, Rose, Fountain, and Arbor terraces. Simonds's sculptures were located on three of these terraces, creating a narrative sequence through this section of the gardens. Looking from the Orangery's east doors, a sculpture was just visible on the stone walk at the far end of the Rose Terrace. On approach, the piece proved to be a large terracotta-colored head with a grimacing face. Cast in plaster from a clay original that was allowed to crack as it dried, the sculpture evokes a disturbed landscape. But it is also an anguished self-portrait, with blank eyes, parted lips, and a tongue that seems poised in an expression of rage or nausea. Titled *Head (from I, Thou)* (1993, pages 60–61), the sculpture was once part of a yoked double portrait of the artist and his father, which together suggested an effort at exorcism of intergenerational conflict. Here was the artist's signature psychoanalytic content, expressed through exaggerated physiognomy.

From the Rose Terrace, stairs lead down to the Fountain Terrace, where a sculpture called *Stugg* lay on the grass. Cast in cement from a clay original and finished with several shades of clay-colored paint, this is a narrative sculpture, depicting a desiccated earth pod that sprouts a pubescent torso and terminates in the same conflation of clown face, goat head, and death mask as the *Head* on view in the museum. As such, the piece recapitulates themes encountered in figural images elsewhere in the exhibition: cycles of birth, growth, and decay; transitions between plant, animal, and human worlds; the generative force of sexuality; and the mocking image of death's grin.

The final work in the installation was encountered on the adjacent Arbor Terrace: a piece titled *Growth* (2009, right) made specifically for the exhibition. Fabricated in polyurethane and clay and finished with the same clay-colored paints as the other outdoor works, the sculpture seemed to sprout from an enormous, ancient wisteria that sprawls over the vaulted structure that gives the terrace its name. The sculpture was fashioned over a broken wisteria branch given to the artist by one of the gardeners; it rose from a cleft in the plant, wired to the arbor like an errant vine. Here again were the suggestions of tuberous plants that resembled body parts, the twisted earth, and the spiral dwellings—all of which evoked the image of rampant growth entirely compatible with the irrepressible energy of the wisteria that was its host.

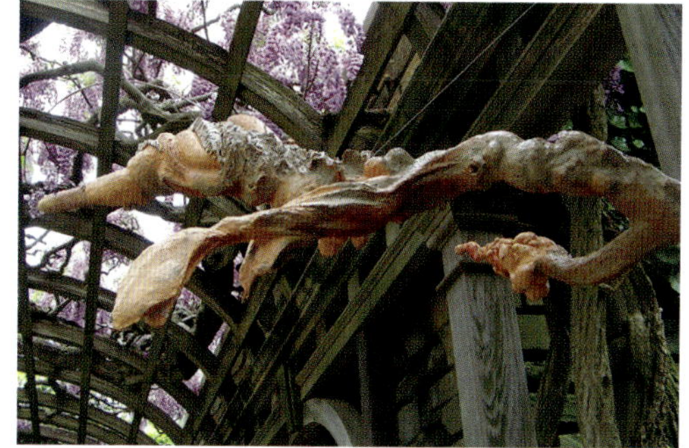

Public reaction to Simonds's work at Dumbarton Oaks was mixed.[2] While the sculptures in the museum and the various materials in the cabinet of curiosities were generally received with enthusiasm, the sculptures in the garden incited some controversy. To some extent, this might be explained by the fact that garden visitors sometimes encountered the sculptures without the benefit of first seeing the introductory and interpretive materials in the museum, although an explanatory handout was available at the garden entrance. In a larger sense, the discrepancy might have been an expression of the different contexts in which the sculptures were seen. Museums are widely understood as curated spaces; people expect to encounter objects collected, presented, and interpreted by professionals, and typically yield to their expertise. Moreover, as sites of temporary exhibitions, museums are associated with change. Gardens, by comparison, are more apt to be thought of as natural rather than curated, managed by biological processes rather than artistry. Where their designs are recognized, they are likely to be regarded as frozen in time—notwithstanding their seasonal aspects, which are assumed to repeat themselves in predictable cycles. (Gardeners at Dumbarton Oaks report constant phone calls in the spring requesting precise information about bloom times, as if these never varied.) Assumptions of an unchanging aspect are associated especially with gardens like those at Dumbarton Oaks, which have attained such stature that they seem to be regarded as finished works of art that should not be altered in any way. But these gardens—like all gardens—are far from fixed: as plants age and die, they are replaced by others, sometimes of a very different sort. As the principal designer of the Dumbarton Oaks Gardens, Beatrix Farrand, herself wrote, "a garden is not a static object . . . it must be constantly not only weeded and cared for, but . . . replanted from time to time in order, like the Red Queen in Alice, to stay in one place . . ."[3] Moreover, the designs are transformed: Dumbarton Oaks itself changed significantly when

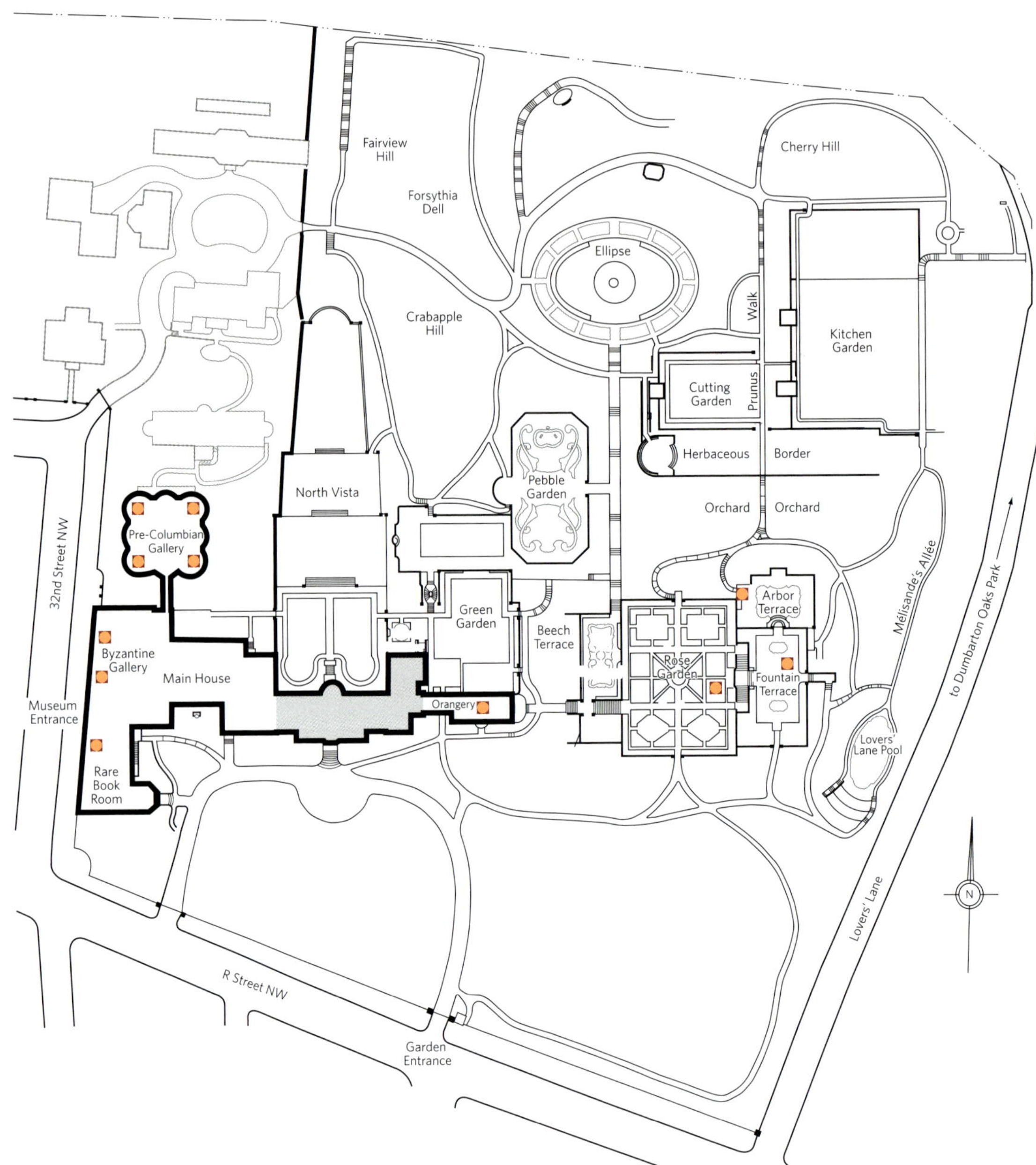

Dumbarton Oaks
Museum and Gardens,
locations of installations
shown in red.

Farrand retired after the Second World War and her place was taken by her former associate Ruth Havey. The latter was responsible for some of the more decorative elements of the gardens, including the transformation of the tennis court into the Pebble Garden and the stone scrollwork on the Arbor Terrace, which changed the character of these areas of the garden significantly and permanently.

Gardens are also transformed by changes in ownership and mission. Dumbarton Oaks was designed as private garden, but became part of an educational institution when its patrons, Mildred and Robert Woods Bliss, donated the house, collections, and gardens to Harvard University in 1940. Farrand herself realized this would have profound impacts on the gardens, as detailed in a prescient report she wrote to the administrative board of the newly established Dumbarton Oaks Research Library and Collection in 1941.[4] "The transfer of ownership from an intimately personal control to a necessarily more impersonal but an enduring educational institution must alter the point of view from which the gardens are considered," she wrote. Paramount in this shift from personal to institutional is the emergence of an educational mission: "It is not necessary to emphasize that the first duty of an educational institution is to use its resources for the benefit of its students." As a research rather than a teaching facility, Dumbarton Oaks serves scholars rather than students, but the point is the same. Further, Farrand recognized that the gardens would have a role in intellectual development: "The training of the eye to an understanding of outdoor beauty should be recognized as a vital part of the student's life at Dumbarton Oaks. The composition of the views from the windows at which they may study, the unconscious infiltration into their minds of daily familiarity with garden problems and their solution must be important."

Farrand thus hoped that "the larger lines of the design may remain approximately unchanged, as none of them have been established without much thought." As examples of those larger lines, she singled out such features as the entrance roads, the wide lawns to the south and southeast of the house, the North Vista, the flower terraces, and the Lovers' Lane Pool. She also asked that the main principles of the design be respected: the sense of withdrawal from the surrounding streets, reinforced with perimeter plantings of evergreens; and the sense of spaciousness, provided by contrasting lawns within. She asked that signature trees be cared for and replaced, and the understory of shrubs maintained. In sum, she said, "there is no intention implied or suggested that the design be kept exactly as it was given to Harvard, but the suggestion is made that if alterations are considered they be made after careful study and with a reasonable hope of their fitting into an already established scheme."

Temporary installations of contemporary art certainly fit into the educational mission of Dumbarton Oaks. But are they compatible with Farrand's "established scheme"? One might argue that temporary changes—like art installations—do not have to rise to this standard, that the alterations Farrand referred to were permanent ones. But Farrand's scheme—her design—still merits deep respect, and it is clear that part of the controversy surrounding the presence of Simonds's work in the garden was its perceived incompatibility with Farrand's aesthetic sensibilities. The sculptures in the garden were more challenging in some respects than those in the museum: the latter were more fanciful, revolving around the myths of the Little People; the former were more emotionally and psychologically charged, with disconcerting overtones of sexuality and death. The anguished self-portrait on the Rose Terrace was a special target of antagonism; several visitors complained that it dishonored not only Farrand, but also the Blisses, who are interred there.

But these sculptures share a deep connection of their own with garden history and aesthetics, especially through their connections with the grotesque. Although the term now signifies anything especially odd, unnatural, disturbing, or deformed, it has specific meanings in art history. In the Renaissance, it referred to the incongruous combination of animal and vegetal motifs found in paintings on the walls of underground vaults or crypts (*grotte*) of ancient Roman buildings. Decorative flourishes based on these motifs became widespread in sixteenth-century architectural friezes, engravings, illustrated books, and garden ornaments, especially in Italy. The grotesque later came to denote anything fancifully extravagant or bizarre, in which, as John Ruskin observed in *The Stones of Venice* (1851–53), the ludicrous is yoked to the fearful. The word was applied retrospectively to describe, for example, hybrid monsters in the stone carvings of medieval cathedrals. In the contexts of art, in other words, the grotesque denotes combinations of animal and vegetal forms that are both serious and playful, fanciful and horrible.[5]

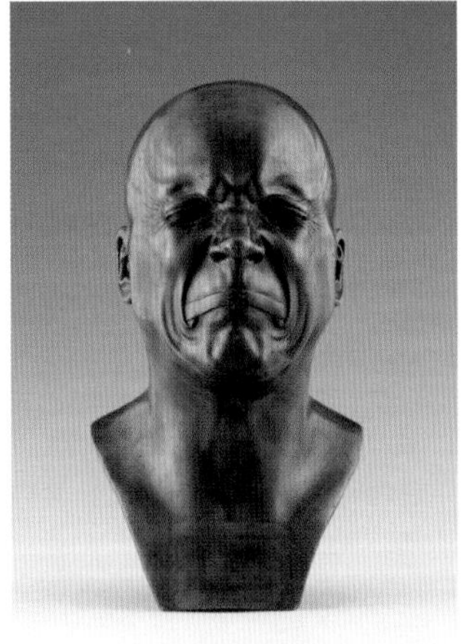

It is these specific meanings of the grotesque to which Simonds is heir. He creates implausible conflations of human, animal, and vegetal forms; at times they are witty, at others, disturbing. The various heads in the Dumbarton Oaks installation are examples of the latter—monstrous hybrids of landforms with human and animal physiognomy, at once ludicrous and loathsome. Like the eighteenth-century Austrian sculptor Franz Xaver Messerschmidt, known for a series of grimacing heads—mostly self-portraits—that reveal how the face changes in response to different emotions (left), Simonds deploys the grotesque to explore the states of his own psychic history; it seems to provide him with the license to think or make almost anything, be it arcane, discomforting, or embarrassingly self-revelatory. In the context of the Dumbarton Oaks Gardens, it evokes associations often glossed over in the discourses of garden history, especially those of sexuality and mortality—associations that were evidently unwelcome to some of the garden's visitors. But these associations are already there. The garden is full of intimations of mortality—including the crypts of the Blisses and numerous memorial inscriptions—and suggestions of surreptitious sexuality, like Lovers' Lane. And although it is not widely recognized, the grotesque is also a subtext at Dumbarton Oaks: Simonds installed *Growth* under the wisteria arbor, right next to a nineteenth-century French lead fountain mask (top right) that is said to represent a river god, with a scallop-shell diadem, pointed animalistic ears, and an open mouth that trickles water into a pool. Acquired by the Blisses in 1927 and incorporated by Farrand into the design for the arbor, the mask occupies the wall opposite the central arch of this three-bay structure. Farrand drawings from the early 1930s suggest that this space was imagined for some sort of fanciful emblem—a lion's or a satyr's head—before becoming home to the river god, who is framed by sheaves of wheat, the Bliss family emblem.[6] Its incongruous combination of human and animal features resonated with Simonds's *Stugg* on the adjacent Fountain Terrace; its open mouth and prominent tongue, with his self-portrait on the Rose Terrace (bottom right). More generally, its fanciful combinations of human, animal, and plant forms were reiterated by the sculpture with which it shared the shady arbor.

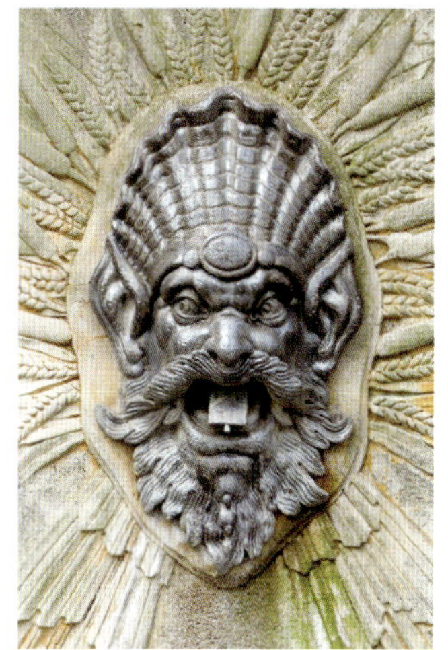

In sum, Simonds created at Dumbarton Oaks a moment unique in his work and in the life of Dumbarton Oaks. While his installation was not universally loved, it was creative, provocative, and revealing—both of his imaginative life as an artist and of the intellectual and aesthetic traditions to which Dumbarton Oaks is heir. In the ever-swelling repositories of human history, we seldom have time to deal with more than generalities; as Ann Reynolds and Germano Celant both observe in their essays in this volume, we create various shorthand systems to make connections through time and across cultures. Sometimes it takes an insistent, even irritating, character to make us pause and look beneath the surface of things—to see hidden details, to ponder meanings, to grasp allusions. Sometimes it takes a fresh set of eyes to enable us to look anew at that which we have become inured to seeing— or to reconsider things about which we think we know everything already. It was Simonds's point to bring new perspectives and even controversy to Dumbarton Oaks; with respect to the gardens especially, he sought to reveal them as a living and evolving place, where the past literally grows into the present and future. In some eyes, he unearthed discomforting themes: he was briefly the serpent in our Eden. But he demonstrated without question the ways that contemporary culture can connect us to the past, reinvigorating historical tropes

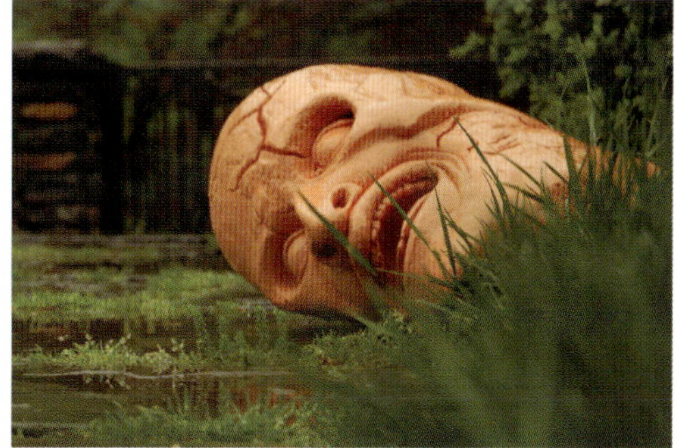

while enlivening the institutions that continue to speak them. In both the museum and the garden, he found ways to make the past alive in the present, even as he challenged people's assumptions about both. As we look forward at Dumbarton Oaks to future installations of contemporary art, we can only hope that they will be as revelatory and transformative as Charles Simonds's has been.

NOTES

1   On Dion's project, see *Mark Dion: Travels of William Bartram Reconsidered* (Philadelphia: Bartram's Garden, 2008).

2   My reading of the responses to the Simonds project come from several sources: a comment book in the museum, casual conversations with visitors, observations made to Dumbarton Oaks docents during tours, and telephone calls.

3   Beatrix Farrand to John S. Thatcher, June 27, 1944, Beatrix Farrand file, Rare Book Collection, Dumbarton Oaks Research Library and Collection, Washington, D.C.

4   Beatrix Farrand, "Report Submitted to the Chairman of the Dumbarton Oaks Administrative Board, on the Grounds of Dumbarton Oaks Research Library and Collection," November 24, 1941, Beatrix Farrand file, Rare Book Collection, Dumbarton Oaks Research Library and Collection, Washington, D.C.

5   For more on the grotesque, see E. H. Gombrich, "The Edge of Chaos," in *The Sense of Order: A Study in the Psychology of Decorative Art* (Oxford: Phaidon, 1979). The reference to John Ruskin, *The Stones of Venice* (London: Smith, Elder, 1851–53) is from vol. III, chap. III, par. XXIII.

6   For more on this plaque and the design of its setting on the Arbor Terrace, see Linda Lott, with James Carder, *Garden Ornament at Dumbarton Oaks* (Washington, D.C.: Dumbarton Oaks Research Library and Collection, 2001), 16–19; and Linda Lott, "The Arbor Terrace at Dumbarton Oaks: History and Design," *Garden History* 31, no. 2 (Winter 2003): 209–17.

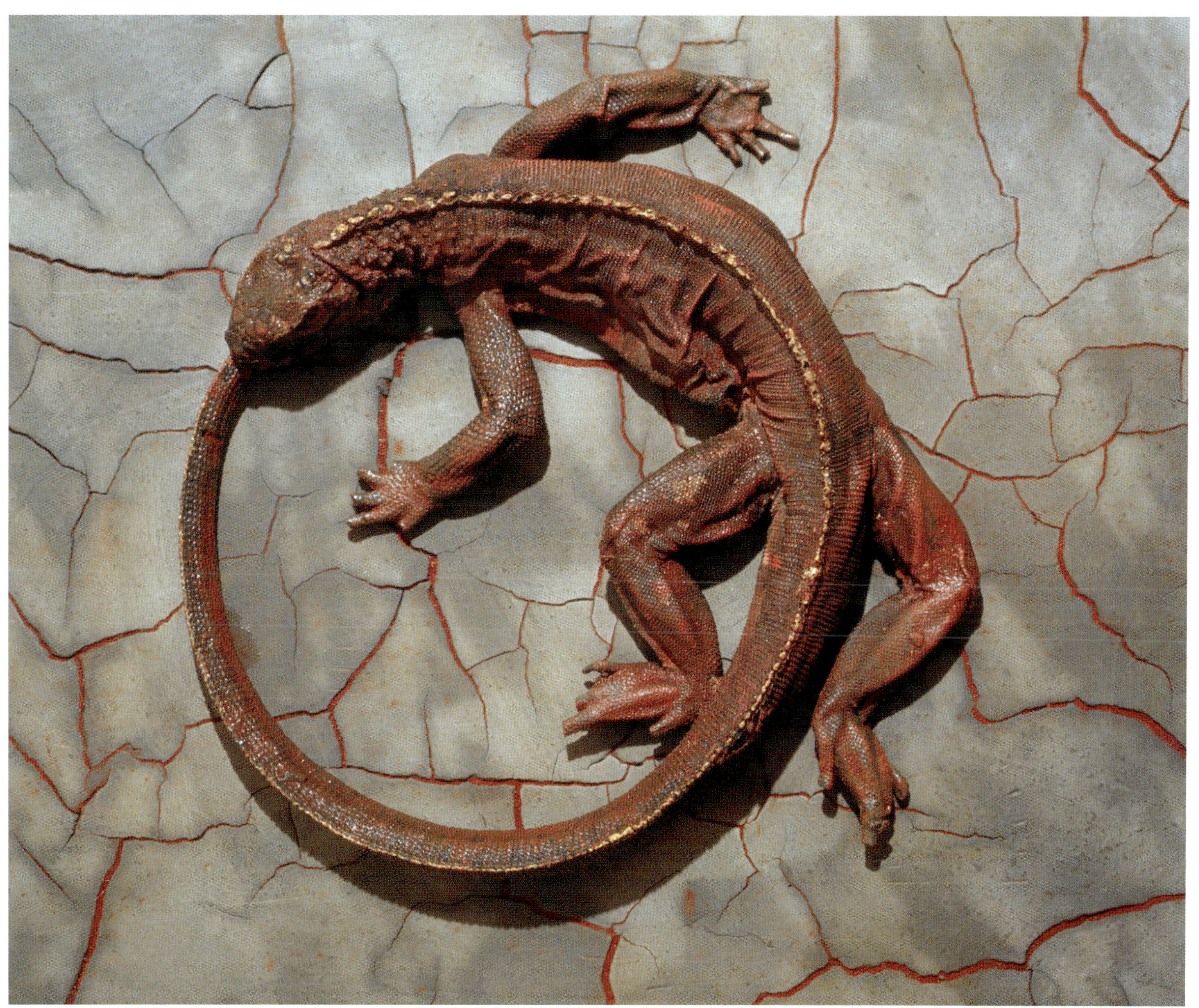

Uroboros, 1973 | Resin, 12½ x 12½ x 2¾ inches | Collection of the artist | 15

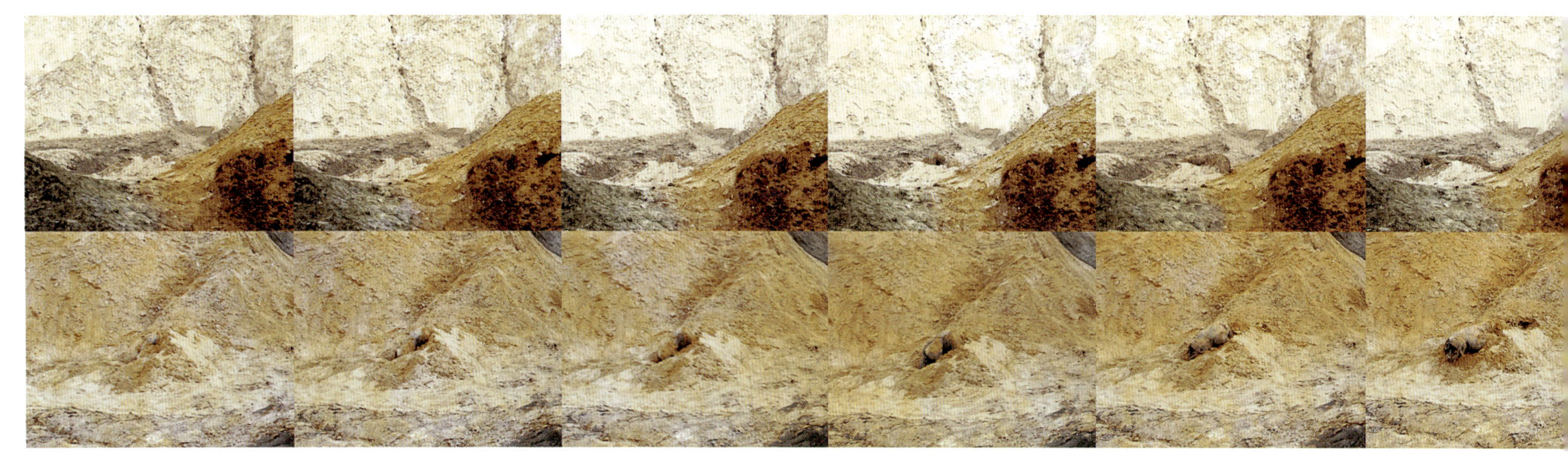

Birth, 1970
Twenty-two color photographs, 16 x 103 inches
Collection of the artist

Landscape/Body/Dwelling, 1973

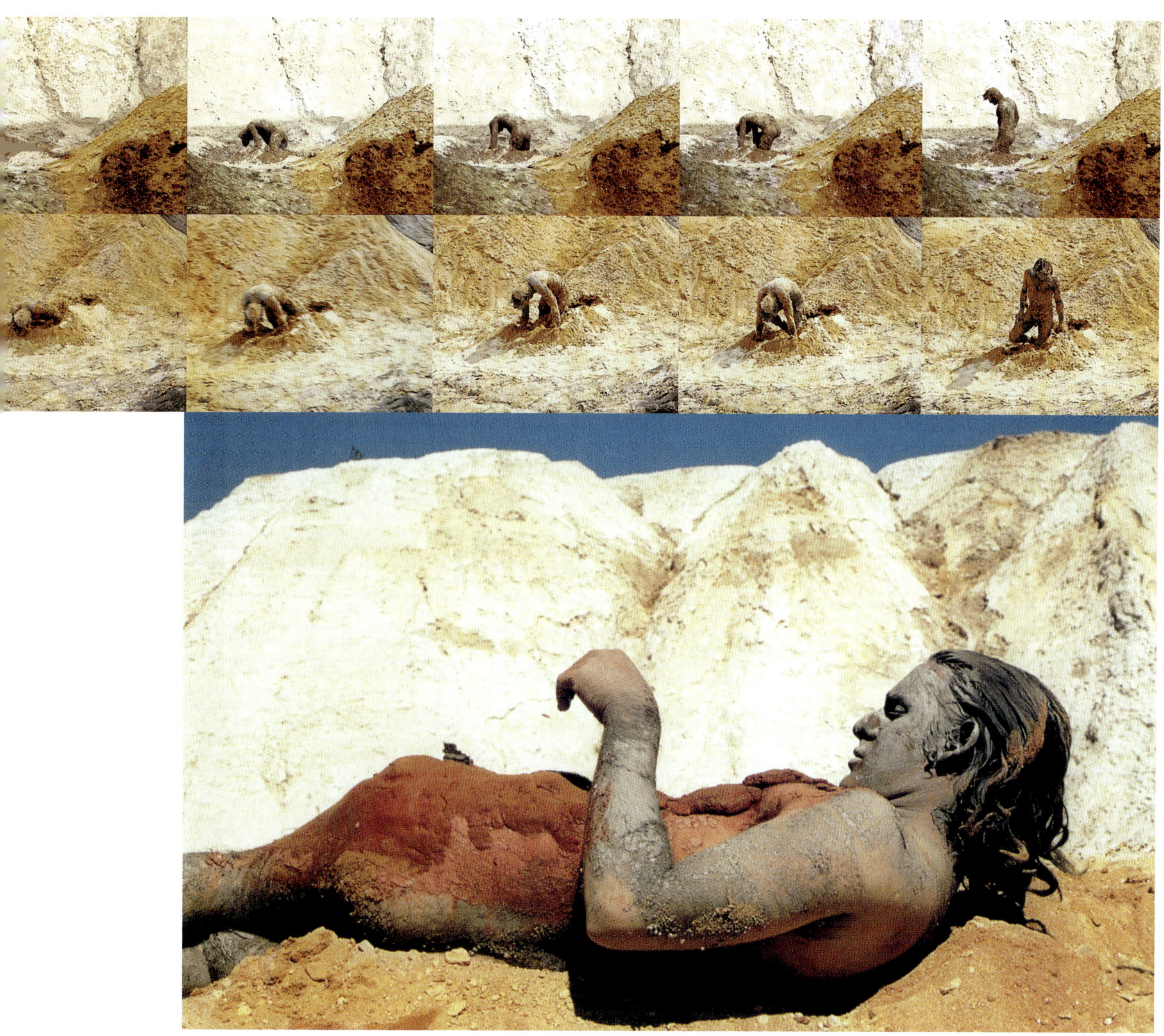

Top left: Simonds's proposal for a Lower East Side tenement museum, an abandoned building in Manhattan to be covered with wisteria (1976); top right: Simonds's installation "Three Trees" for the Architecture Museum in Basel, where support columns were covered with hollowed trees that protruded through windows and the roof (1985); bottom left: Simonds's photograph of the Arizona desert in bloom (1980); bottom right: planting the kitchen garden at Dumbarton Oaks (2009).

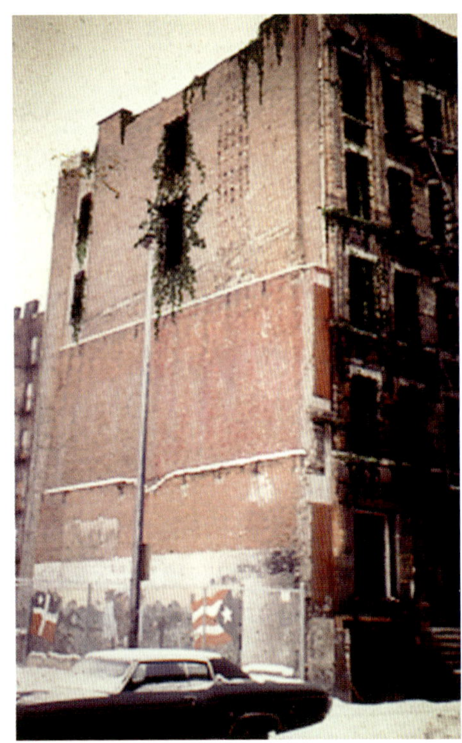

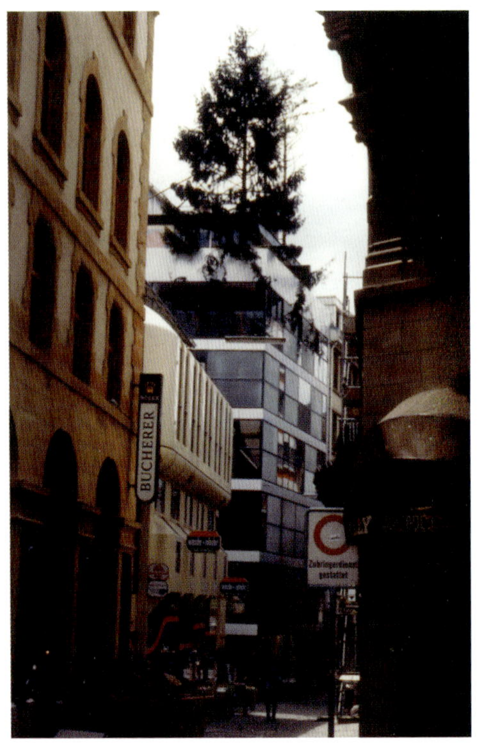

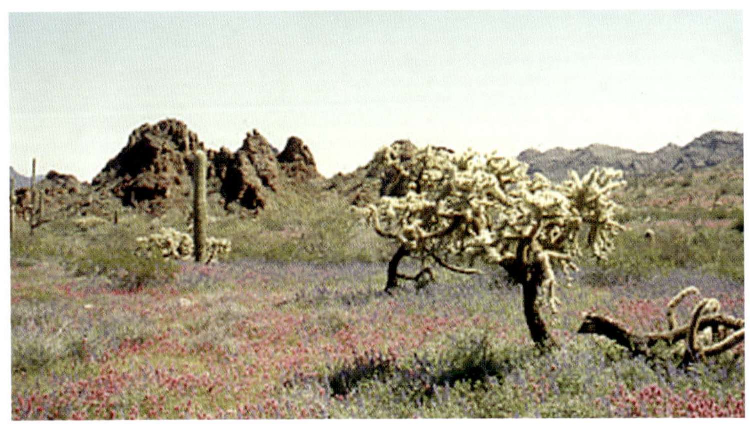

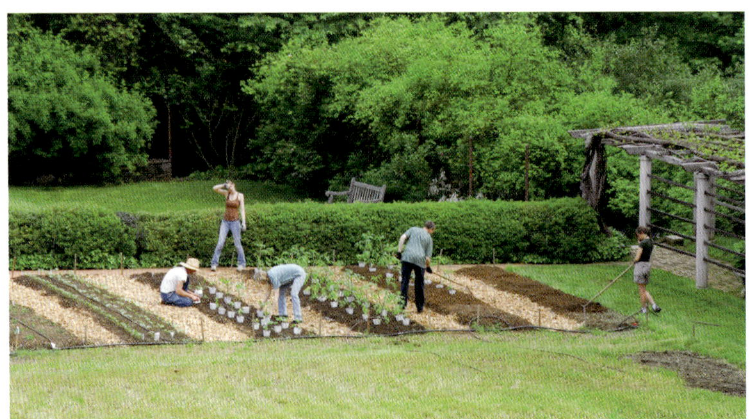

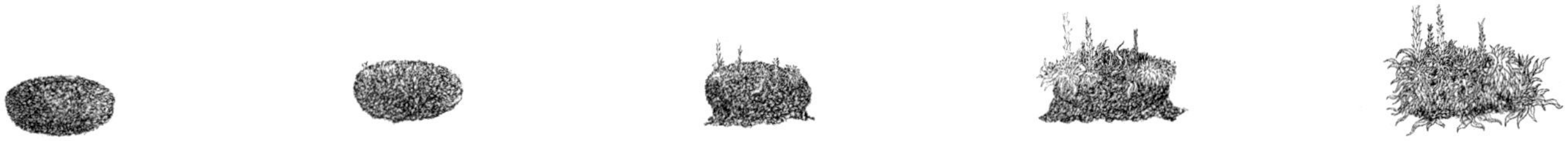

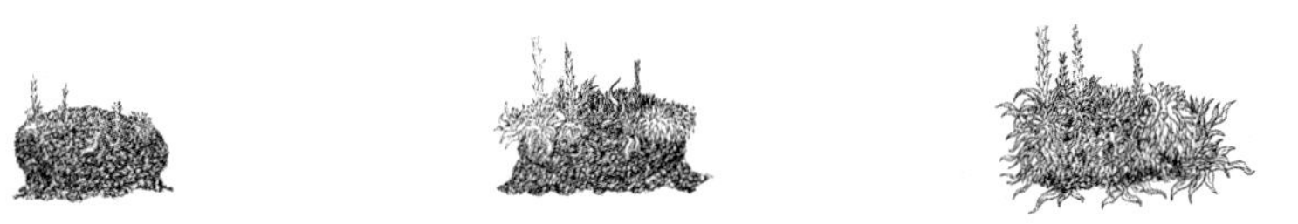

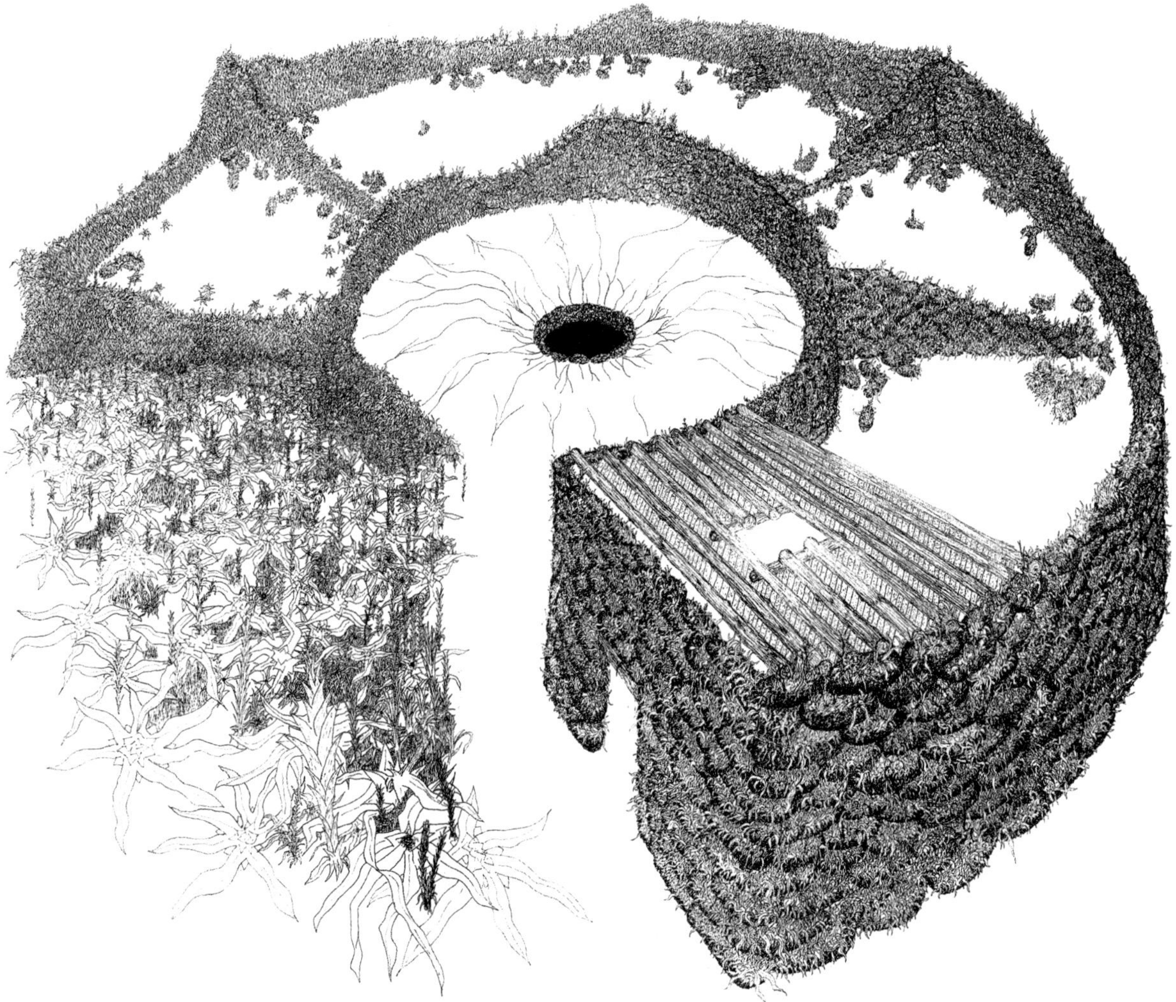

Growth House, 1975
Photo print, 25¾ x 29½ inches
Collection of the artist

This seasonally renewable dwelling is built with earthen bricks that have seeds planted inside. As the seeds sprout, growth transforms the built structure—the dwelling is converted from shelter to food and is harvested and eaten. It is then re-seeded and rebuilt by its inhabitants. Simonds considers this dwelling to be hermaphroditic, marrying building and shelter (male) with growing and food (female).

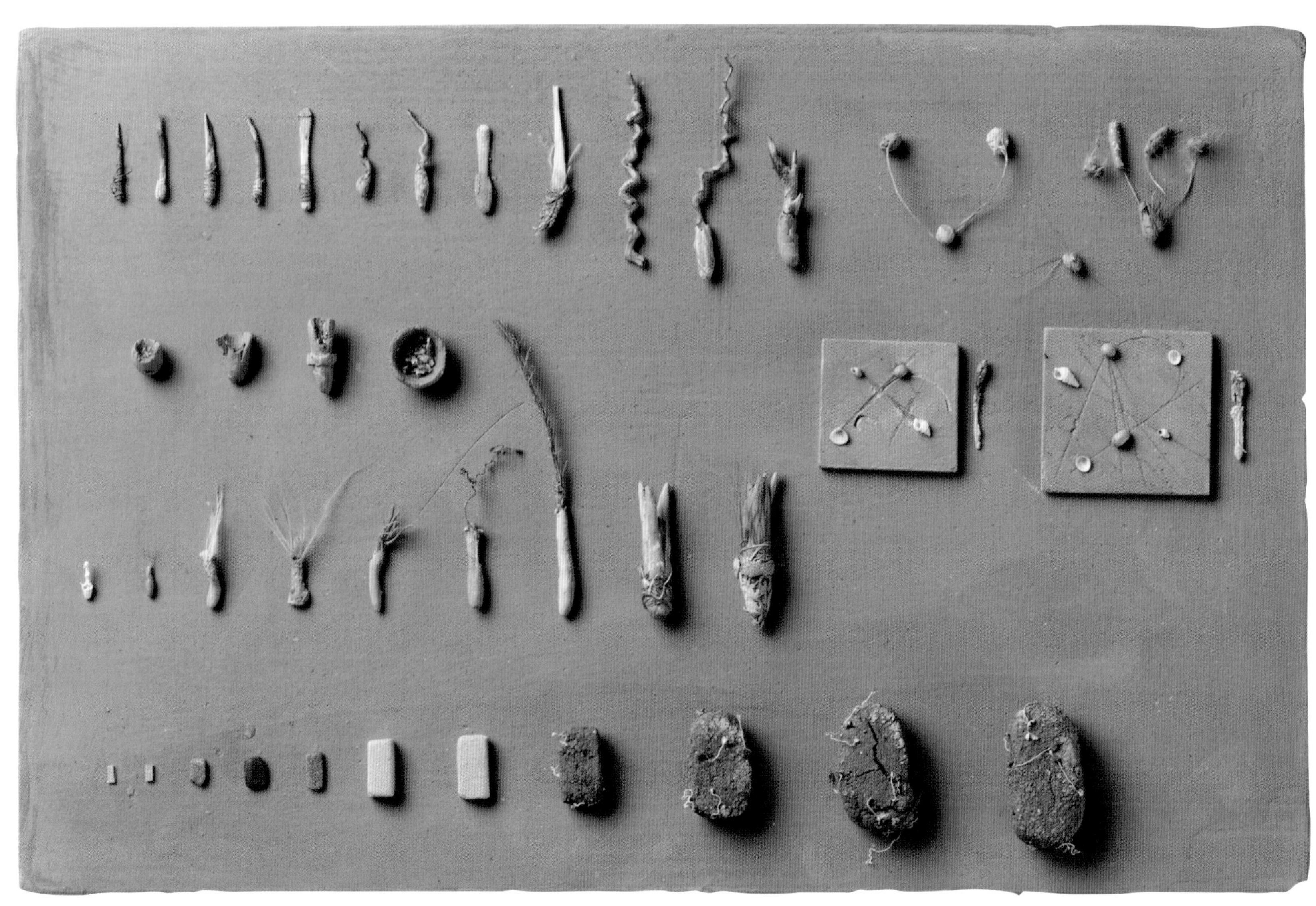

Ritual Objects, 1987
Mixed media, 7½ x 9½ x 1 inches
The Lola and Allen Goldring Collection

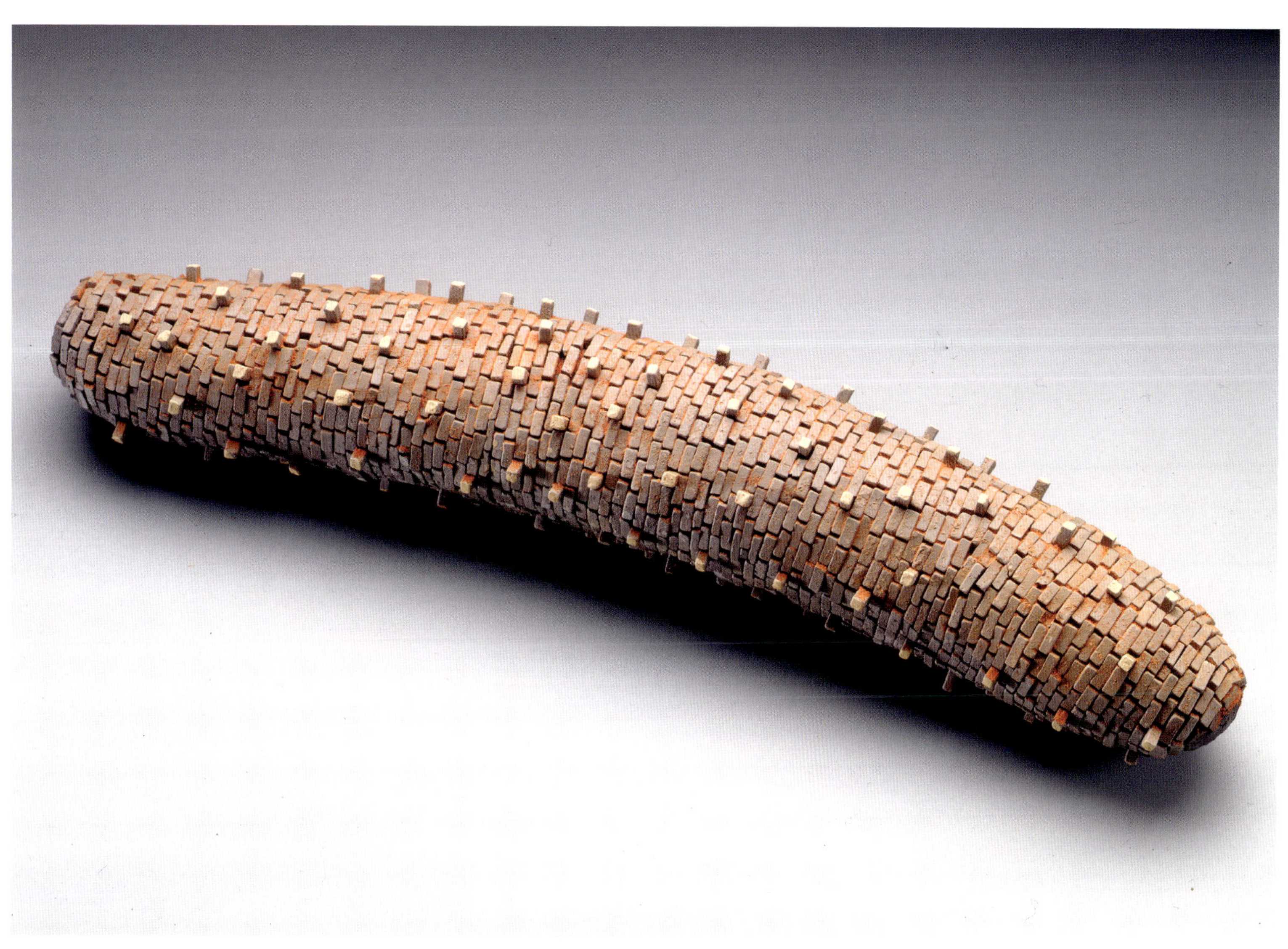

It, 1993
Clay and plaster, 3½ x 17 x 3½ inches
Collection of the artist

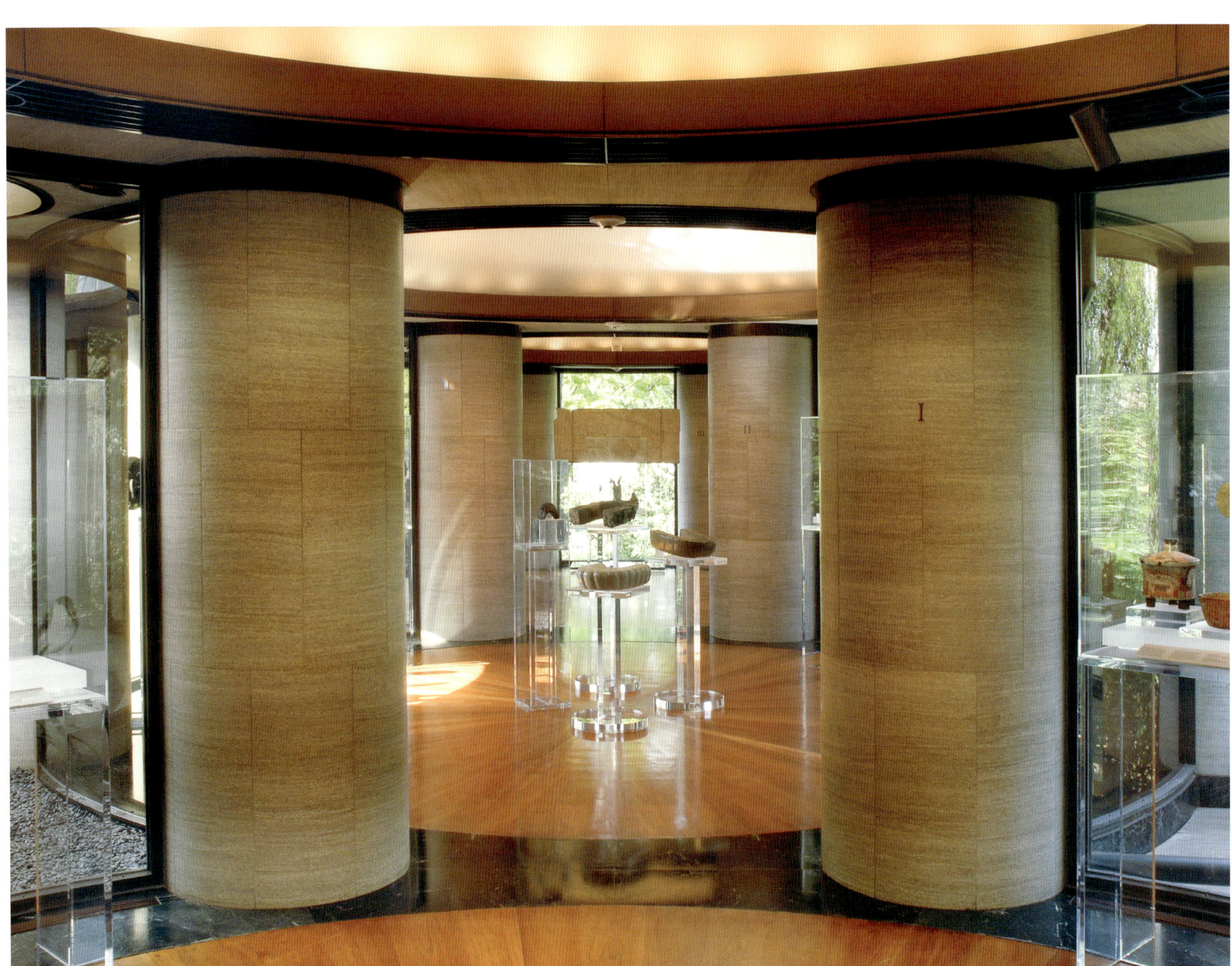

 Charles Simonds In Situ in the
Dumbarton Oaks Museum
Joanne Pillsbury

When Robert Woods Bliss, one of the founders of Dumbarton Oaks, began collecting Pre-Columbian art in earnest in the 1930s, the art of the ancient Americas was only rarely on display in art museums and exhibitions. At that time, stone sculptures, ceramics, textiles, and other objects created before the arrival of the first Europeans in Latin America were more commonly shown in natural history museums, where such works were viewed in the context of anthropological exhibits. But Bliss sought to create a collection that emphasized the aesthetic aspects of Pre-Columbian art, and to show it at the world's leading art—rather than anthropology—museums before creating a permanent gallery for the collection at Dumbarton Oaks. Bliss focused on objects of rare materials and high craftsmanship, generally avoiding ceramics unless they were of particular interest iconographically.

The Robert Woods Bliss Collection of Pre-Columbian Art was installed in its permanent home in 1963, in a wing off the preexisting Byzantine galleries (left). The wing, designed by Philip Johnson, was conceived as a small garden pavilion. The unusual building features eight interconnected circular galleries, with floor-to-ceiling glass walls, arranged in a square around an open courtyard with a fountain. Surmounted by domes reminiscent of those Johnson knew of from Istanbul, the building is known for its low-key but luxurious use of materials, from teak floors to bronze soffits, that echoed the discernment evident in the collection itself. Johnson designed the building to be as transparent as possible; he wanted the "garden to march right up to museum displays and become part of them."[1] This sense of transparency is heightened by the use of Plexiglas cases and stands to display the Pre-Columbian Collection. The objects seem to hover in space, untethered by either mounts or extensive labels, or by the architecture, which seems to melt away.

In 2009, a series of striking intrusions—both architectural and material—appeared in the Johnson pavilion at Dumbarton Oaks. Charles Simonds's interventions in the museum

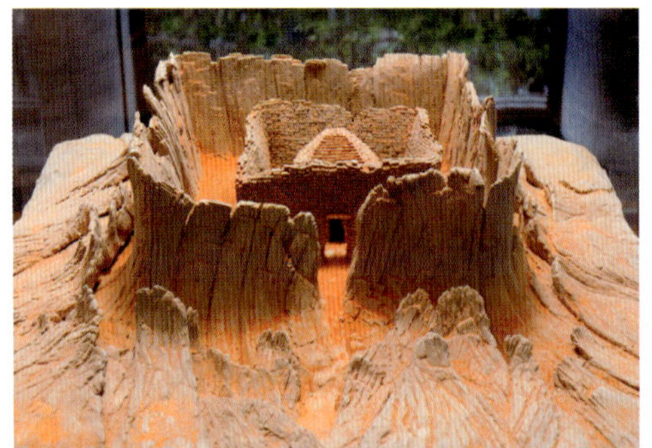

galleries produced startling juxtapositions, but in a subtle way also filled voids. Although the amount of supporting text providing a background for understanding Pre-Columbian cultures has increased in the galleries in recent years, the installation at Dumbarton Oaks has long been considered to be an extreme example of the display of "decontextualized" works of art, the minimalist setting and presentation far from the detailed explanatory texts and dioramas of anthropology museums. Simonds's interventions in the Johnson pavilion, particularly works such as *Rock Flower* (1986, top left) and *Wilted Towers* (1984), provoked in the viewer a sense of absent contexts, both Pre-Columbian and modern.

Indeed, unwary visitors even mistook *Rock Flower* and *Wilted Towers* for models of Pre-Columbian architecture, never mind the fact that Simonds's imaginary buildings were closer in spirit to the Native American architecture of the southwest United States than to the ornate splendor of Maya palaces and temples, the likely original contexts of many of the Pre-Columbian sculptures surrounding *Rock Flower* in the Johnson pavilion. Viewers would peer into the structures and search for explanatory texts nearby, but then return to Simonds's works again and contemplate them in a new way, once they were assured that their purposes were not strictly didactic.

Mistaking the contemporary for ancient is understandable, as numerous architectural models are known from the Pre-Columbian Americas. Some of the most complex were made by the Moche, a culture that flourished on the North Coast of Peru in the first eight centuries of the Common Era. Unfired clay models were included in burials at San José de Moro[2] (bottom left), and ceramic vessels with elaborate miniature temples can be found in many museum collections. These too presumably came from burials, though the majority of such vessels lack known find sites. Rarely populated, many of these vessels are also simple musical instruments or whistles, indicating the ritual nature of these representations and suggesting the possibility that such architecture was considered animate.[3] Curiously, works such as *Rock Flower*, with its barklike walls, and the detumescent *Wilted Towers* speak of an organic, animate architecture as well, but in terms more biological than spiritual.

Rock Flower, with its biomorphic palisade implying limited access to a small ritual space, seems to echo aspects of Pre-Columbian architecture, particularly Maya, Chimu, and Inca buildings designed for the observance of certain solar and celestial phenomena. Simonds's miniature architectural installations are often referred to as dwellings for a mythical population, yet the striking aspect of *Rock Flower*, *Pyramid*, and *Y* (in 2009, the latter two works were on display in the Byzantine galleries, facing page) is the very lack of domestic, seemingly inhabitable spaces. A limited access to interiors and an emphasis on solid forms

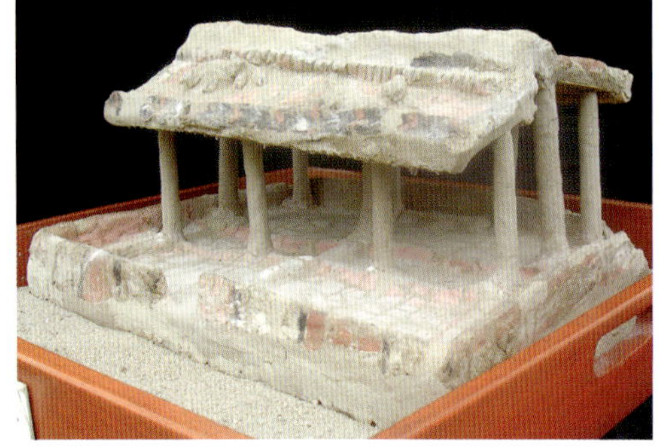

over enclosed spaces speak of concerns about defense or a celebration of ritual rather than the mundane matters of cooking and sleeping. It is architecture as symbol rather than as shelter. In *Wilted Towers*, for example, Simonds appears to be overturning, quite explicitly, our expectation of, and deep desire for, architecture that provides stable and enduring shelter. Its apparent organic flaccidity and untrustworthiness invokes the ineluctable transience of its erstwhile but vanished inhabitants.

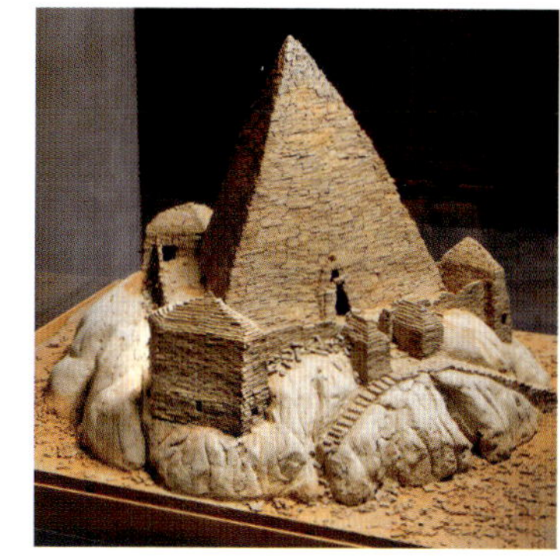

The presence of Simonds's architecture in the Dumbarton Oaks Museum also provoked considerations of epistemology, calling to mind the profound differences in knowledge about the ancient American past between Bliss's time and our own. When Bliss made his first purchases of Pre-Columbian objects in 1912–14, little was known about the complex societies of the ancient Americas. The Aztecs and the Incas were the best known of the Pre-Columbian cultures, as they were the dominant empires in North and South America at the time of the Spanish conquest. But little was known about the thousands of years of history that preceded these two late societies. Simonds's works, as acts of reconstructing an imagined past, remind us of the extraordinary growth of Americanist archaeology in the twentieth century. In this day of mass tourism to archaeological sites in the Yucatan Peninsula and elsewhere, it is worthwhile to remind ourselves of the inaccessibility of most Pre-Columbian sites to individuals outside of Latin America at the beginning of the twentieth century. Knowledge of the actual architecture of these sites was available only through a small number of books; some books, such as John Lloyd Stephens's *Incidents of Travel in Central America, Chiapas, and Yucatan* (1841), were widely disseminated, but most were of more limited circulation.[4] Our understanding of ancient American society—and the broader context of the Pre-Columbian Collection—has increased dramatically with the number and scale of archaeological projects from the 1930s to the present day.

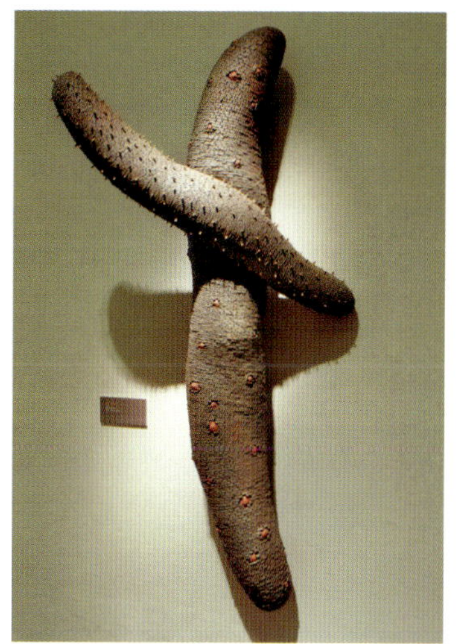

Simonds's art offers tantalizing glimpses into the residues of a hitherto unknown yet seemingly knowable civilization, and in doing so stimulates our cognizance of the almost magical sense of continuing discovery that is a significant characteristic of contemporary Pre-Columbian archaeology. The early works of Simonds parallel the dramatic rise in archaeological knowledge, particularly about Latin America in the late 1960s and 1970s. These discoveries became part of a broader public dialogue and were ultimately refracted in contemporary art. Simonds's colleague and friend Robert Smithson was also responding to such currents, albeit it in different forms. Smithson's essay "Incidents of Mirror-Travel in the Yucatan" and installation *Yucatan Mirror Displacements (1–9)* of 1969 were, in part, oblique responses to Stephens.[5]

The presence of *Rock Flower* and *Wilted Towers* in the Pre-Columbian galleries did more than remind us of epistemology, however, and Simonds's sculptures became sites for reflection on broader concerns of duration, both the lifecycles of individuals and the fates of entire cultures. Simonds's work in the context of the Dumbarton Oaks Museum makes present the idea of ancient lost civilizations. *Rock Flower* and, to a greater extent, *Wilted Towers*—both strikingly depopulated—force us to step back and reflect on the once-thriving cities where the objects in the Pre-Columbian Collection were created, used, feared, and treasured. Many, but not all, Pre-Columbian cities were gradually or abruptly abandoned at some point in the past, and these sites are now quiet reminders of the rise and fall of civilizations. We prefer our ruins empty, and in this sense the absence of figures in Simonds's architecture, and the nonspecific nature of the architecture, allow an opportunity for unimpeded reflection and imagination.

Wilted Towers, with its deflated, fallen brick structures, speaks to the melancholic aspect of archaeology and its chronicling of the ceaseless march of time. A memento mori in the galleries, it parallels the biological metaphor that archaeologists use to distinguish periods of time in pre-Hispanic Mesoamerica: Preclassic, Classic, Postclassic, reflecting earlier beliefs about the transition from nascent, unformed cultures, to the florescence of a middle period, and ultimately to an inevitable decline. Simonds's mysterious works provide sites for thinking about these enduring, structuring cycles of birth, maturation, and decay, in a setting where such questions are particularly resonant. This idea continues in the garden, where *Head (from I, Thou)* (1993) appears almost like a fallen architectural tenon, its grimace and cracks seemingly reflecting the impact of the fall as much as the specific inherent psychological complexity of the work itself.

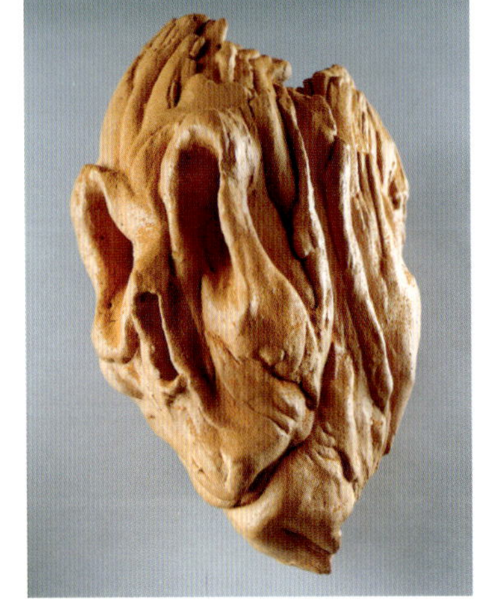

The other resonant presence in the Pre-Columbian galleries supplied by Charles Simonds is the very material of *Rock Flower* and *Wilted Towers*: clay. After entering the first gallery in the Johnson pavilion, visitors generally turn to the right and proceed into a second gallery containing Aztec and Mixtec objects, along with works from one of their ancestral cities, Teotihuacan. These Central Mexican works flanked Simonds's *Head* (1991, left), a work of ambiguous anthropomorphic/zoomorphic characteristics. Made of clay and plaster, its rich red hue is a reminder of the earth from which it was made. Depending upon a viewer's interpretative inclination, it could equally be read as gradually achieving form (i.e., coming into existence) or losing form (i.e., eroding, decaying, and dissolving).

Clay was one of the foundational materials of Pre-Columbian material culture, yet it is notable for its relative absence in the Bliss collection. Clay, as a material, figures prominently in Pre-Columbian origin myths, particularly the Maya *Popol Vuh*, where man is first created out of clay, just as it does in Simonds's own early works, particularly *Birth*, a film and photographic series from 1970.[6] Bliss himself, however, considered clay objects to be in the realm of anthropological collections and largely eschewed objects of this material, unless they were very finely crafted, fired works with interesting iconographies. *Head* stood out as a primordial form, the inchoate ambiguity of its human/animal characteristics creating tension and unease in a gallery filled with disturbing objects.

Head's companions in the gallery included a necklace with shell beads in the form of human skulls and a necklace with gold ornaments in the shape of either human skulls or spider monkey heads (with moveable mandibles, top right).[7] These Mixtec-Aztec necklaces echo the themes of the transformation/decay of flesh and the disconcerting ambiguity of Simonds's sculpture. Across from *Head*, in its own case, was a small ornament fashioned from the shell of the thorny oyster, *Spondylus* (bottom right). The ornament represents the Aztec god Xipe Totec, "Our Lord the Flayed One," a deity associated with fertility. The priests of Xipe Totec wore the flayed skins of sacrificial victims, symbolically replicating the new corn emerging from dying husks. In Aztec belief, sacrifice was essential for fertility and the continuation of life. The flayed skin served as a metonym for the concept of death and rebirth. In the carved ornament, one can observe the mouth of Xipe below the mask of flayed skin.

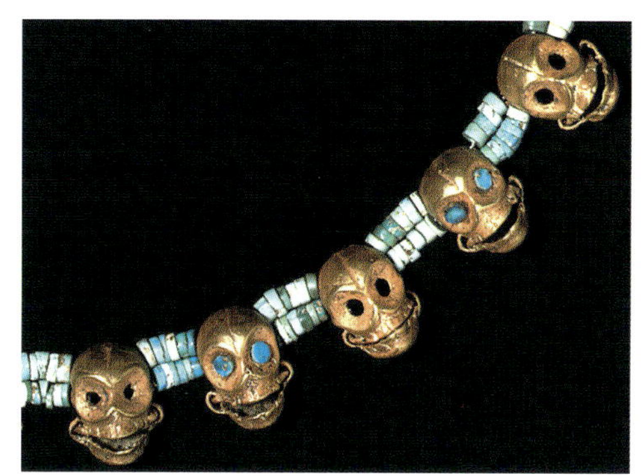

Spondylus, which was highly valued and closely associated with concepts of fertility and sacrifice in the ancient Americas, was a ritual material of great importance. Difficult to obtain and work, the shell ranges in color from white to orange, with some specimens and species achieving a rich red or purple. The variegated red-orange used for the Dumbarton Oaks Xipe Totec underscores the connection between blood, sacrifice, and fertility. The skull necklace was similarly fashioned from *Spondylus*, but it also reveals the addition of a sprinkling of red pigment, possibly cinnabar, as an allusion to the blood of sacrifice. Cinnabar was also sprinkled on bodies in tombs, possibly as a synecdoche for the ritual of blood sacrifice in an enduring form. *Head* itself was encircled by a light sprinkling of red clay dust in its temporary entombment in the museum case, an unanticipated connection to a long-standing funerary tradition in ancient Mesoamerica, and one that invokes further unease if one reads *Head* as a decaying form.

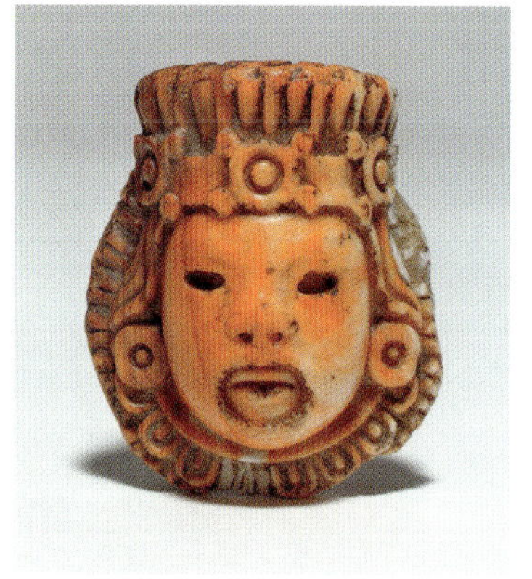

The disembodied *Head* also prompted comparisons with the next gallery, where the Gulf Coast collection is displayed.[8] The Gulf Coast region is known for the early and elaborate articulation of the Mesoamerican ball game. In Classic-period Veracruz, the

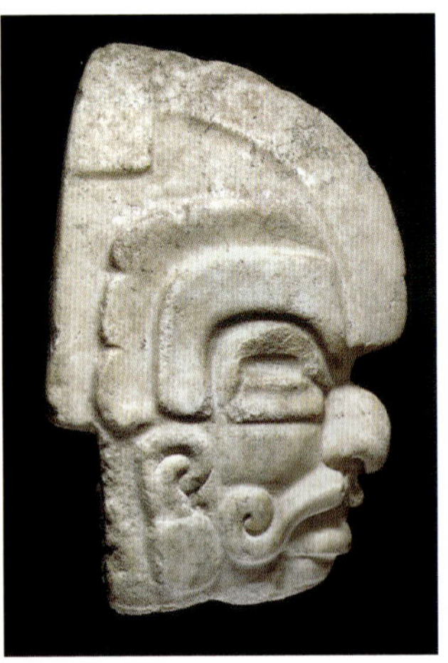

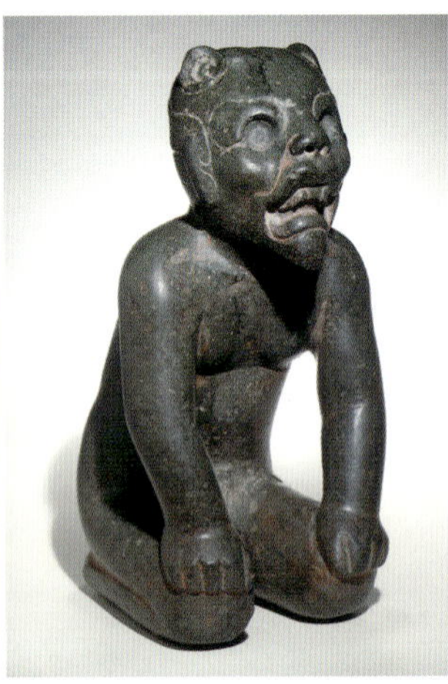

ballgame was closely associated with sacrifice, and thin stone heads—really just profile heads, known as *hachas*, the Spanish word for axe—are thought to represent the severed heads of sacrificial victims (top, far left). But the anthropomorphic/zoomorphic ambiguity of *Head* also encouraged comparison with sculptures associated with the Olmec culture, one of the earliest complex societies of Mexico. Dating to the first millennium before the Common Era, Olmec "transformation" figures are among the most striking works from the ancient Americas (top left). These small-scale greenstone figures seem to represent beings in the process of metamorphosis. Human bodies sprout jaguar heads and paws, or jaguars adopt the stance of human boxers. The intriguing figures speak of animal strengths and potentials, giving them a power that belies their small scale. As with *Head* and *Stugg* (1991), a large-scale work on view on a garden terrace, there are strong resonances between the ancient and the contemporary, particularly concerning ideas about transmutation and transmogrification.

Very different affinities and associations were prompted by the siting of *Tumbleweed* (1993). Placed across the pavilion from *Head*, in a gallery featuring Pre-Columbian art from the Andean highlands, this delicate work in dazzling white porcelain invokes a hybrid, imaginary botanical form. *Tumbleweed* is formally similar to the structure of its namesake, desiccated remains of desert plants blown from their root systems. But unlike tumbleweeds, the work features the promise of new life in the form of tiny leaves emerging from the dead plant. As with Xipe Totec, it offers an idea of rebirth from death.

In an unexpected way, *Tumbleweed* (facing page) seemed at home in the Andean galleries. As John Beardsley notes in this volume, this imagined desert plant was consonant with the Andean landscape itself, particularly the hyperarid region of the coast, home to the Moche and Chimu objects in the next gallery. Formally, its bright, spiky forms echoed not only the mother-of-pearl of the inlay of a Wari mosaic mirror with a zoomorphic handle, but also that other marine creature so highly valued in the ancient Americas, *Spondylus*, especially in the delicate/threatening parallel between the spiky white spines of the bivalve and the points of *Tumbleweed*. The idea of recreating botanical forms in precious materials was one the Inca explored in spectacular detail (bottom left). The Coricancha "golden enclosure," in Cuzco, a temple dedicated to the sun, included a garden of full-size replicas in gold of plants found in far-flung regions of the Inca Empire.

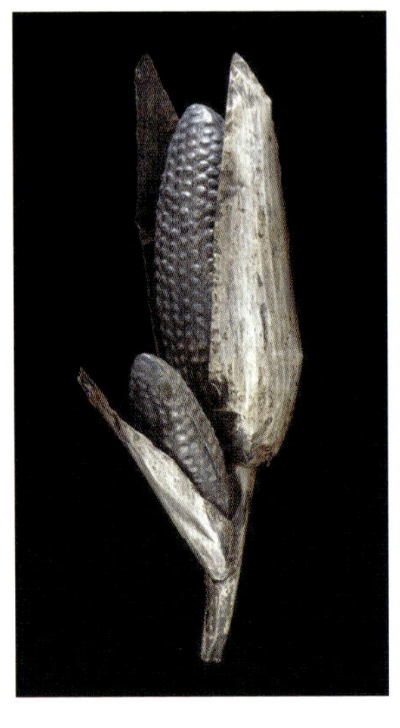

Tumbleweed not only plays with ideas of cyclical existence but also presents another formal tension between vulnerability and strength. Porcelain, a clay with a high kaolin content, requires great skill to manipulate the balance of water to mineral. When fired at a very high temperature, however, it achieves full vitrification; its surprising tensile strength makes possible works of breathtaking thinness and translucency. *Tumbleweed* was created at the Manufacture Nationale de Céramique, Sèvres, where Simonds was part of the program of distinguished artists in residence. In some ways, the work is a descendent of the tour de force porcelain rooms of the eighteenth century with their abundant floral imagery. But *Tumbleweed* takes the material in a new direction, referencing not the refined species of palace gardens but the undomesticated wild west, its sprouts of new growth reading more as barbed wire than as inviting blossoms. Although it initially appears to be a work quite apart from *Wilted Towers* and *Rock Flower*, it shares with both not only biomorphic forms but also a sense of abandoned sites and desolation. A sense of play also infuses the piece, particularly in the very idea of a tumbleweed—its abiding characteristic one of rootless, aimless movement—rendered in a material at once hard and yet so easily shattered. It is this tension between the ephemeral and the enduring, delicacy and strength, the very purposefulness behind the creation of a solid object the name of which invokes something that we have come to regard culturally as the veritable cliché for the quintessentially random and transient, that imbues the work with its remarkable power.

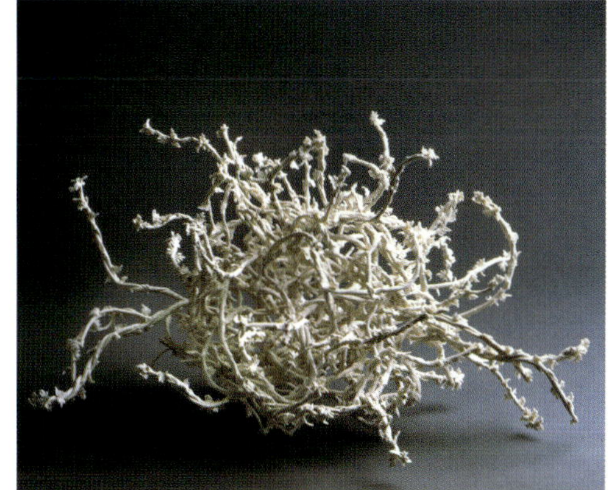

Beyond the Johnson pavilion, Simonds's works continued to provoke and provide a subversive counterpoint to other museum collections and the gardens. *Pyramid*, in a corner of the main courtyard of the museum, was a quiet counterpoint to the classicism of the surrounding architecture and collections. Again a primordial presence, *Pyramid* stood as an allusion to a far more ancient architecture that preceded the creation of the Greek, Roman, and Byzantine objects nearby. *Y*, installed in the "altar" area of the Byzantine gallery, was in many ways at home in the ritual setting, conceptually and even formally, with its cross form echoing the Christian imagery on the liturgical silver from the Sion Treasure, a sixth-century Byzantine hoard from the south coast of Turkey. But the humble material of *Y*, clay and plaster, seems to be a reminder of a more modest ritual tradition, even a sly rebuke, to the ostentation of Byzantium.

One of the intentions of Johnson's pavilion was to bring the outside in, to make the boundaries between the garden and galleries disappear. Charles Simonds's installation at Dumbarton Oaks worked in this spirit, with the sculptures in the galleries recalling the natural world and the works in the garden bringing us back to objects in the Bliss collection. *Stugg*, the large-scale work on the garden terrace, depicts an anthropomorphized botanical form, a stem from which the torso and head of a figure sprout. The head is again ambiguous, between human and animal, between animation and decay. *Stugg* presents one of the

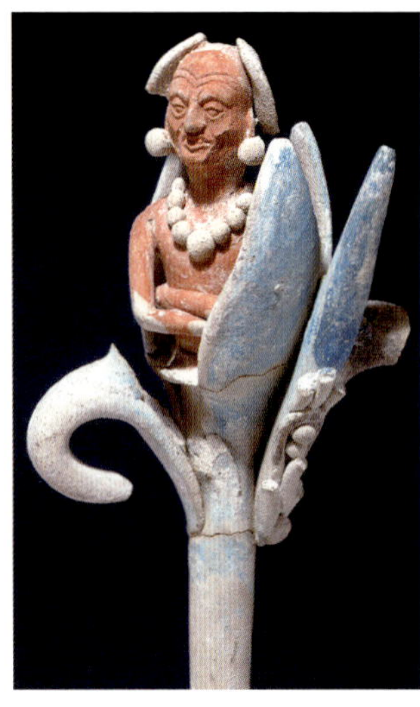

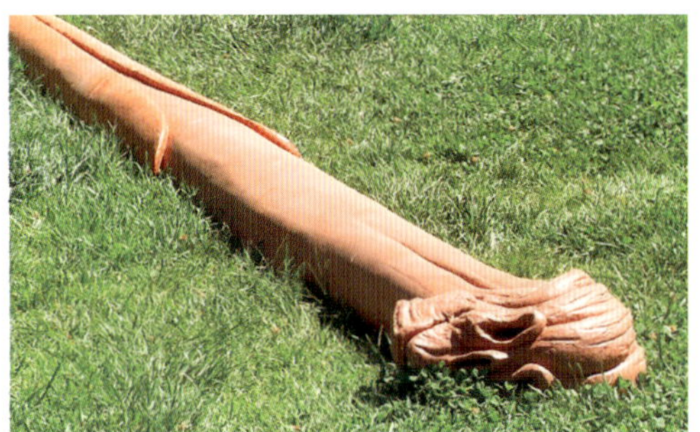

striking affinities—similarities without direct links—of the exhibition *Landscape Body Dwelling* at Dumbarton Oaks. One of the treasures of the Pre-Columbian Collection at Dumbarton Oaks is a small Maya Jaina-style polychromed ceramic whistle (top left). Recalling the anthropomorphism and phytomorphism of Simonds's *Stugg* (bottom left), this whistle features an aged man emerging from the stem of a flower.

Jaina is the name given to a class of Maya figurines from the Late Classic period (600–900 CE).[9] These figurines are most closely associated with the island of Jaina, in the Gulf of Mexico, off the western coast of the state of Campeche, where they have been found in burials. Some scholars believe that the number of burials on Jaina exceeds the number that would be expected for a population of such a small island and argue that the island served as a necropolis. The Maya conceived of watery places as portals to the underworld, suggesting that the island was a particularly auspicious place "to enter the water," to use the phrase the Maya used to signify death. Figurines of the Jaina style have also been found on the mainland, at sites in the states of Campeche, Tabasco, and Chiapas. Jaina figurines were created as individual figures and as male/female and animal/human pairs.[10]

Another type of Jaina figurine is represented by the Dumbarton Oaks whistle. There are at least six other examples of figurines with an aged man emerging from a blossom. Occasionally a younger male is represented, in which case he is usually identified as the beautiful young maize god, his metamorphosis echoing the growth of this essential Mesoamerican crop. The Dumbarton Oaks figure may not be a young maize god, but he may still be divine. For example, in a Lacandon Maya creation myth, gods, lineage founders, and their helpers were born of plumeria blossoms. Whatever the precise meaning of the figure, the piece was undoubtedly used in some sort of a ritual before its eventual interment. As a whistle, its potential for sound links it to a broader world of flutes and other instruments terminating in a floral shape, a synesthesiastic allusion to music emitted as aromatic sounds and to the breath of the soul.[11]

The parallel phytological metamorphosis of *Stugg* and the Jaina whistle was one of the many unanticipated affinities of the exhibition *Landscape Body Dwelling* at Dumbarton Oaks. Hundreds, if not thousands, of years separated the Pre-Columbian and Byzantine collections from the sculpture of Simonds, yet the juxtaposition of the works provided unique opportunities for reflection on enduring themes. One of the greatest pleasures of Simonds's intervention in the galleries and gardens, and in the life of the residential research institute of Dumbarton Oaks, were the conversations that the work elicited, conversations that continue today among those who experienced the installation.

NOTES

1   Philip Johnson, quoted in James N. Carder, "The Architectural History of Dumbarton Oaks and the Contribution of Armand Albert Rateau," in *A Home of the Humanities: The Collecting and Patronage of Mildred and Robert Woods Bliss*, ed. James N. Carder (Washington, D.C.: Dumbarton Oaks Research Library and Collection), 110.

2   Luis Jaime Castillo, Andrew Nelson, and Chris Nelson, "'Maquetas' Mochicas: San José de Moro," *Arkinka* 2, no. 22 (1997): 120–28.

3   Juliet Wiersema, "The Architectural Vessels of the Moche of Peru (CE 200–850): Architecture for the Afterlife" (PhD diss., University of Maryland, 2010).

4   John Lloyd Stephens, *Incidents of Travel in Central America, Chiapas, and Yucatan* (London: John Murray, 1841).

5   Robert Smithson, "Incidents of Mirror-Travel in the Yucatan," *Artforum* 8, no. 1 (1969). See also John Beardsley, *Earthworks and Beyond: Contemporary Art in the Landscape*, 4th ed. (New York: Abbeville Press, 2006); and Jennifer L. Roberts, *Mirror-Travels: Robert Smithson and History* (New Haven: Yale University Press, 2004).

6   For a recent translation of the *Popol Vuh*, see Allen J. Christenson, *Popol Vuh: The Sacred Book of the Maya* (Norman: University of Oklahoma Press, 2007). For a more detailed discussion of *Birth*, see Beardsley, this volume.

7   Susan Toby Evans, ed., *Ancient Mexican Art at Dumbarton Oaks: Central Highlands, Southwestern Highlands, Gulf Lowlands* (Washington, D.C.: Dumbarton Oaks Research Library and Collection, 2010).

8   For more information on the Gulf Coast collection, see Evans, *Ancient Mexican Art at Dumbarton Oaks*. For the Olmec transformation figures, see Karl A. Taube, *Olmec Art at Dumbarton Oaks* (Washington, D.C.: Dumbarton Oaks Research Library and Collection, 2004).

9   Megan O'Neil, "Jaina-style Figurines," in *Ancient Maya Art at Dumbarton Oaks*, eds. Joanne Pillsbury, Miriam Doutriaux, Reiko Ishihara-Brito, and Alexandre Tokovinine (Washington D.C.: Dumbarton Oaks Research Library and Collections, forthcoming).

10 The male/female pairs include older males with younger females, possibly representing specific deities and ideas of fertility, although some scholars have suggested that the sexual play represented is of a decidedly earthier nature, and that such figurines represent burlesque theatrical performers.

11 Karl A. Taube, "Flower Mountain: Concepts of Life, Beauty, and Paradise among the Classic Maya," *Res: Anthropology and Aesthetics* 45 (Spring 2004): 69–98.

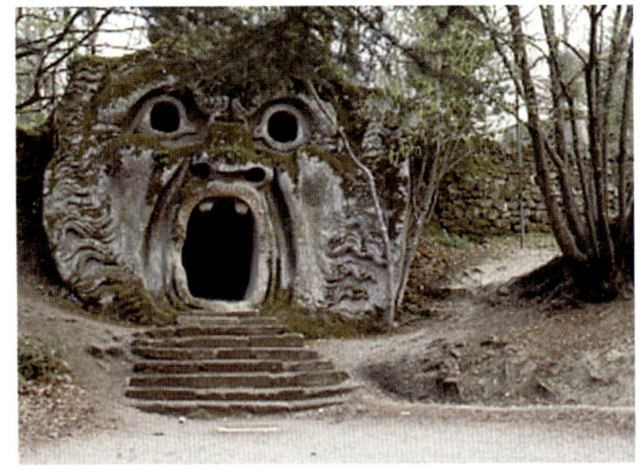

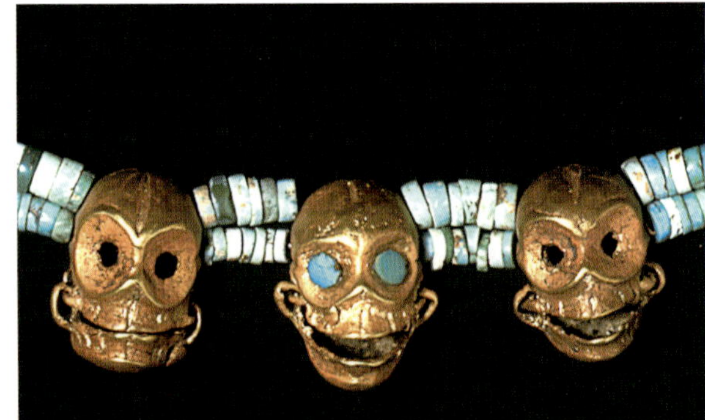

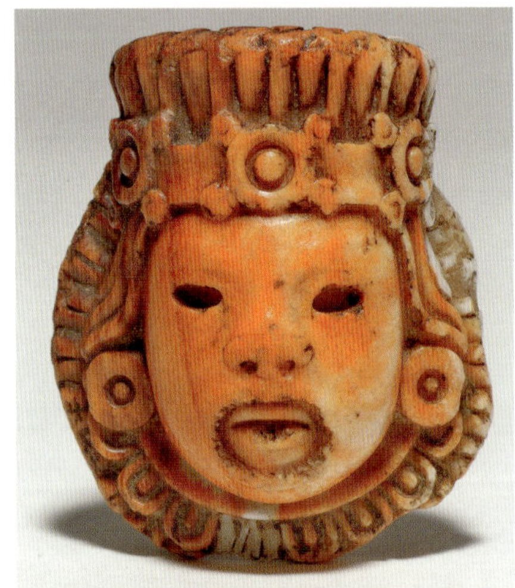

Top left: Colossal head in the *sacro bosco* at the Villa Orsini, Bomarzo, Italy (late sixteenth century)

Bottom left: Simonds's photograph of a goat head in South Carolina (1984).

From the Dumbarton Oaks Collection
Top right: Mixteca-Puebla–style necklace with ornaments in the shape of human skulls or monkey heads, 900–1520 CE, cast gold and turquoise

Center right: Aztec ornament representing Xipe Totec wearing the flayed skin of a sacrificial victim, 1500 CE, carved *Spondylus* shell

Bottom right: Mixtec-Aztec necklace with beads in the shape of human skulls, 1200–1520 CE, carved shell

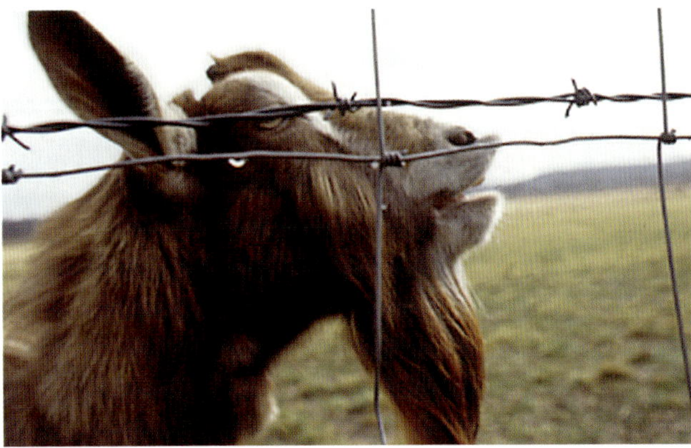

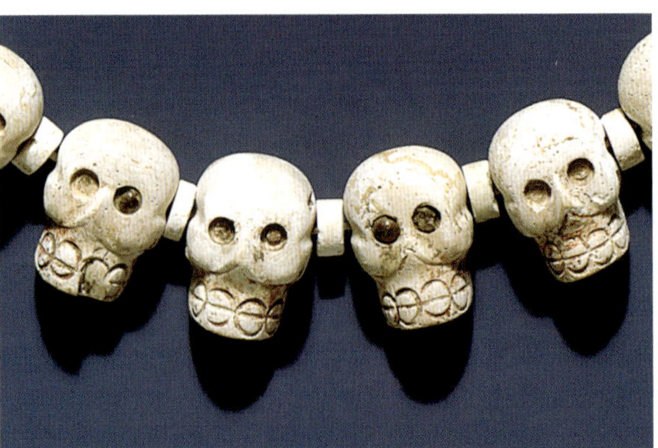

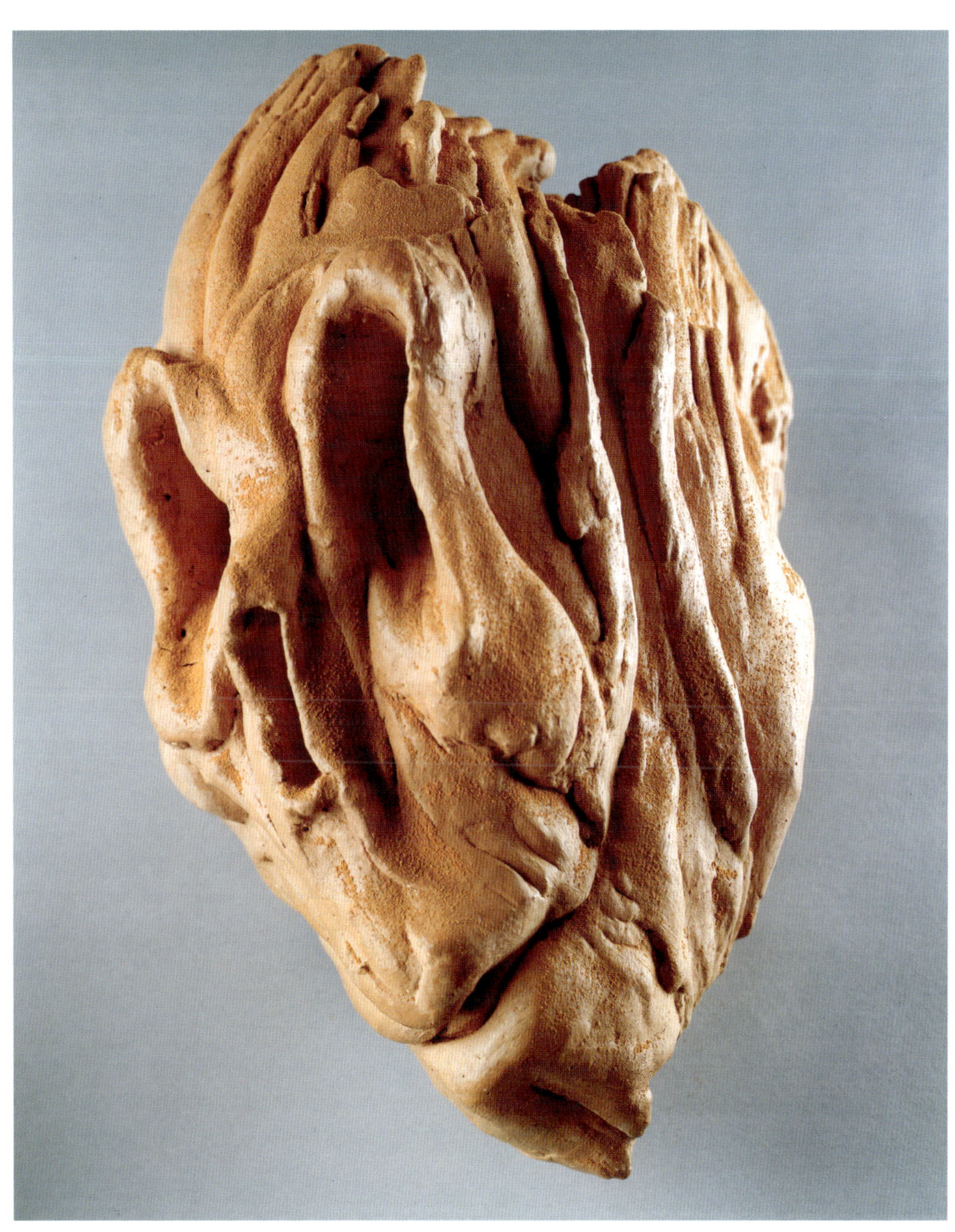

Head, 1991
Plaster and clay, 8 x 15 x 11 inches
Collection of the artist

Detail of a nesting porcelain plate service
with carved mountain imagery, created
by the artist (along with *Tumbleweed*) at
Manufacture Nationale de Céramique,
Sèvres, in 2009.

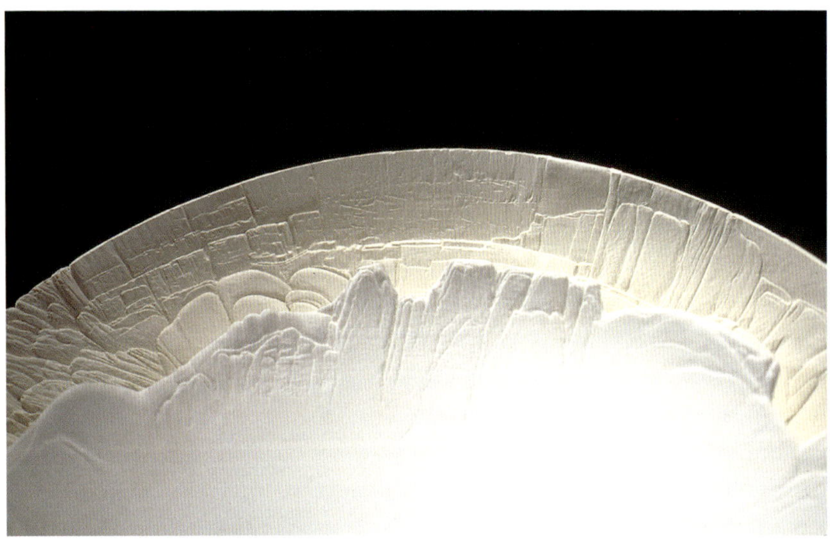

Wari mosaic mirror, 650–1000 CE,
shell, pyrite, and turquoise

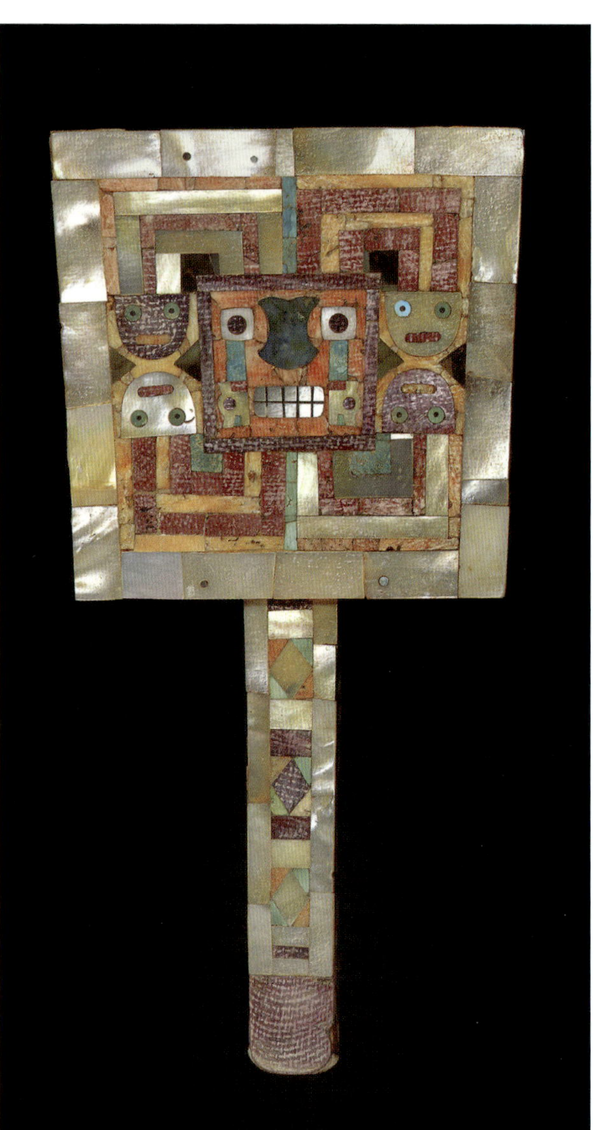

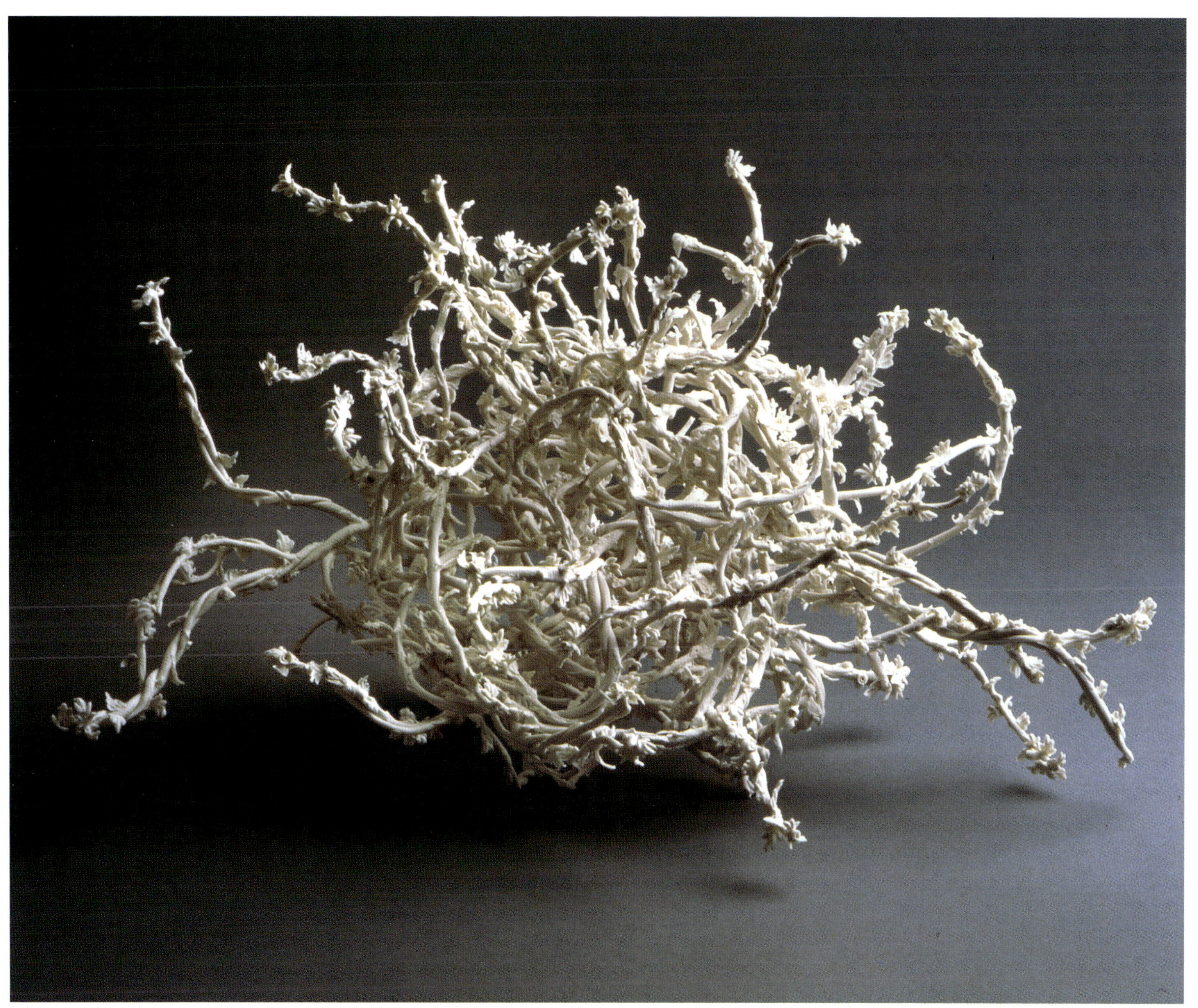

Tumbleweed, 1993 | Porcelain, 9 x 16 x 17 inches | Collection of the artist

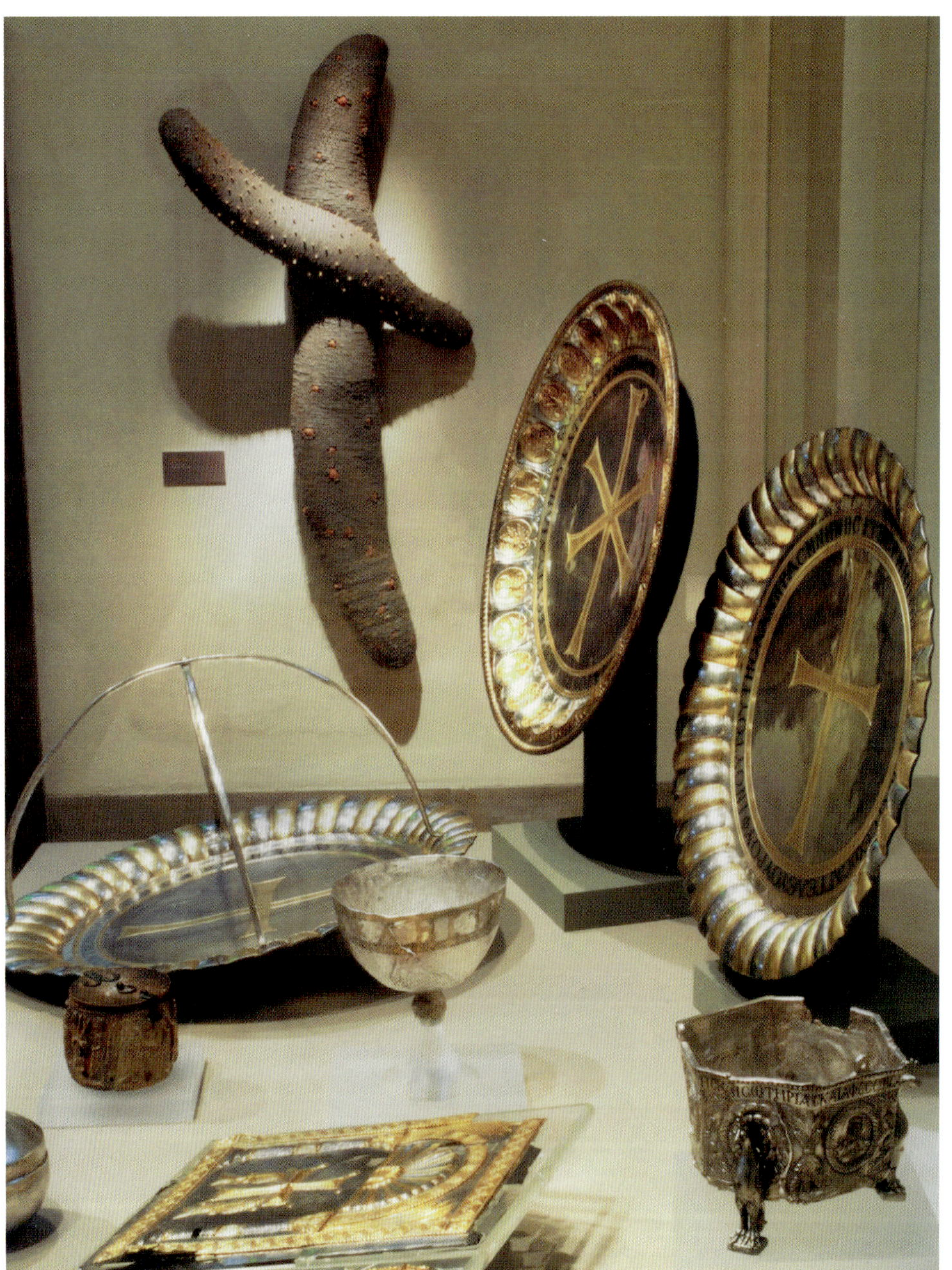

Y installed in the Byzantine gallery, Dumbarton Oaks.

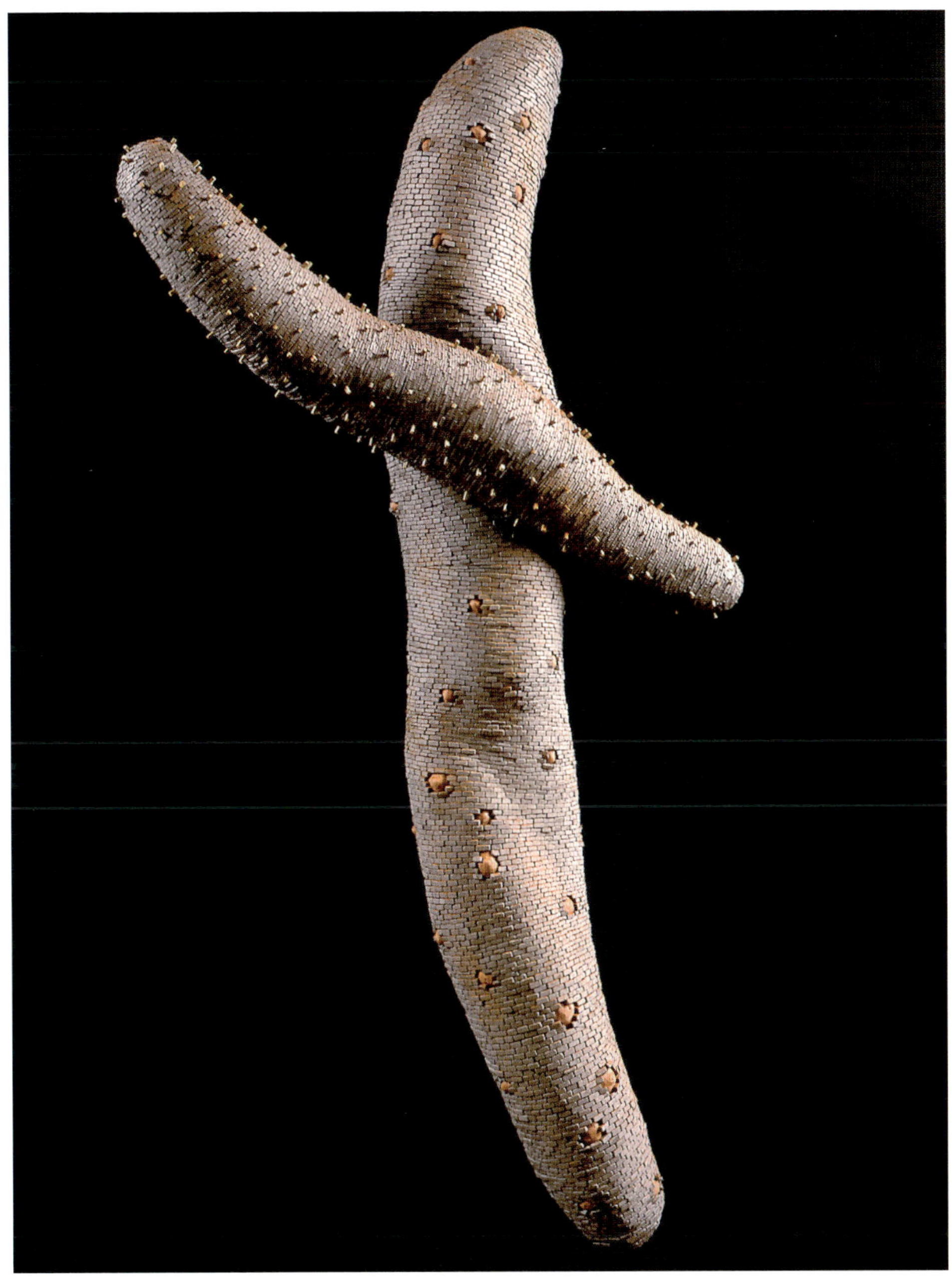

Y, 2001
Clay and plaster, 60 x 35 x 11 inches
Collection of the artist

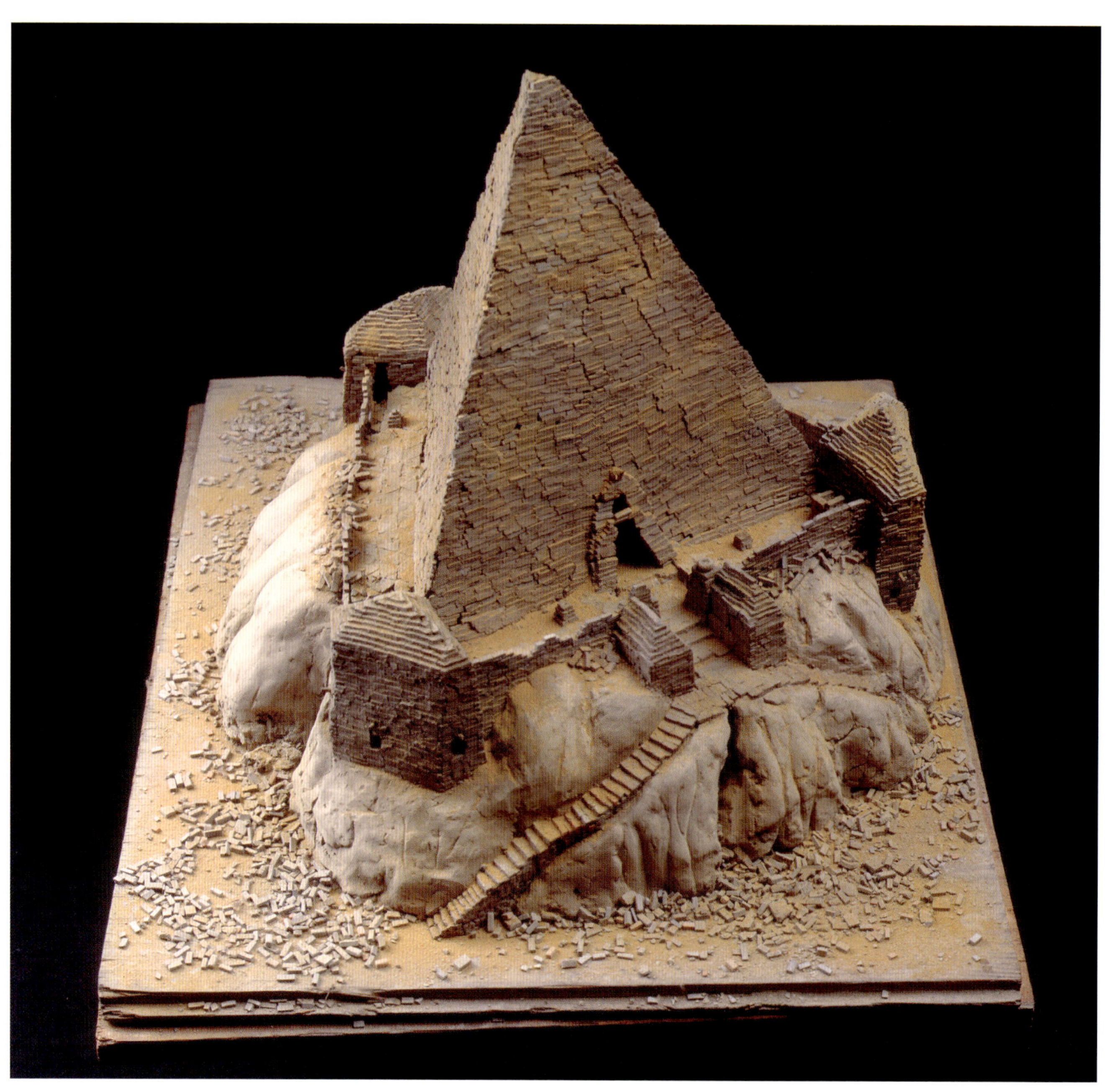

Pyramid, 1972 | Clay and wood, 15¾ x 24 x 24 inches | Private collection

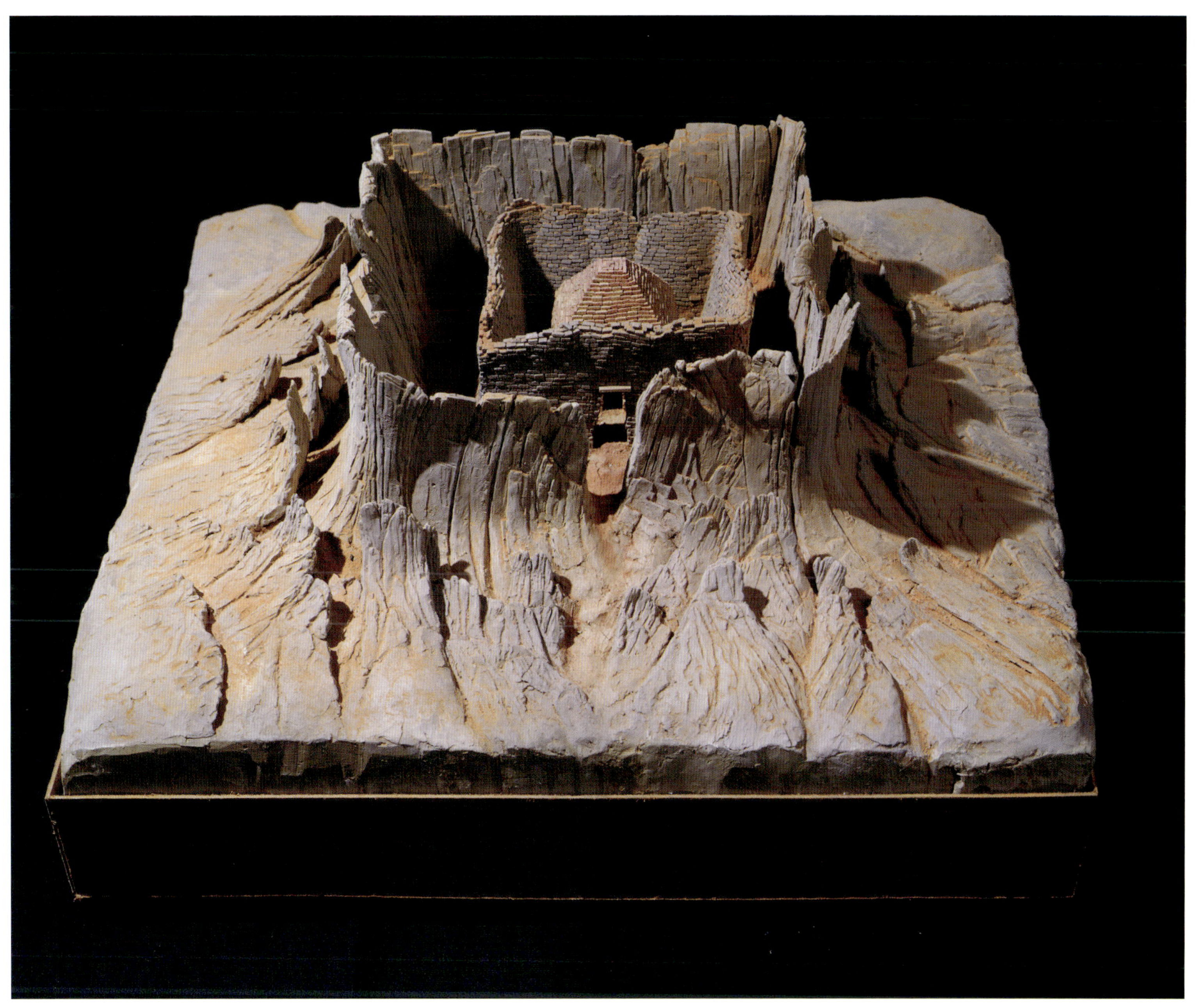

Rock Flower, 1986 | Clay and wood, 10 x 24 x 24 inches
Hirshhorn Museum and Sculpture Garden, Smithsonian Institution, Museum Purchase, 1999

Top: Photomontages by the artist of imaginary playlots that suggest analogies between the body and landscape (1973)

Center: *Stugg* installed on the Fountain Terrace in the Dumbarton Oaks Gardens.

Bottom left: *Stump* (1984, clay and wood, 15 x 24 x 24 inches, collection of the artist); bottom center: Simonds's photograph of a blossom at the botanical garden in Berlin (1978); bottom right: Simonds's photograph of Antoni Gaudí's *Basilica de la Sagrada Família*, Barcelona (begun 1882).

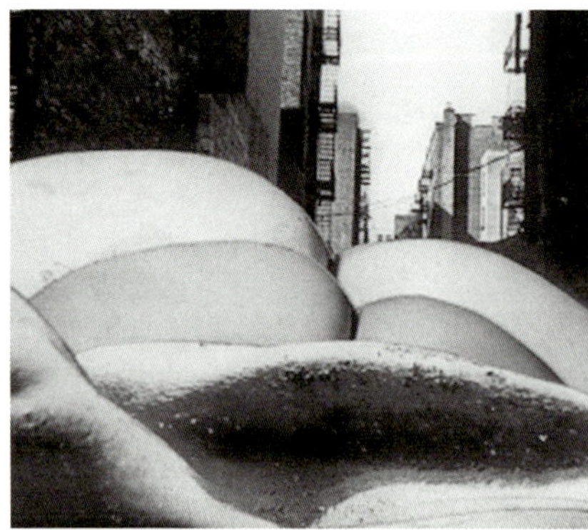

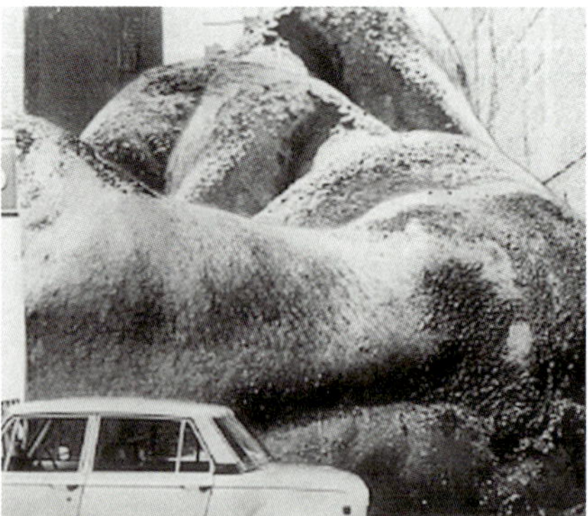

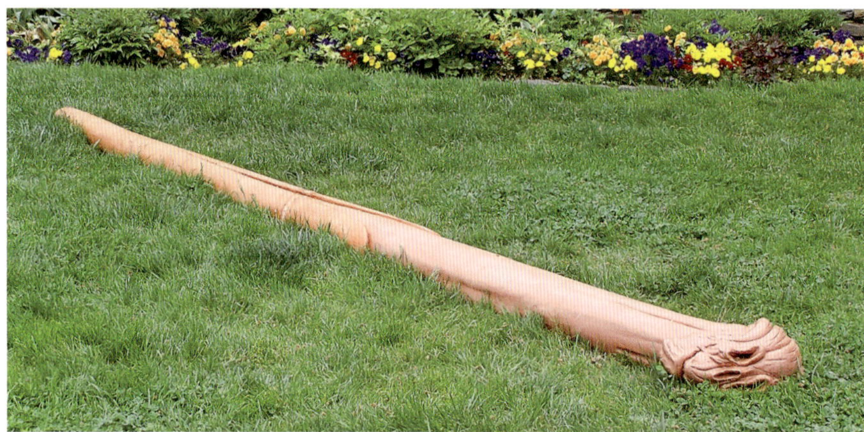

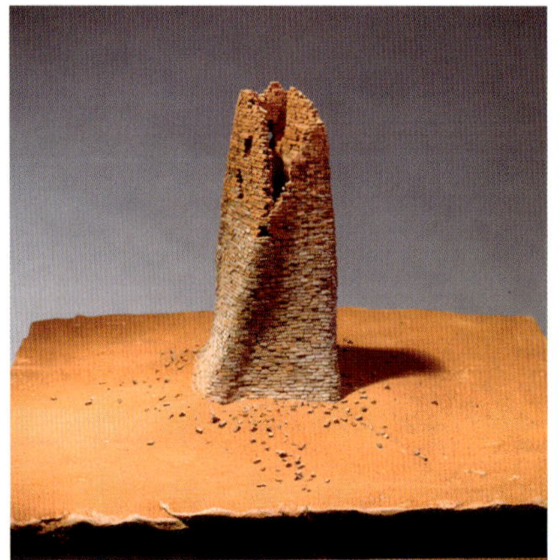

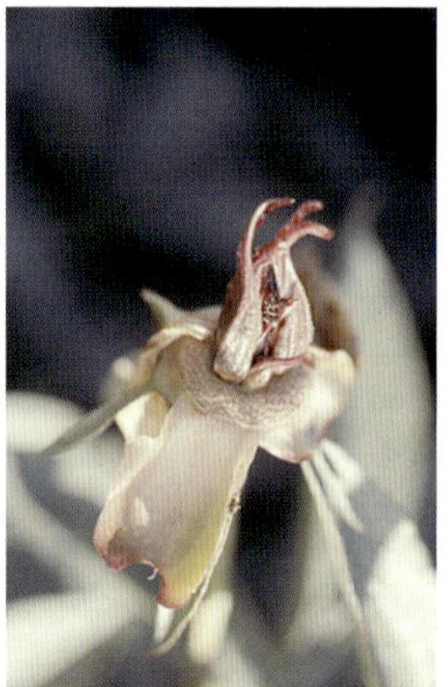

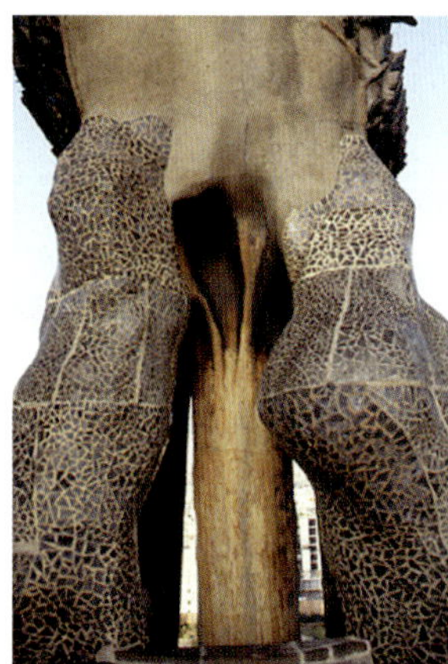

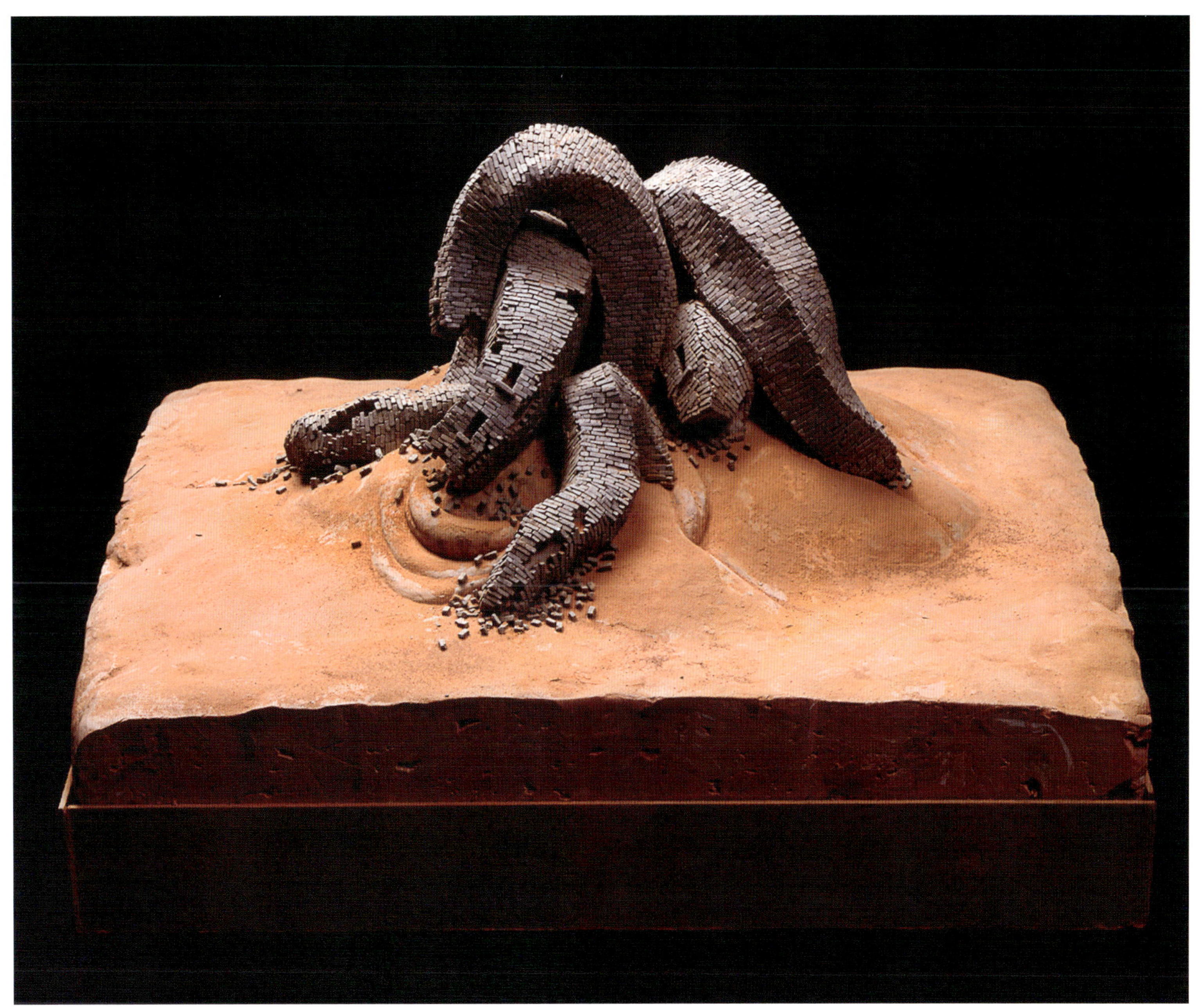

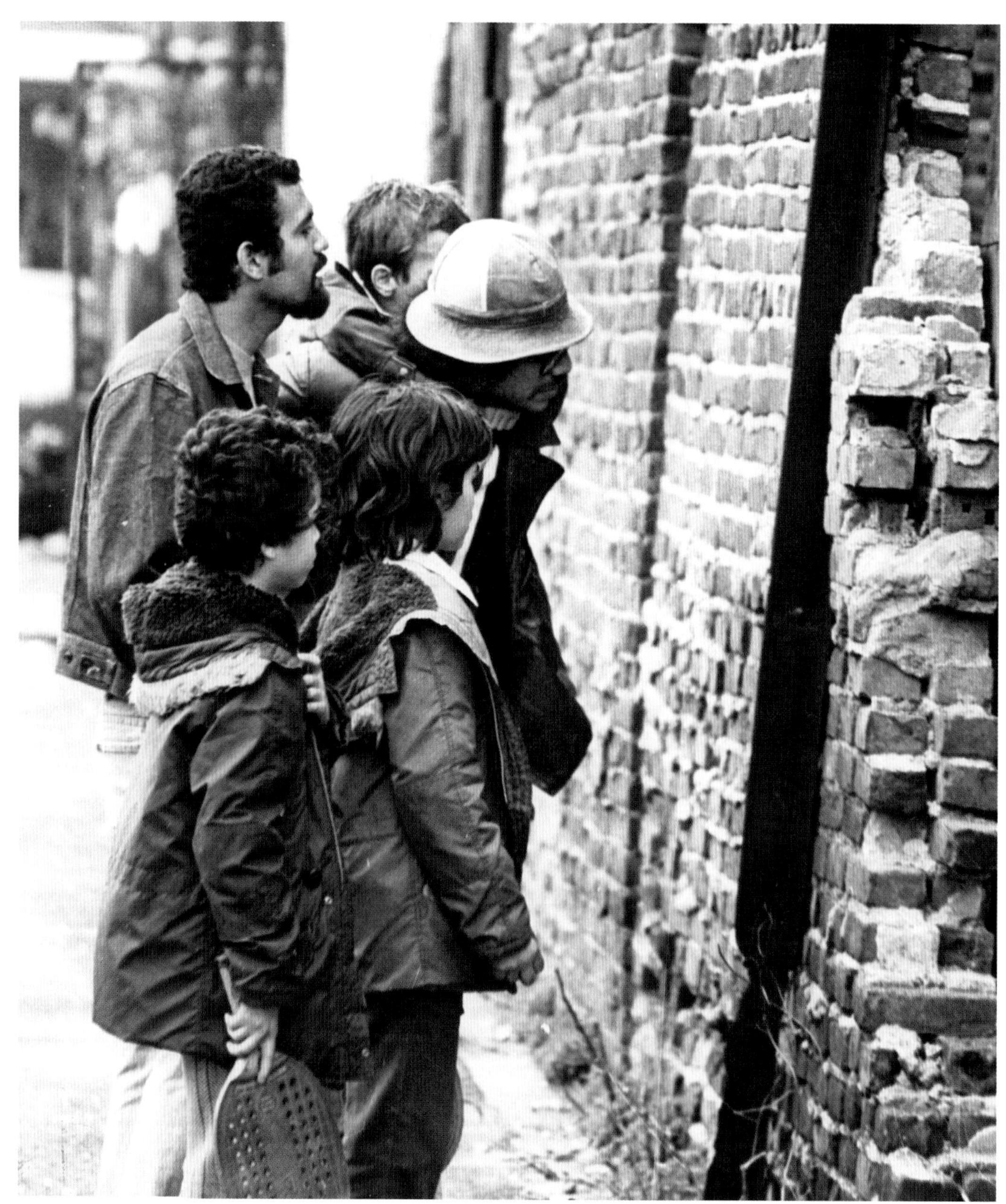

A Nomad in the City

Germano Celant

When Charles Simonds embarked on his artistic career between 1969 and 1971, he operated in a setting that lay outside the traditional bounds of art: the street. He immediately sought to make his interventions burst from a context experienced and shared by others, by people outside of the world of art. His intention was to create art everywhere, in all kinds of settings. Ever since his first interventions in the streets of New York (1972, facing page and top right), he has managed to avoid the distortions of the pristine and aseptic space of the gallery or museum, creating works that have blended into the landscape of the city—a setting where the public is not inveigled by the communicative power of the sacred place, which makes the artistic object a separate entity; where instead the work is immersed in the chaos of life; and where the poetic and visual impulse is entrusted to its autonomous power of persuasion, without any defense. Urban space, with all of its communicative characteristics, is taken on for its centripetal force, prior to any artistic intervention.

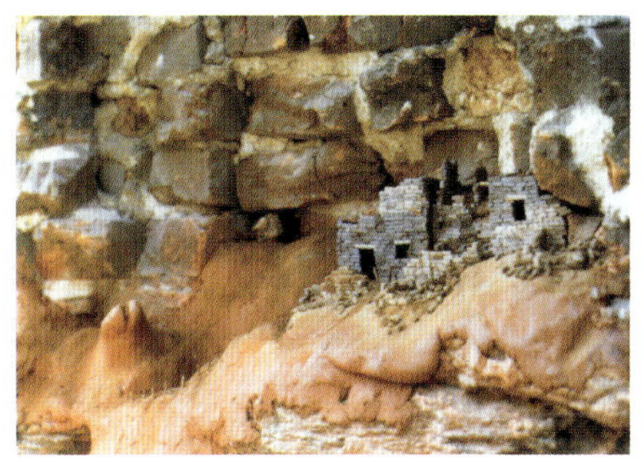

   Simonds chose the urban landscape for its tension and its secret power, which is not the repetitive power of the "white cube," but one of drama and tragedy, of magic and singularity. His choice, which he shared with artists such as Gordon Matta-Clark (bottom right), questioned the abstract and ideal dimensions of minimal art.[1] His aim was to reject the environmental homogenization of the intervention and to enter the reality of the urban and architectural configuration, thus introducing the notions of hazard, risk, and chance and plunging into real life. To understand the boldness of this move away from the lifeless event and toward a regenerative immersion into a territory where forces come from below, it is necessary to describe the minimalist tendency, with its mystical fascination with the absolute dimension of forms and materials, of lines and colors.

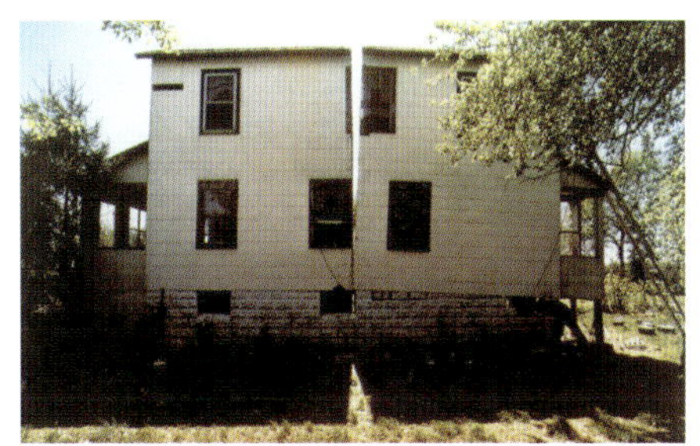

The advent of minimalism in 1963–64 marked the first attempt by artists to under-mine the idea of the object as an entity connected to the subjective impulse, typical of both nonrepresentational and figurative art after the Second World War, and to transfer it into a limited processual territory reduced to its specific terms.[2] Responding to a belief that the acquisition of personal values is fundamental to understanding the motives of the artifact, minimalism presented a technique of verification that followed the logic of construction alone. Part of this constructive procedure was the control of the whole of the environment, whether inside or outside architecture, which spurned any reference to the real and everyday context in order to determine its spatial logic operationally. While deriving from the self-evident truths of the architectural, volumetric, and superficial data, it treated them as only part of a reductive and elementary process of formation. Thus minimal research concerned the factual and primary analysis of space.

Investigation was carried out by detailing, in a logical and rational manner, con-crete entities concerning, first (in the period from 1964 to 1969), the location of the works of art, and later, the structure of the setting itself, understood as a place with four walls, a floor, and a ceiling. The definition and practical enumeration of the volume, color, surface and support, and material and process of construction led to the cognitive formulation of a series of fundamentally aniconic settings. In a period still dominated by the chaotic assemblage and the free gesture, as well as by the pop use of imagery, the minimal art-ists—whether sculptors or painters—rehabilitated a rigorous formalism, impersonal simplicity, and tightly controlled technique. Their adoption of formalism and their reductive attitude shifted the focus from what was made and found to the construction and forma-tion of an object, while their choice of simple and monolithic forms was a move away from the haphazard fragmentation of their surroundings.

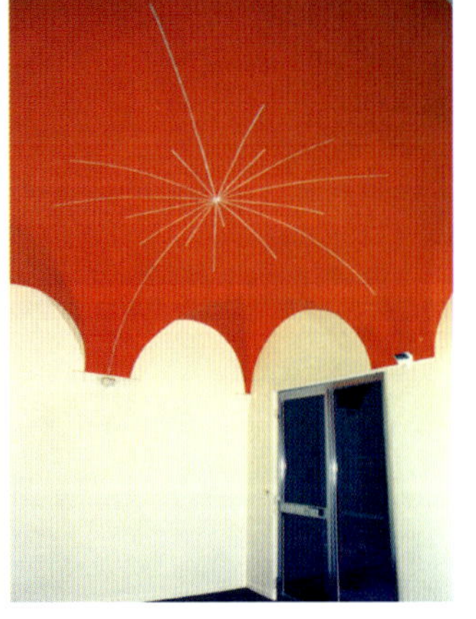

The move from symbolic and metaphorical composites to constructive ingredients and from complex results to elementary entities was inspired by the ideas of John Dewey and Ludwig Wittgenstein, who applied empirical and logical methods instead of romantic and abstractly irrational ones. The analytical tendency of minimal art coincided substantially with empiricist tendencies, restricting its investigations to observable facts and to the rela-tion among those facts. For the minimalists, the only way to intervene in the material was to consider it from the perspective of quantitative measurement and logical structuring. This structural reading takes into consideration the possible linguistic "intersections" of the indi-vidual setting and the systems of subdivision and partition, which are determined by its own two- and three-dimensional characteristics, and applies them to the given space, so that every spatial or artistic practice has to be studied in situ. The minimalists sought a greater critical awareness of the phenomenon of the "environment" seen as a monolithic whole. Between 1967 and 1970, the environment was defined through a series of new terms, which established an equivalence of significance between architectural structures and artistic compositions. This procedure is illustrated by works set in environments by Dan Flavin, Carl Andre, Donald Judd, Sol LeWitt (installation at Saman Gallery, Genoa, 1975, facing page), and Richard Serra in the United States and Daniel Buren (installation at Galleria Apollinaire, Milan 1968, top right) and Blinky Palermo in Europe. Alternately, the definition was established with descriptive enunciations of environmental structures already in use. Examples of this practice, which is based on the tautology between artistic intervention and the factual truth of the architectural space, are provided by the creations of Michael Asher, Robert Irwin, James Turrell, Doug Wheeler, Bruce Nauman, Eric Orr, and Maria Nordman.

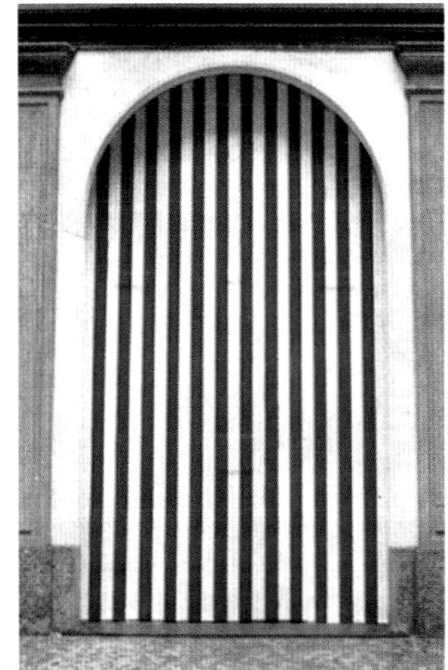

It was into this climate of research that Simonds entered, understanding, in part after his encounter with Christo, that art is not a free zone, an antagonistic space wedged into the social organism, an almost magical hollow, or a limbo that grows out of and feeds on "another" breath, as proposed by minimal art. Rather, art is something that concerns a total spectacle of life and that avoids the absolute and virtual space in order to come into direct contact with a more real reality. It is a coming into the world that starts in the bowels of the earth, as exemplified in *Birth* (1970) and *Landscape/Body/Dwelling* (1973, right). These works are permeated by a passion for location and by an energy and force of gravity that nails the artifact (the artfully made object) to the ground. The birth, in order to take place, has to emerge from the womb of a specific place; it formulates an attitude that avoids the inhuman, that is, technological and scientific, sources of minimalism.

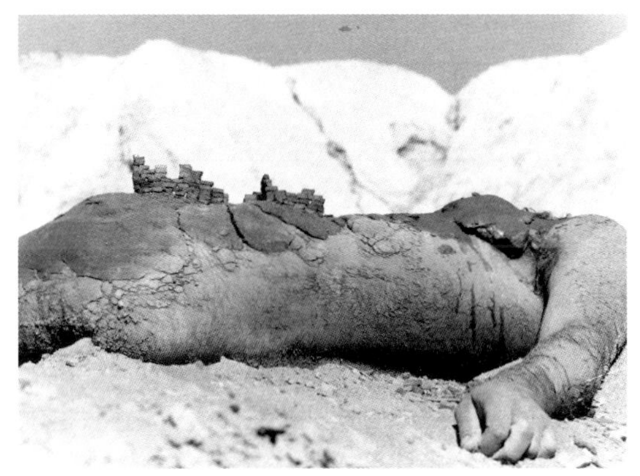

When an artist is invited by a museum or an institution to exhibit one of his works, he is provided with a series of "prepackaged" settings and times whose meanings are complex and varied—they are metasigns of the artistic sociocultural system. Normally he neither questions nor considers them; he passively and simply places and arranges within them a number of aesthetic and linguistic fillings, often of an architectural character. He displays his work in accordance with the prearranged grids and, even if he alters the microstructures of the artistic object with minimal variation, he does not disrupt or question the generalized and approved macrostructures of the given spaces and times. Only Daniel Buren in France and Michael Asher in California—who were conscious that it was not just the theory and practice of art that organized and produced linguistic modifications in its context, but also the plane of the environmental and temporal arrangement and location of the work—rejected the passive role and proposed a process that, utilizing spaces and times (although in an altered sense), brought into question the prefigurations imposed by the art system as a social and cultural, as well as ideological, framework.

They systematically refused to submit to configured environmental schemes and temporal processes. Instead of passively accepting an operative vision and practice that had been shaped over the years by exhibition venues, these artists cut down every established environmental system, breaking it to continually weaken the constituted norms and to leave room for alternative uses. The breakup was achieved by making the relationship between the environmental structures and the variations of forms and sequences dialectical, so that they could circularly impose their logic on the preexistent architectural configurations. In this way, in relation to the different architectural and chronological conditions, a preestablished definition of the work of art cannot exist. Each intervention and location is dialectical. Unlike the disintegrating hypotheses and practices, they occupy an environmental space and a time, but are simultaneously occupied and determined by them.

Since 1969, Simonds has also made his action hold a dialogue with context. But his action is not projected onto the traditional system of art—the museums and galleries, with their ascetic and metaphysical approach that negates the desire to interact with the real and the everyday. From 1971 onward, he opted instead for the jagged landscape and the urban ruin, starting with the Lower East Side in New York, a tragic and ruinous theatrical setting where life was scarred by violence and poverty. Here the artist entered into dialogue with the worn and flaking walls of decrepit buildings, with their walled and neglected gardens. He made reference, with his imaginary civilization of Little People, to the kids of East Houston Street, and he tried to communicate to everyone the unprecedented and magical character of his microconstructions of villages and houses, which were the quintessence of and a metaphor for a nomadism that also defined the artist himself. And while he has continued to create sculptural "islands" on which he erects fantastic buildings, his action has always been centered on the street. In 1975, he infiltrated areas of Genoa with bad reputations as haunts of prostitution, while in Paris he marked his passage onto the decaying scene of the Passage Julien Lacroix and the Rue des Cascades.

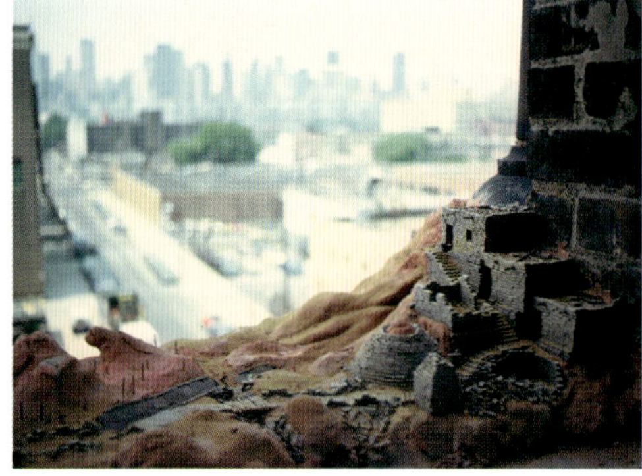

He has also ventured into the American landscape, erecting several dwellings and a *Growth House* (page 19) at Artpark in Lewiston, New York, in 1974, and agreeing (though only rarely) to make use of the environmental panorama offered by museums and institutions such as PS1, Long Island City (left), or the Whitney Museum of American Art, New York, in 1975. While doing so, however, he tried to break out of the traditional exhibition scene. He displayed

the constructive energy of his Little People on an open part of the terrace at PS1, and he found
a way of emphasizing their nomadism by locating their dwellings in a recess of the inner stair-
case, outside the galleries, at the Whitney Museum of American Art. In 1976, at the American
Museum of Natural History, New York, he established a relationship with archaeological and
historical objects, such as models of Aztec temples, presenting the "'Linear People,' who live
in a line and leave the past behind like a museum." Alongside them were the "'Circular People,'
who live in a circle, excavating the past and rebuilding it into their present," and the "'Spiral
People,' who bury the past and use it as building material to try to make their dwelling higher."[3]
Yet the course he took was not always so official. In 1978, he went to East Berlin to create
clandestine artistic constructions, as the city was still under the control of the Russians and
the sway of a realist art, an expression of ideology and the state.

In 1981, he halted his descent into the negative and the vacuum of the city in an
attempt to construct something that was not threatened from the outside. Instead of accepting the transience and the fortuitousness of his locations, Simonds "cut" his landscape into
walls and settings, so that it no longer appeared to be a lost power but aspired to be a power
that remained. On the wall of the cafeteria—an "off space"—in the Museum of Contemporary
Art, Chicago, he created a canyon, where the architectural traces of the imaginary civilization
of the Little People became permanent; this creation marked a shift from the fleeting to the
lasting that seemed to be a metaphor for the oscillation between death and life, a coming and
going between the two. As an effort to take on the world without submitting to it—to consent
to a reappropriation of his work so as not to leave it to others or in an unknown elsewhere—
this led the artist to enrich his production of islands, on which pyramids, ritual towers,
fortresses, mazes, and wilted towers appeared. These elements were no longer related to the
desolate landscape of streets and stairways—filled with the sinister and violent, the troubled
and precarious life of the city—but embodied "organic" life. From *Priapus* (1984) to *Succulent*
(2001, right), seething energies of a markedly erotic character began to appear that condi-
tioned the bustle of the architectural movements of the Little People. Compared to the more
controlled and arid constructions of the 1970s, these dwellings seemed to have taken on new
life. Having passed through a process of settling into and interacting with the frenzied urban
scene, they now focused on themselves in order to incorporate the psychological and orgias-
tic aggregates of a different way of being in the world. From *Pod No. 1* and *Pod No. 2* (1984) to
House Plant No. 1 and *House Plant No. 2* (1998), erotic exultation became manifest. Inner drives
were reflected, as fertilizing forces, in the articulation of the architecture, and the plunge into
the sensual and sexual evoked a vortex that permeated the fabulous life of the Little People.

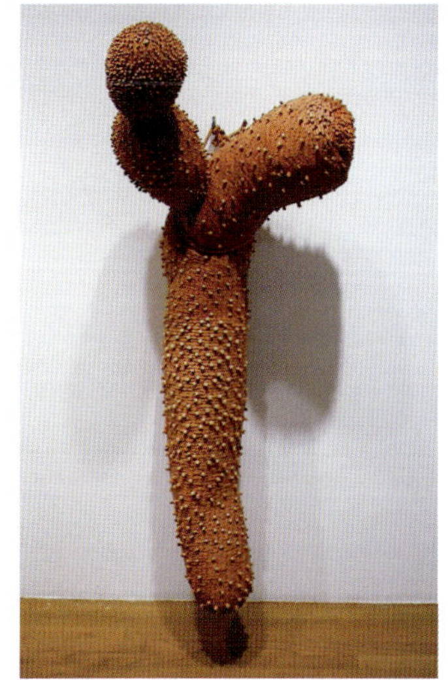

Simonds does not oppose his practice to the tradition of sculpture in a simplistic manner, but cultivates it with the idea of a living and mobile mode of action that contrasts with the inactivity and immobility of objects produced as art. His work draws its life from the pneuma of the setting and the animating power of the location, as can be sensed from the fact that his dwellings have a lifetime related to the social life of the city. Far from forming absolute and eternal entities, his constructions are linked to the flow of public reactions to them. Sometimes defended and preserved by locals and sometimes obliterated by locals because of their desire to possess them, the dwellings register both an attraction to magic and a yearning to destroy.

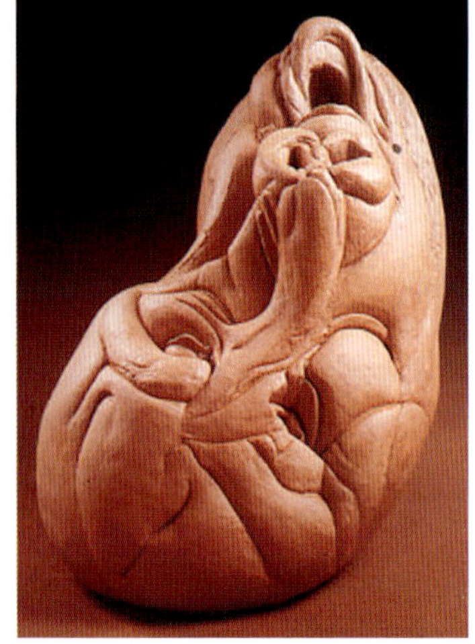

In both cases, the public brought the constructions to life. If this was an essential part of the practice of art, then it was inevitable that Simonds would make his architectures breathe by giving them a carnal and a human dimension. Starting with *Head* (1991), *Singing Monkey* (1991, top left), *Head (from I, Thou)* (1993), and *Man and Fish* (1993), he transformed clay into flesh, crammed with portions of body, head, and mouth and congealed to frame a movement of dance and contortion. This phase no longer dissociated the presence/absence of the bodies of the Little People, but gave them concrete form in landscape and architecture. In 1995, he eliminated the double of the artifact so as to let the public speak and express themselves. At the Centre d'Étude de l'Expression, Clinique des Maladies Mentales et de l'Encéphale in the Centre Hospitalier Sainte-Anne, Paris, the artist created a sculpture in collaboration with the patients, jointly constructing a sort of clay "cake" with imaginary figures (bottom left). It was another way of holding a dialogue and bringing art into life, thereby obtaining an identity that was neither fictitious nor unfounded, but rather linked to the flow of a different energy that found power in its larval character.

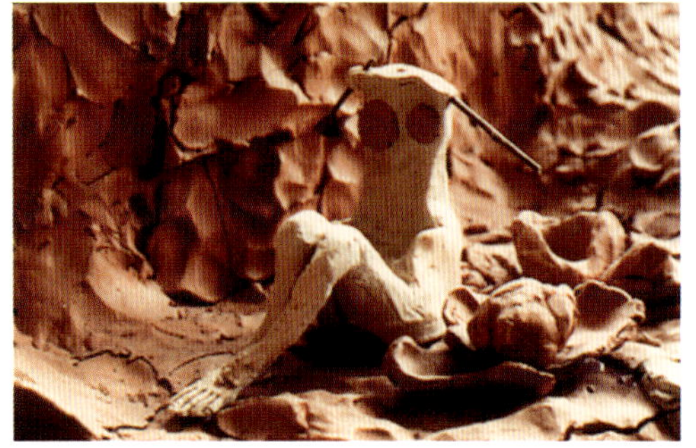

In rejecting the false reality of art, Simonds passed through the threshold—be it a school, a city, a hospital, or a park—that the nomad crosses to enter the world. His work relied on the pact of mutual involvement that was established in the interval between the two territories and environments. In the new landscape that was opened up to the gaze, it is not hard to see the mixing and interweaving. Everywhere fragments of constructions and mountains, of panoramas and valleys, of dismembered organs and figures, of rocks and plants form extensions, flames, and eruptions that spurt from the ground and wall. They are stalactites and stalagmites—dispersions of a curious ambivalence formed out of love and sensuality as well as rigidity and aggressiveness—that pour out of their settings, rending the air and space. Swollen and protuberant islands, sparkling with their structural and natural-istic details, they work their way into houses and rooms, museums and galleries, to present themselves as combinations of the volatile and fixed, as places that are magnets for energy and the gaze (top right).

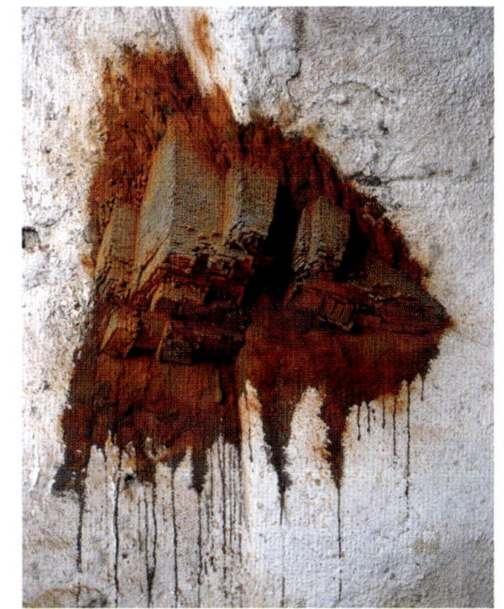

By connecting with various real contexts, Simonds counters the unreality of art, seen as an illusory and fictitious entity with no aspiration to establishing a relationship with the circumstances and situations in which it finds itself operating. He continually gets in direct touch, without mediations and without filters, with the concrete and sociocultural entities of a place. As a consequence, his response has always been to take a stand with regard to the given situation—often doing so outside of the traditional art world. Frequently risking the solitude and isolation that stem from an independent operation that does not pass through the gallery and the art market, the artist is almost always attracted not by the display of his works but by their integration into a specific context that is not the "white cube." Thus, when invited to present his work at Dumbarton Oaks, he had to deal with its history and its character as a museum—as a splendid historical complex with grounds laid out by Beatrix Farrand, with nineteenth-century buildings standing alongside a modern structure by Philip Johnson, and with collections of Pre-Columbian and Byzantine artifacts and an extremely important library of rare and antique books.

As in his other interventions in situ, Simonds tried to communicate directly with the cultural and social character of this prestigious location, developing angles of approach in such a way that his work was perceived as an element unified with the buildings and their natural settings. He sought this connection so that his art would not appear as separate and different, but as a full participant in the historic complex of Dumbarton Oaks. He did not iso-late himself, but worked in a location that—owing to its character as a "nomadic" complex, spread out in time and space—seems to have been deliberately created for his sculpture. The result was that his installation shared in the conditions of existence of the architec-tural and natural ensemble, and the two never stopped echoing and responding to one another. The artist, in fact, looked for a correspondence between his figures and the forms hidden among the lawns, hedges, fountains, paths, and flowers; he inserted himself with the urban articulations of the Little People into the real topography of the environmental routes. He made his work the meeting place from which to read the visible and invisible of Dumbarton Oaks in a different way. He revealed the coincidences and intersections of signs and images inscribed in the collections and in his sculpture. All of this turned into a fusion that, in the Orangery, took the form of *Mental Earth* (bottom right), a climbing sculpture that

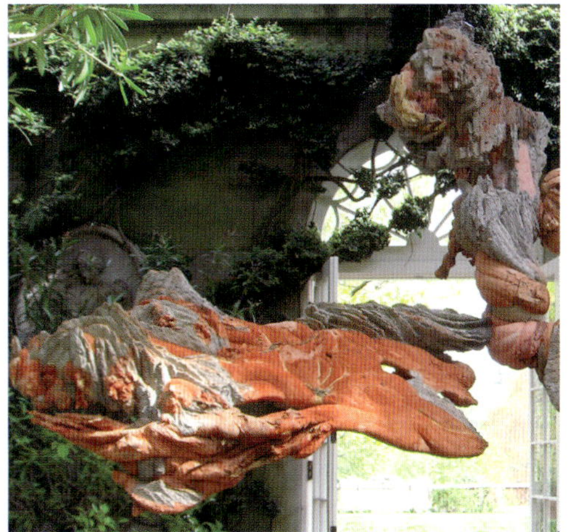

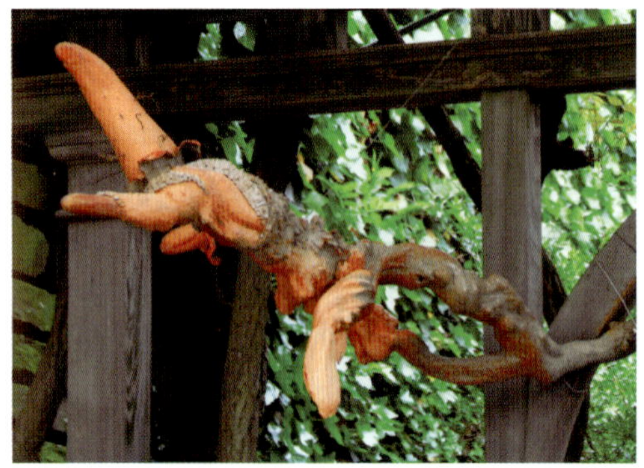

blended into the plants and creepers growing inside the conservatory. Like a cloud of mist that floated, poised in the air, without touching any of the walls, it mixed up their reciprocal textures. An airy architecture in which faces and masks, pieces of body and architecture, were merged, it was a sort of "dream material" that created a tension between natural and artificial, as it seemed to tackle the discontinuity between nature and the imaginary activity of the Little People, who are also a metaphor for human civilization. This process of osmosis was repeated with *Growth* (top left) in the wisteria arbor, where the flows of the branches of the old vine found an extension in the mixture of nodes and joints, the mixture of plant and architecture, with which Simonds sought to demonstrate that the coexistence of art and nature is possible, without either predominating over the other. Then the dwellings became acts of a singular anthropology of inhabitation. They strolled about in the ramified city and consented to contamination by the ancient and profound branches of the vine. It was a way of treating nature as if human beings and landscape were one and the same, forming a new whole that represented a new civilization.

Locating the sculptures on the grass or on branches was also a way of neutralizing the narcissism of the artist, whose presence disappeared in order to propose again a full condition of creativity, between the natural and the artificial. In this sense, a walk around Dumbarton Oaks was also an exploration of an alternative vision of its existence—one that was not only historical, but contemporary. It could be said that Simonds set out to give the place an anthropomorphic connotation in order to construct a human image of it, so that its physiognomy would assume the character of a body in flesh and blood. In addition, by scattering figures with a ruddy surface that had organic connotations—such as *Stugg* (1991, bottom left), on the Fountain Terrace, with its almost sexual coupling of petals, body, and head, itself a mixture of mask, phantom, and goat's head—the artist invited an almost erotic interpretation of the water and the fountain, turning the garden into a territory of desire. Elsewhere, he introduced a grim and menacing presence into the route through the garden by having a head peep out unexpectedly from the bushes in the Rose Terrace (facing page, top); he uncovered the gloomy nature of the place, which is revealed to be the location of a cemetery where the ashes of the Blisses (the creators of Dumbarton Oaks) are buried. By making the real world of Dumbarton Oaks and the imaginary world of the Little People coexist, the artist misdirected the traditional systems of perception and made the environment poetic, relating it to a different civilization of dream and thought.

But the quest for a correspondence between the imagery of the place and the artist's sculptural interventions (which were linked to his "conquest" of Dumbarton Oaks) has a

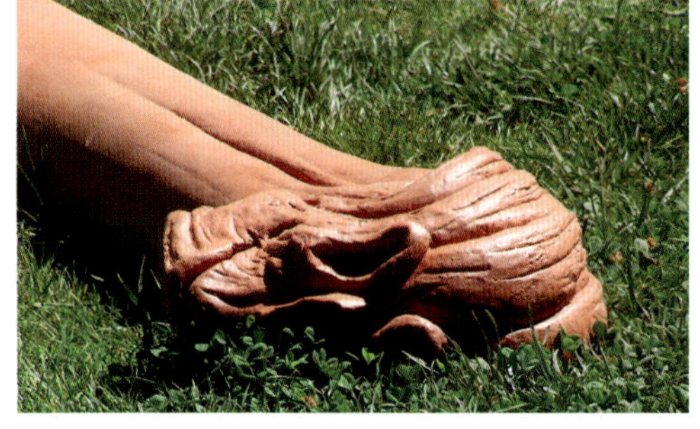

mirrorlike effect. When exploring the museum's architecture and rich collections, Simonds's gaze inevitably fell on archaeological objects of Pre-Columbian cultures (from the Maya to the Aztecs), on Christian jewelry, and on Byzantine mosaics. This led him to examine the similarities between his action and a range of iconic histories, discovering complexities that opened up unexpected and surprising analogies and relationships that are not immediately decipherable. The artist assembled them in a cabinet of curiosities—a series of display cases in which he juxtaposed postcards, artifacts, small sculptures, catalogues, and copies of illustrations from old books that he collected over the course of his career. The cabinet of curiosities was another "situation" that opened up in front of the artist, as if it was a further territory of movement and settlement for the Little People. Only now the journey was inside the world of Charles Simonds, whose artistic life has been permanently cultural, where the traces of the present and the past are mixed up, becoming vestiges and remains, steeped in ideas and psyche, the social and the political. Entering Dumbarton Oaks was analogous to being invited to adopt a philological and iconological attitude to his own work. It was another construction of the memory of forms and figures that, though latent and unconscious, survived to become the fundamental premise of his action. His pioneering research into its singularity involved the use of a method that unconsciously followed in the footsteps of the great art historian Aby Warburg; the method entailed the construction of tables based on the iconographic interweaving of repetitive images of gestures or actions, of motifs or decorations, that, even if apparently discontinuous and anachronistic, represented a symptom of historical knowledge (bottom right). This method has been described as a "psychotechnics" of history, in which the historian becomes a seismograph and a "sensor of the pathologies of time—without distinction between the latencies and crisis—a researcher guided by scientific self-denial" (*wissenschaftliche Selbstverleugnung*), a thinker attentive to the unity of the "basic problems," a scientist alert to the specificity of individual objects.[4]

Thus, the entire course followed by Simonds can be seen as having been touched by history, as a deluge of energetic and iconic moments that form a spiral harking back to the tradition of ancient art. The various interventions and symbologies to which the Little People have had recourse are revealed to be caught up in the vortex of past civilizations, almost becoming elements of a transmission of remote polarities subjected to the metamorphosis of contemporary language. *Mental Earth* can be understood as an artificial mimesis of natural truths, as an illusionism turned on its head. It represents the revival of a "naturalism" of the visual arts, dear to the painters and sculptors of the sixteenth century, reexamined the other way round: the reemergence of a vegetable aspect through a material,

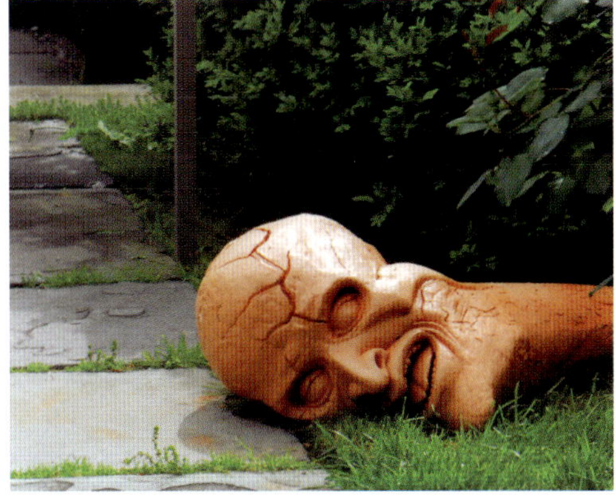

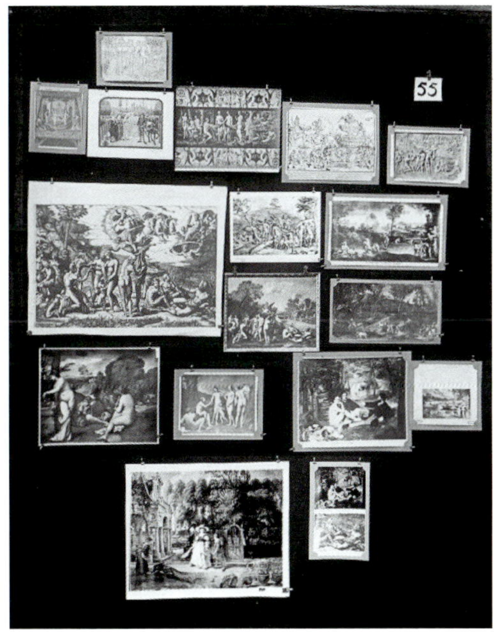

clay—a material dream. Installed in a "hut," surrounded by vines, the sculpture leads into a world of naturalness that is typical of the sixteenth-century rustic style.[5] An exaltation of sturdiness and strength, of humility and simplicity, that invites art to be less concerned with the decoration of the middle-class home, a setting that feeds the art market, and to see itself instead as a possible intervention in the context of the real and the natural, one that set out here to create a delicate balance with urban ruins and the sublime layouts of the garden. A search for equilibrium that modestly and simply considers the artistic intervention as an intellectual distillation and a metaphorical instrument of a reunion with the identity of places. In *Stugg* and *Growth*, this harmony between natural and artificial can also be seen in the coherence of the nodes and the veins, between the vine branch and the crust of the Little People's landscape, which are both pervaded by endless bumps and cracks that make explicit their origin in the same universe. They almost seem to be off-spring of the same culture—the interwoven and heavy culture of agricultural and pastoral civilization that is stifled by the advent of urban culture.

The meeting that takes place between art and nature is represented in the relationship between art and history, which finds an amalgam in the rooms of the Main House, which contains the Byzantine Collection, the Garden Library, and, in a wing designed by Philip Johnson, the Pre-Columbian Collection. Here, the artist brought together distinct realities and practices, placing his sculptures in relation to the historical artifacts or laying out in display cases the possible iconographic resemblances between his representations and the documents produced by seventeenth- and eighteenth-century artists/scientists, from Francesco Colonna to Claude Duret and Giambattista della Porta, on the themes of the similarity and the connection between nature and the human figure.

The ritual and ceremonial products of Byzantium—especially the bowls, dishes, basins, and monstrances with crosses—are associated by the artist with *Y* (2001, left). The sculpture stems from the same erotic and sensual motivations as *Head (from I, Thou)* and *Succulent*, but takes on an ambiguous connotation that connects it to the other objects on display, so that it looks like a pregnant cross whose body is covered with a mixture of blisters and small bricks in the form of cactus thorns. It seems to bring about an identity of opposites, sacred with profane, logical with illogical, male with female, becoming a sacred receptacle, almost a cathedral with a long nave and two transepts, that is brought to life by sexual potencies. A relationship with the architecture of life as well as death has been present ever since his first sculptures, including *Pyramid* (1972), which was displayed nearby.

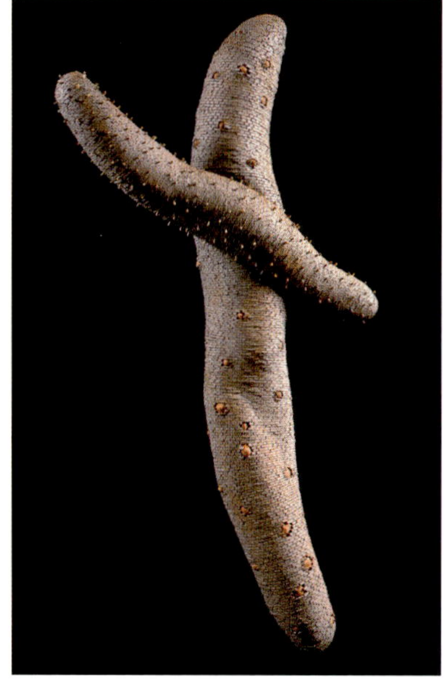

By investigating the roots of Simonds's early activity, we can sense the unearthed value of a subterranean and ritual quantum that is the lifeblood of all his production: "when this whole thing started with me, I was pretty crazy, and everything that I did was very ritualized and all the behaviors were very esoteric, very strange behaviors. Some of it I don't really need to talk about, peculiar things . . . for instance all the bricks in the beginning had my blood in them . . ."[6] The ceremony of impregnating the architecture of the Little People with his own blood is further evidence of the artist's desire to enclose his action in the space of the body, to bring art into the living core of everyday existence. Testimony to this was provided in the cabinet of curiosities, by *Brick Cutting Board* (1969, page 82), which includes a plaster cast of a relief that held a test tube of the artist's blood. The inclusion of *Brick Cutting Board* in the exhibition, as well as of blood in the bricks, is a declaration of his intent to clear his own narcissism away and to pour his energy into the underground current of an imagination that is not personal, but that belongs to the memory and the social order of a new culture—that of the Little People. It is a metaphor for his desire to give a voice to a society that is weak and fragile as well as an acknowledgment that he (the artist), with his blood, is an integral part of that society. Thus, Simonds opens his gaze to an inner eye; this brings him into tune with the exaltation of the life-giving force of the soul in Byzantine painting and decoration.

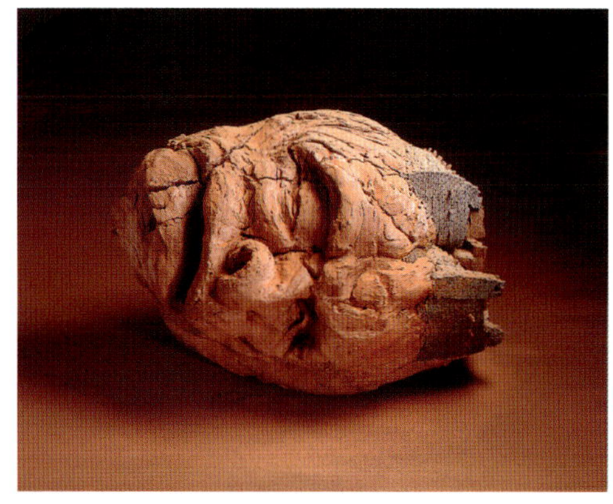

Other parallels are found with medieval culture, where it is possible to discern an affinity with the fantastic imagery of the Gothic *grylles*, composite monsters typically made up of heads or faces with multiple limbs.[7] In Simonds's work, there are many weird chimera made up of buildings and heads, human beings and animals, and genitals and landscapes, from *Ritual Garden #9* (1978) to *Head* (1993, top right), from *Priapus* to *Man and Fish*. They form tangled and interlocking entities in which architecture and details of the human body are mixed; they are created by skillfully and expertly adapting the sculptural process, always bold and surprisingly precise, to the anatomy of the living creature. The antagonistic polarities, in which, in the end, we feel the presence of Eros and Thanatos, are also reflections on the religious impulses that have left a mark on his consciousness. Consequently life, and so nature too, instant by instant, threatens to turn into the opposite. Plants are either instruments of positive "insemination" (as seen in Claude Duret, *Phalle Hollandique*, bottom right) or are fertilized by the "negative," regenerating themselves continually by visual metaphors that make them resemble—like mushrooms—sexual organs or snakes. They are, like Simonds's figures, pivots of a dialectic in which what is form or image can be plunged back into the crucible of the vital flow or of mortal opacity. This circular process is symbolized in the display cases by

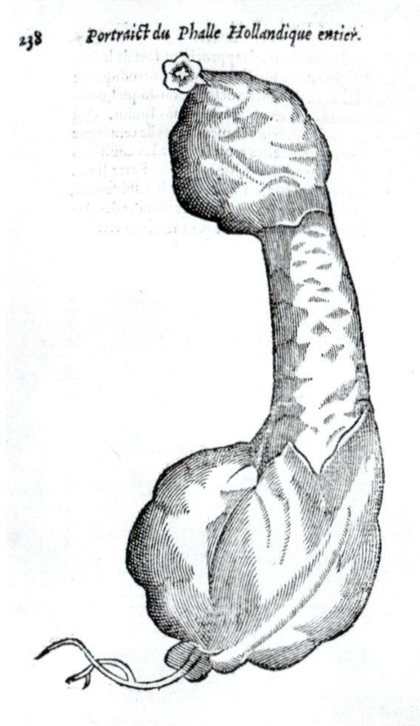

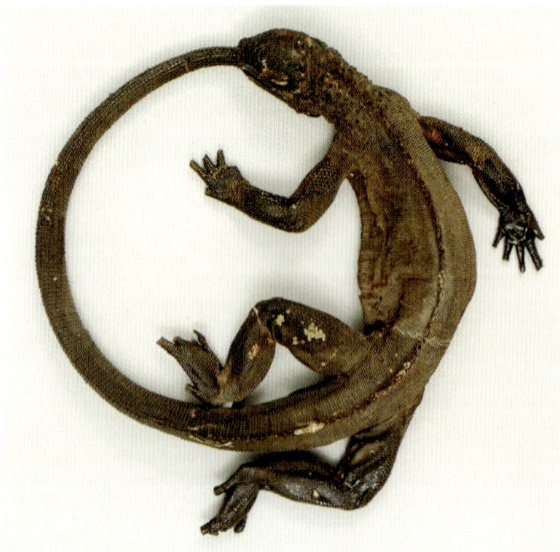

the Uroboros, the serpent of medieval iconography that bites its own tail, thus alluding to eternal return (left). In addition to representing the coupling and interlocking of figures, the symbol is an indication of a personal participation (his private life) and of the renewal and continual resurrection of the Little People.

Elsewhere it is human beings—in the person of Adam and Eve—who allow themselves to be inseminated by plants or animals, thus becoming doubles who regain possession of another truth. They are "awake" in an erotic and intellectual sense, so that the new material passes through the "door" of the male and female sexual organs as well as the head. This alchemical crossing is depicted in the fifteenth-century treatises, as well as in the books of C. G. Jung that reproduce their iconography. In this sense, if Adam, portrayed as source of both life and thought, is the founder of a new regeneration, then the Little People are symbols of the possible resurrection of our society. This vision, which lies somewhere between the alchemical and the Christian, has been present from Simonds's first work, *Birth*; it is the sign of a journey from the earthly to the radiant spirit of art: "all of a sudden I understood what I believed, about my body, who am I, where am I, what am I, and where do I fit, and at the same time all of it is aside from being now, has to do with time, has to do with being born, living and dying and it's all the same time. And it's all of a kind of birth, life, death, resurrection."[8]

The passage from one state of being to another is also linked with the surfacing of obscure and unconscious forms that are as deadly as they are fertile. Under their deluge, the artist discovers poetry and catharsis. For this reason, Simonds calls to mind the educational and emotional depth of the theoretical and behavioral studies of his mother, Anita I. Bell, who investigated the effects of the scrotal sac and the testes on the psychological development of children.[9] She established a link between the parts permeated by blood and those permeated by the mind, seeking a point of contact and relationship between the impulses that govern the body and those that govern the psychology of the adolescent. She has made an anti-Freudian crossing, with the scrotum and the unconscious exchanging roles in the child, without spilling over into impatience and into mature sexual experience. A fluidization that feeds a fire common to the whole body, and with which her son (Charles Simonds) identifies—to the point of "sculpting" a testicle, also exhibited in the cabinet of curiosities—to convey the intensity of the link between real and imaginary, natural and artificial, unconscious and conscious, mobile and fixed, spirit and matter.

Anxiety and emotions are also brought to light through the decipherment of a "dictionary" of ritual and symbolic objects that the Little People have constructed over time.

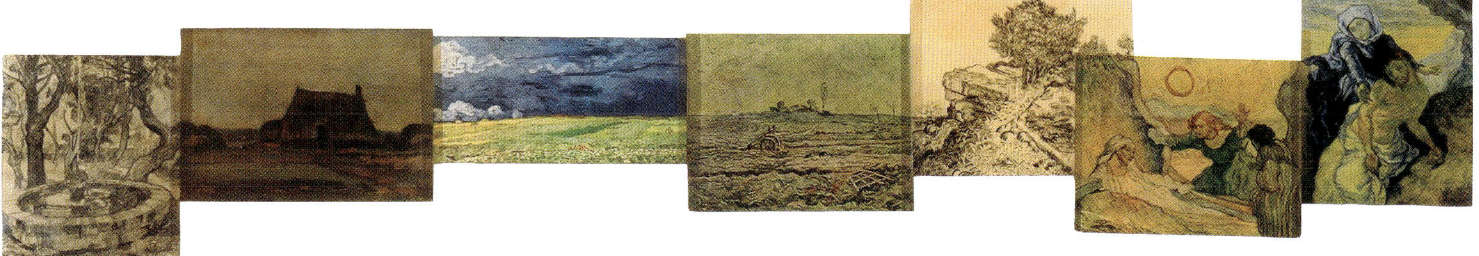

Ritual Objects (1987, page 20) is a "palette" on which appear all the "colors" of their life: "This is their world, and this is how I imagine the evolution of the objects in their world. There are knives, games with shells, sexual autoerotic items, bricks and tools." These objects speak to a continuity that is already recorded in Maya and Aztec rituals (page 32) that instilled life into the anthropomorphic or zoomorphic objects used in ceremonies and daily life. An incarnation that speaks of a demiurge "throwing into the world" the human being, who can spring from things as well as from flowers. A manifestation of the inner realm of a world that is no different from that of the child impregnated with the effects of a mingling between scrotum or testicles and torpor or sleep. The figures that are embedded in one another are the same as the ones in *Stugg* and *Untitled (Three Elements)* (1993), in which they reveal a formal or organic, figurative or abstract fullness that is indispensable nourishment for an existence.

The invisible that becomes visible, or the metaphysical that becomes physical, refers in Simonds's work to a raw material and to a depth that becomes the voice of art, an activating principle and a visual inspiration that circulate in human beings as in nature to animate both the social and the personal. In fact, the journey made through the imaginary civilization is a way of using his own creativity (or his own psychophysical capacities) to expel a flow of experiences and images that can lead to a self-discovery. This feeds on the double of art to bring out those feelings that, once transferred into dwellings, give breathing space and inspiration to other reconstructions of himself. Creating architectures and landscapes to merge with his own sap, if not his own blood, as at the beginning, he arrives at a higher edifice that feeds once again on the material of the context and represents a purified condition of the world. In this perspective, the sequence of landscapes from Monument Valley to the Dutch views of Van Gogh (above) can be reinterpreted as a flow of blazing energy that is able to liquefy, and thus to fluidize all together, through the focus of the gaze, from painting to photograph, the images of the context passed, as vagabond and as nomad, between nature and art. An alchemical transmutation, arranged in succession, that by working on base material—such as postcards—communicates the power to introject opposites that turn into unity. It is on this uninterrupted flow of energy, which appears and disappears, and which is destroyed only to be replaced by another, that the fullness of the Little People is based. Although loath to appear or to be represented, these shadows of art that refuse to yield to the power of the symbolic and the economic are a testimony to a different life: the protest of a nomadic being who, through the misleading power of his fluid and ephemeral action, is able to make the imaginary fit into any context, urban or historic, psychological or social, almost succeeding in taking the place of reality.

NOTES

1   The multiplicity of personal and cultural relationships established by Simonds from 1968 to 1973 included living in a loft on Christie Street in New York with Gordon Matta-Clark, with whom he shared a propensity for finding urban situations in which to intervene and with whom he collaborated on many projects (such as his own *Tarot Cards* and Matta-Clark's *Jacks*). This period was characterized by a range of artistic research that—from antiform to arte povera, from conceptual art to body art, and from pop art to minimalism—brought into question the linguistic and material limits of painting and sculpture. Simonds's attention to these lines of research explains his interest in the writings and exhibitions on the immateriality of art by Robert Barry, Joseph Kosuth, Lawrence Weiner, and Douglas Huebler (promoted by Seth Siegelaub); in the interventions on desert and snow-clad plains made by Michael Heizer, Robert Smithson, Walter de Maria, and Dennis Oppenheim (published in *Newsweek* in 1968); in the energetic intensifications and performances carried out by artists from Joseph Beuys to Mario Merz, from Michelangelo Pistoletto to Richard Long, and from Daniel Buren to Jannis Kounellis in Europe; and in the sensual, personal, and yielding forms of expression that were introduced by the theories of Lucy Lippard and seen in the works of Bruce Nauman, Louise Bourgeois, and Eva Hesse in the exhibition *Eccentric Abstraction*. Simonds's meeting and personal relationship with Lippard dates from 1973, when a tour of the *Dwellings* scattered through the streets of Manhattan. In the end, the awareness that it was possible to intervene in the landscape in a soft and ephemeral manner was one of the motives for the artist's reflection on the "sterility of minimalist white spaces contrasted by the excitement and life in the streets." Charles Simonds, conversation with author, 2010.

2   Here I draw on and rework the ideas on the relationship between art and environment first expressed in Germano Celant, *Ambiente/arte dal futurismo alla body art* (Venice: La Biennale di Venezia, 1977).

3   Charles Simonds, "Earth and Sanity," *International Journal of Art Therapy* 1 (1997): 8.

4   Georges Didi-Huberman, *L'image survivante: Histoire de l'art et temps des fantômes selon Aby Warburg* (Paris: Editions de Minuit, 2002).

5   Marcello Fagiolo, *Natura e artificio: L'ordine rustico, le fontane, gli automi nella cultura del manierismo europeo* (Rome: Officina Edizioni, 1979).

6   Charles Simonds, interview with author, May 2010.

7   Jurgis Baltrušaitis, *Le Moyen Age fantastique: Antiquités et exotismes dans l'art gothique* (Paris: A. Colin, 1955); and Lorraine Daston and Katharine Park, *Wonders and the Order of Nature, 1150–1750* (New York: Zone Books, 1998).

8   Charles Simonds, interview with author, May 2010.

9   Anita I. Bell, "Psychologic Implications of Scrotal Sac and Testes for the Male Child," *Clinical Pediatrics* 13 (October 1974): 838–47; and Anita I. Bell, "Male Anxiety during Sleep," *The International Journal of Psychoanalysis* 56 (1975): 455–64.

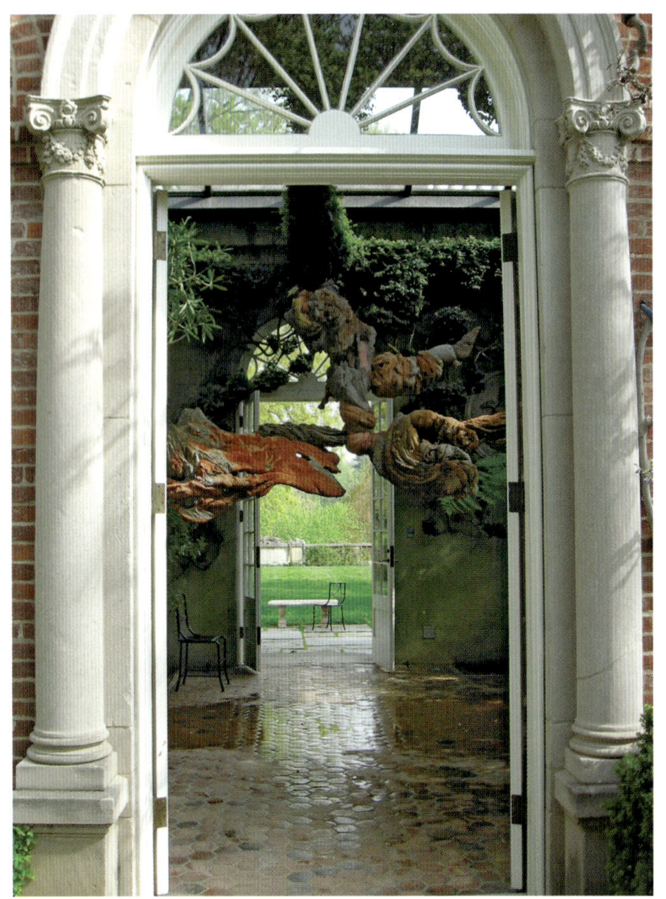 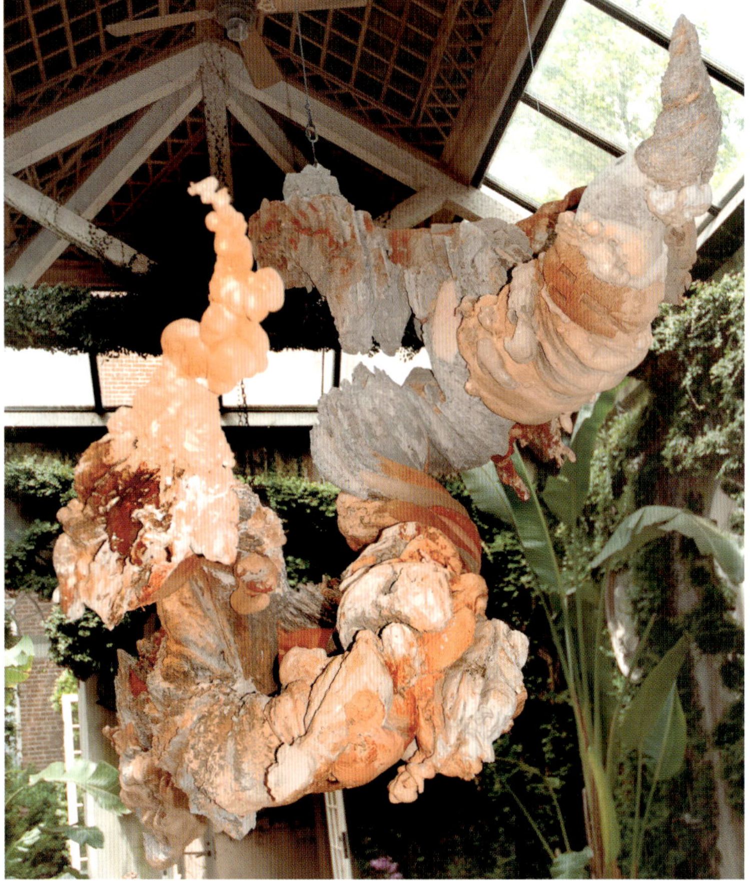

Mental Earth, 2003
Metal, polyurethane, clay, and
wood, 89 x 126 x 80 inches
Collection of the artist

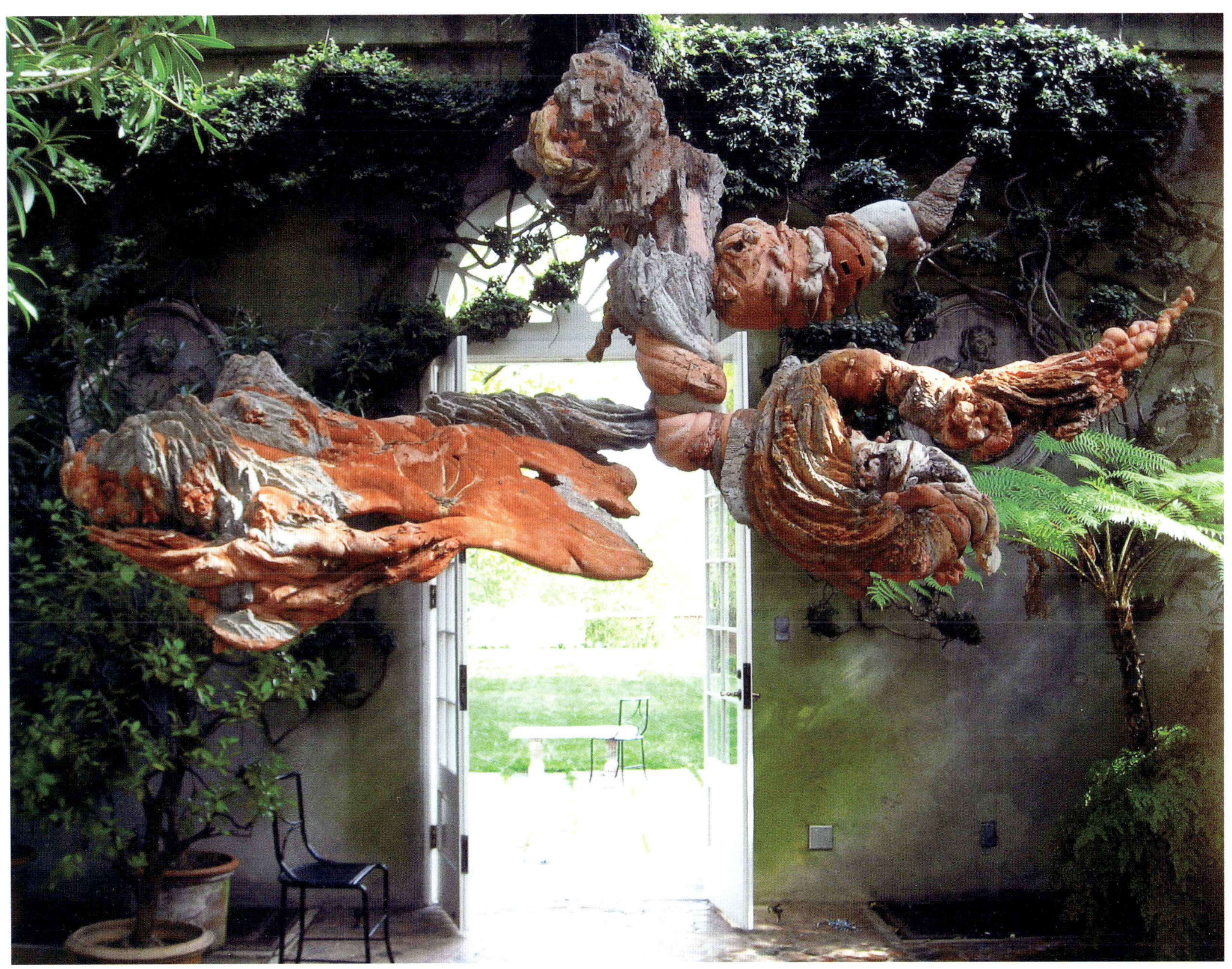

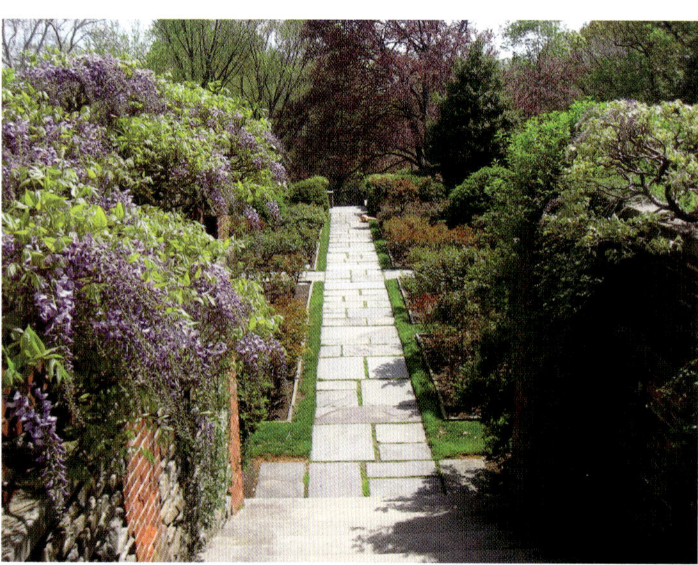

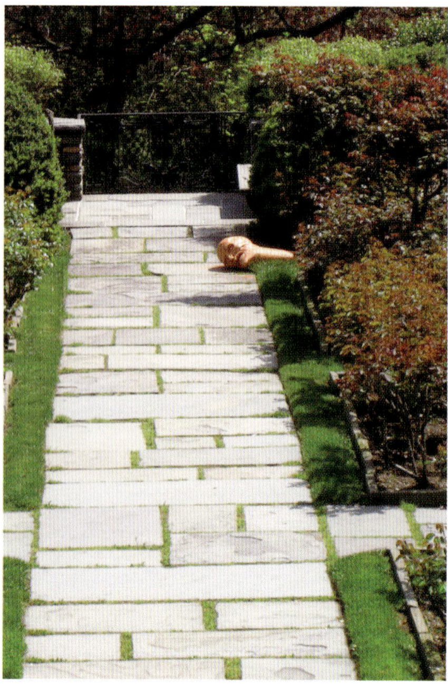

Head (from I, Thou), 1993
Clay and plaster,
10 x 34 x 20 inches
Collection of the artist

Views of the Rose Terrace
(this page) and the installation of
Head (from I, Thou) (facing page).

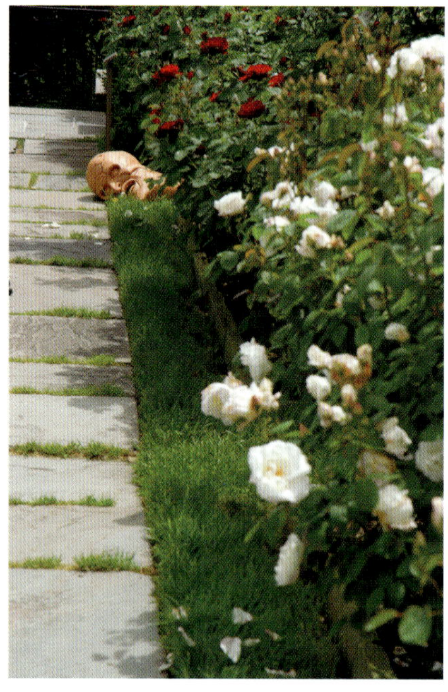

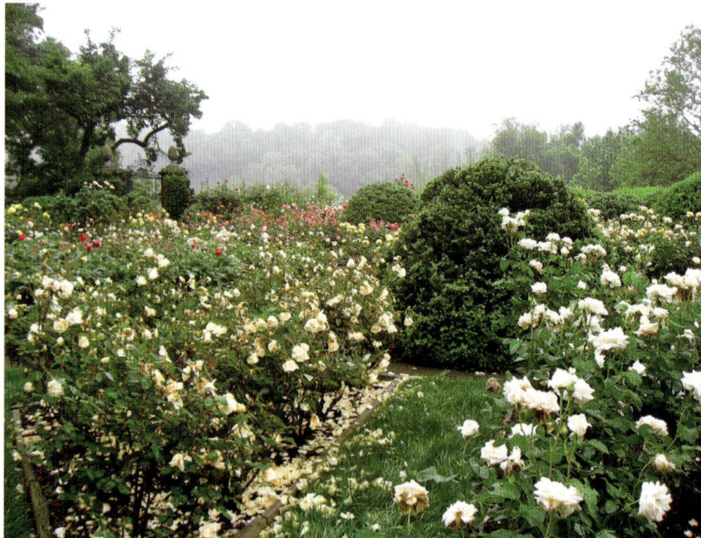

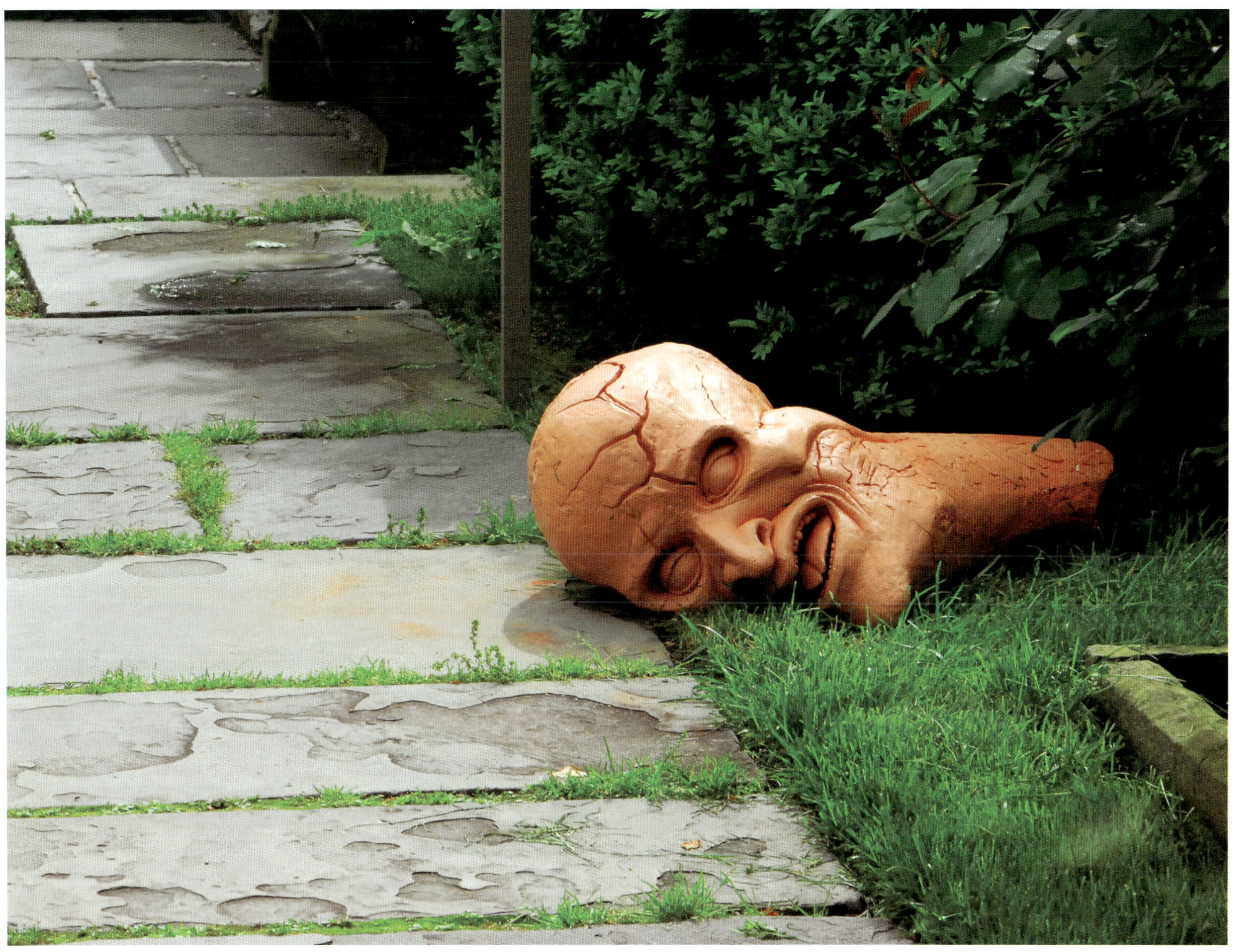

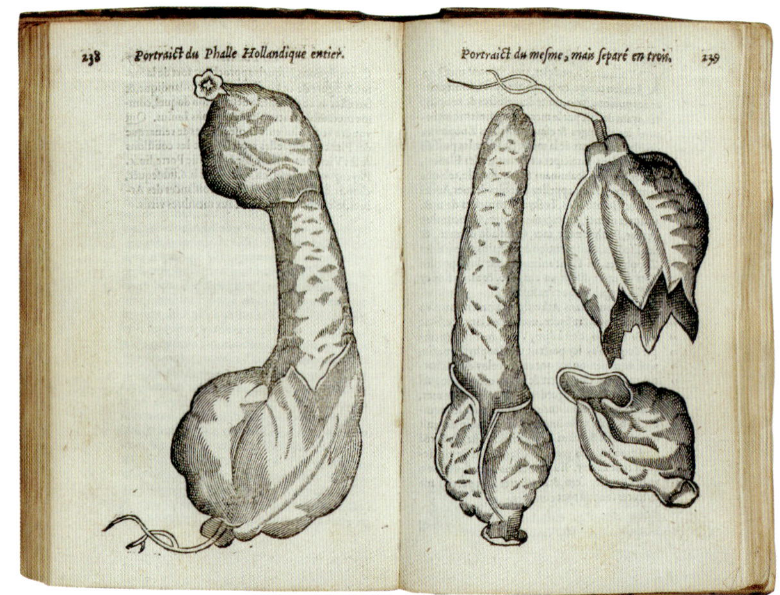

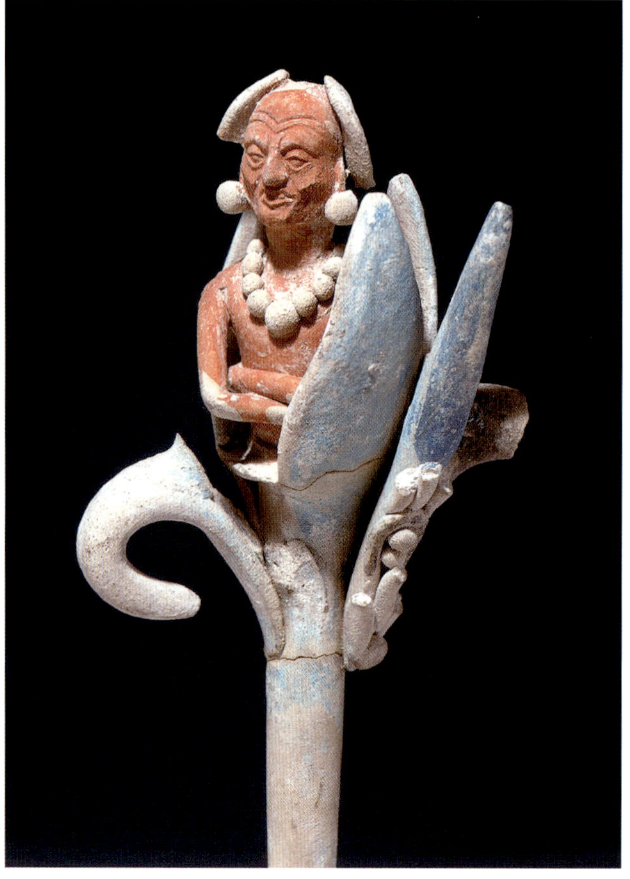

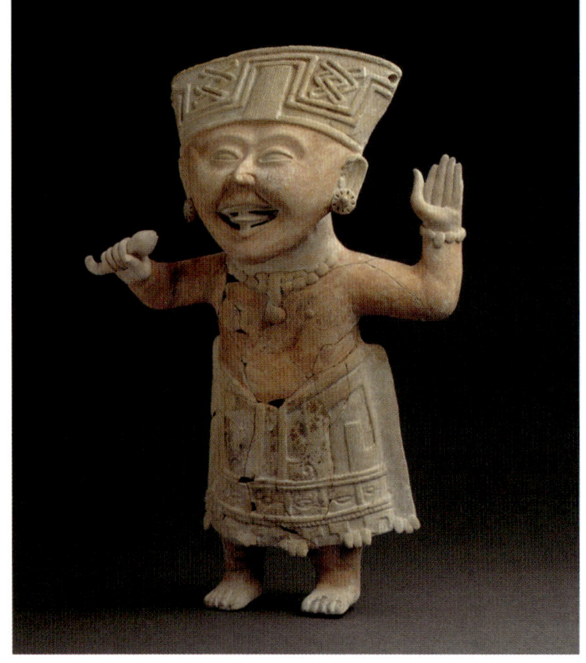

Top left: *Phalle Hollandique*, from Claude Duret, *Histoire admirable des plantes et herbes esmerueillables & miraculeuses en nature* (Paris: Chez Nicholas Bvon, 1605); top right: Maya Jaina-style whistle, 600–900 CE, ceramic with red, blue, and black paint; bottom left: Remojadas "Smiling" Figure, 600–800 CE.

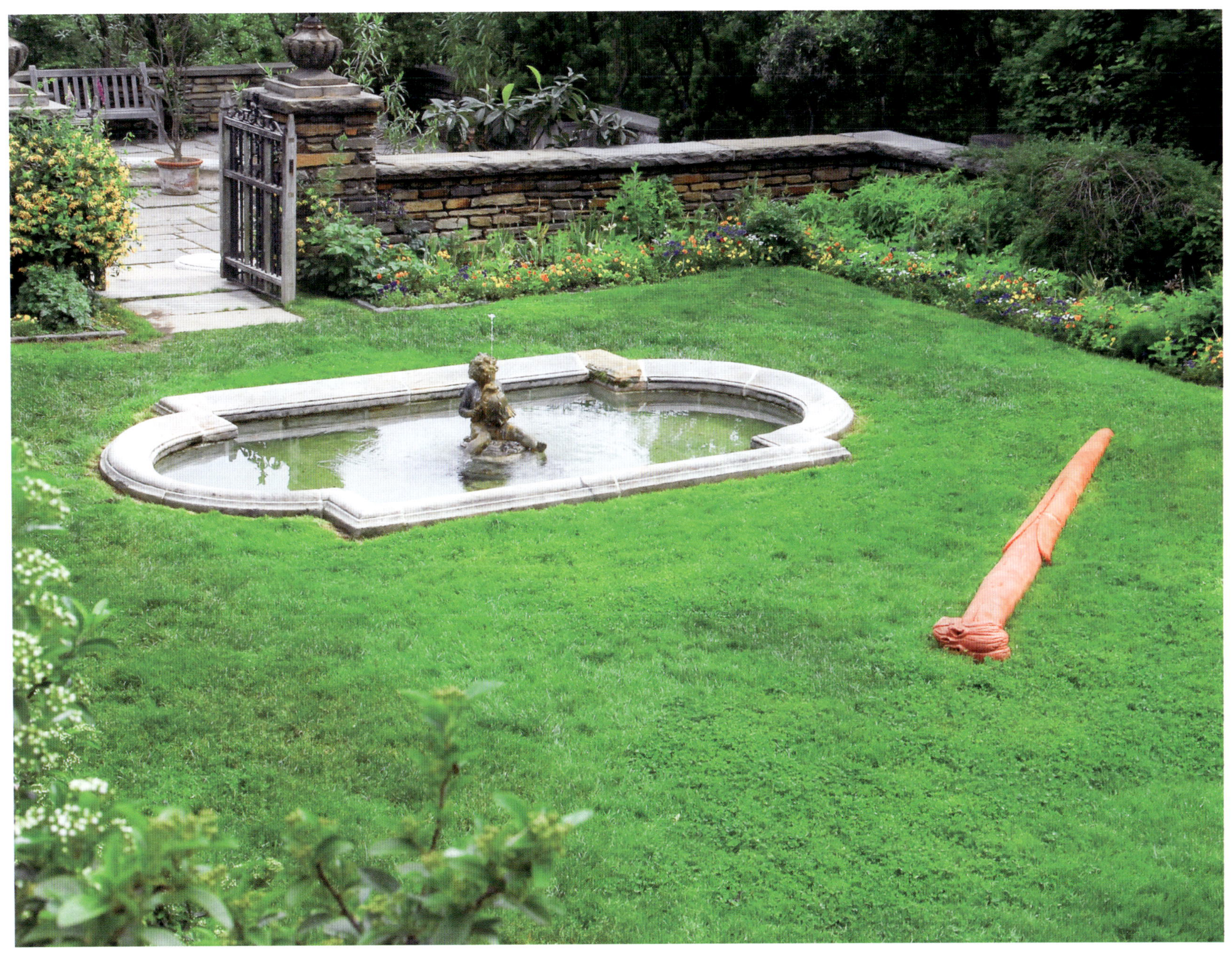

Stugg, 1991 | Cement, 9 x 177 x 15 inches | Collection of the artist

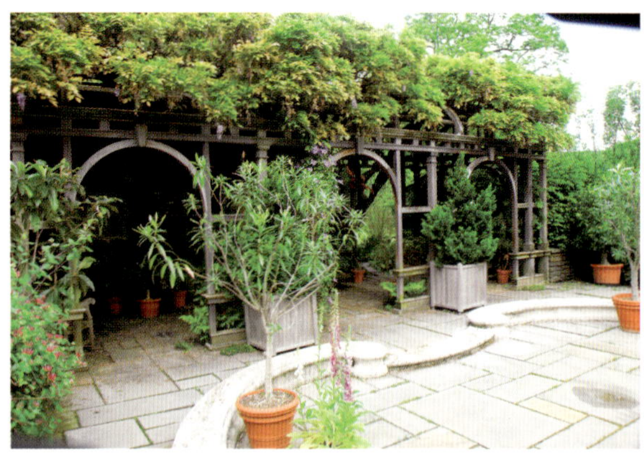

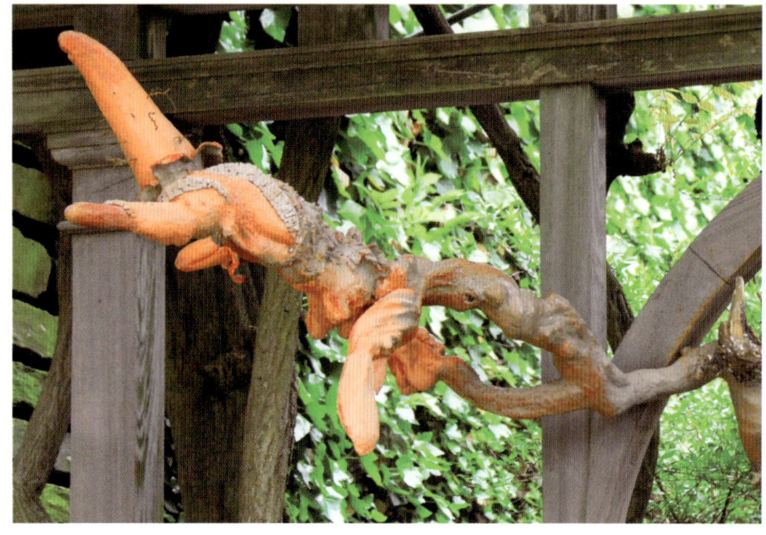

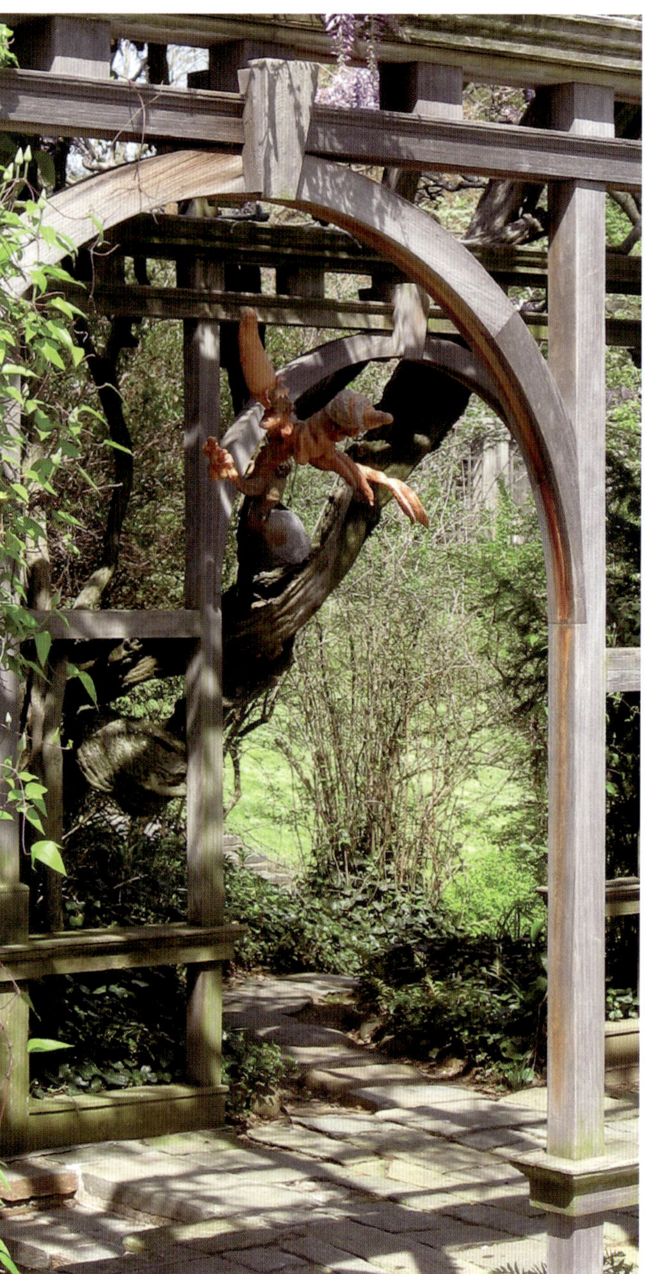

Growth, 2009
Metal, polyurethane, wood, and clay,
28 x 60 x 29 inches
Collection of the artist

The installation on the Arbor Terrace at
Dumbarton Oaks.

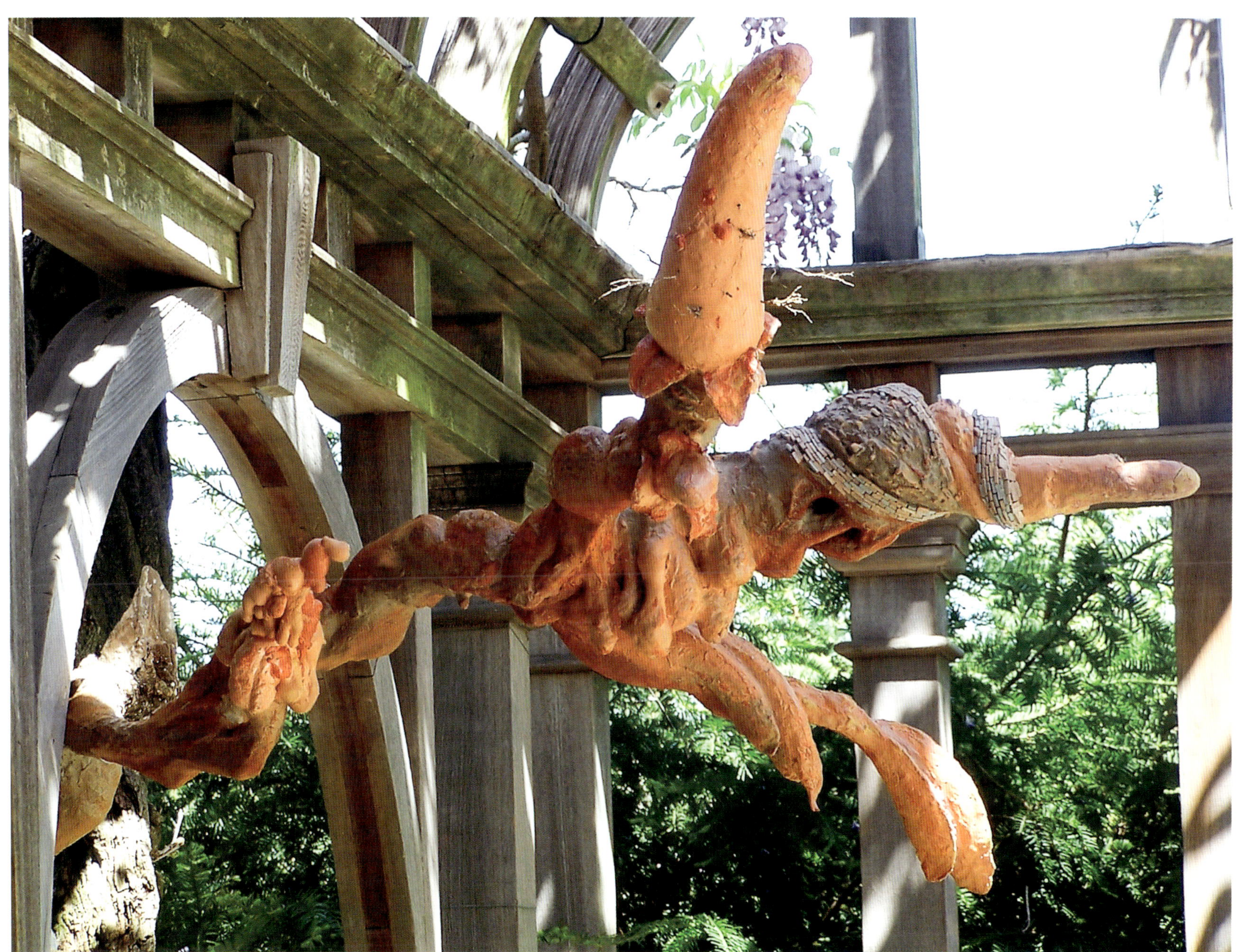

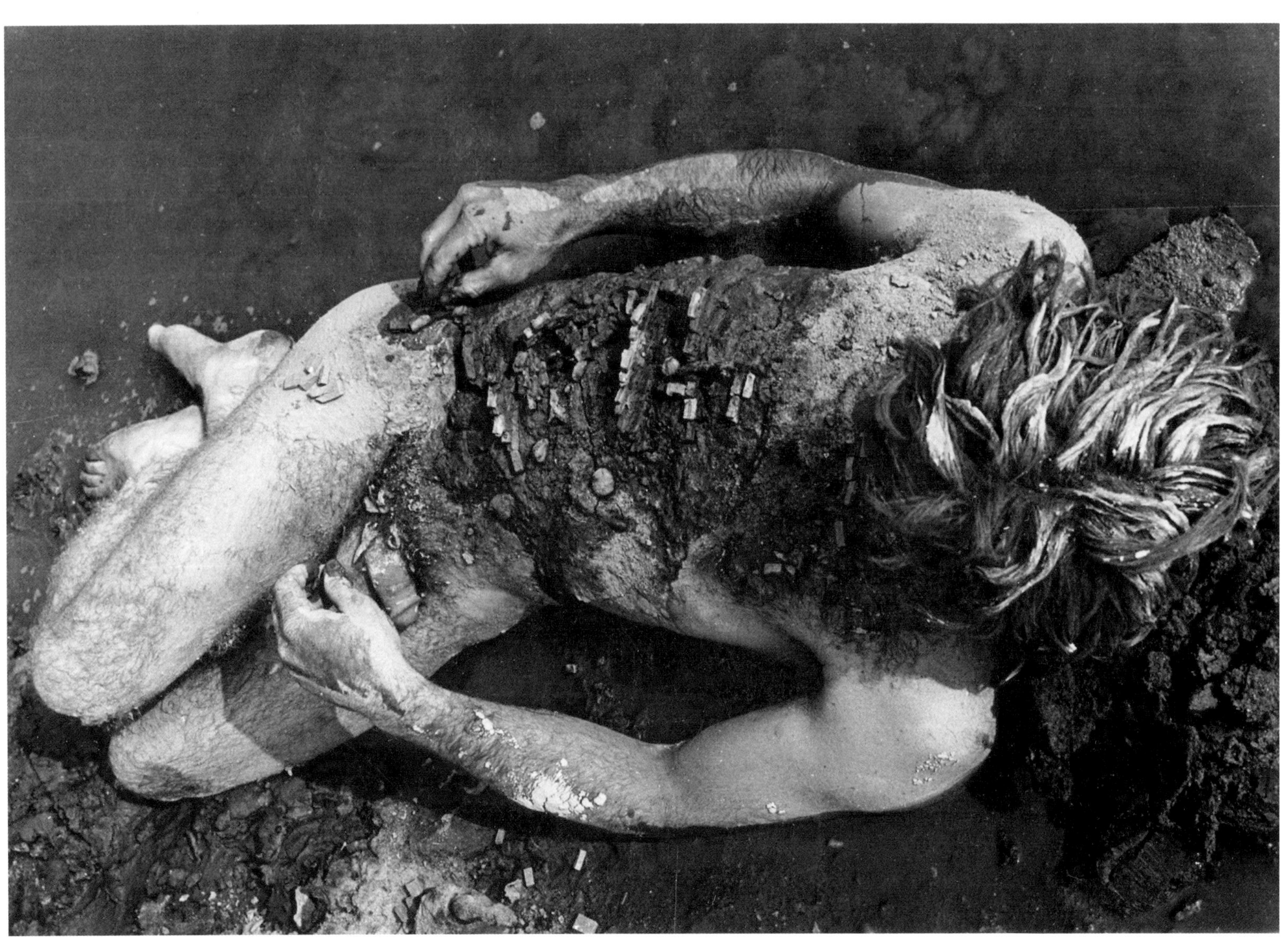

Dwelling as a World

Ann Reynolds

> The significance of cultural behaviour is not exhausted when we have clearly
> understood that it is local and man-made and hugely variable. It tends also to
> be integrated. A culture, like an individual, is a more or less consistent pattern
> of thought and action. The form that these acts take we can understand only by
> understanding first the emotional and intellectual mainsprings of that society.
>
> Ruth Benedict, *Patterns of Culture*[1]

Charles Simonds builds little worlds out of clay and other malleable materials. These worlds consist of carefully detailed miniature buildings or more elaborate, often quite fantastical, architectural and landscape environments. He also creates rather unconventional self-portraits by manipulating his facial features into more generalized or grotesque masks. Scattered throughout the indoor and outdoor spaces and amid the different collections at the Dumbarton Oaks Museum and Gardens during his exhibition *Landscape Body Dwelling*, these miniature worlds and portrait heads slipped into their chosen surroundings, becoming almost at home there. In some instances, individual works were so compatible with their environments as to be initially difficult to discern; in others, an initial surprise encounter led to a deeper appreciation of the preexisting formal, aesthetic, emotional, or pedagogical terms of a work's surroundings. *Mental Earth*, a large landscape of twisted rock formations punctuated with small, intricate dwellings, was suspended from the center of the ceiling of the Orangery, filling this space and echoing the large, creeping fig vine that extends up and along all sides of the room. A long staff with the distorted image of the artist's head emerging from one end lay on the grass within an elegant terrace complete with two shallow,

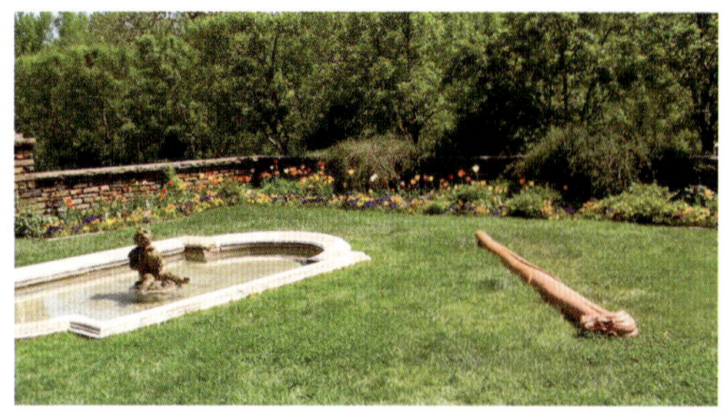

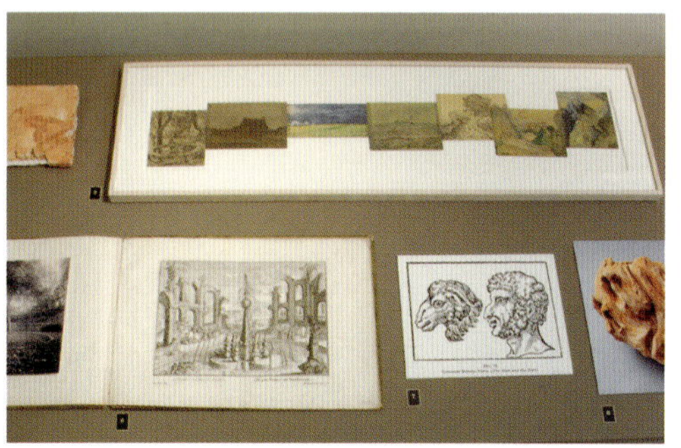

cartouche-shaped pools. The fountains in these pools, which consist of a single putto embracing a large fish that spews a thin, steady, vertical stream of water, provided a humorous contrast to the menacing figure emerging from the horizontal staff (top left). Installed among the collections in the museum galleries, Simonds's clay *Pyramid* and *Rock Flower* suggested didactic models of the hypothetical dwellings of the peoples whose cultural objects surrounded these miniature structures. His *Y*, a crossing of two long, three-dimensional, amoebalike forms whose surfaces are covered with tiny gray bricks studded with spiky or pimply orange protrusions, bore no immediate formal resemblance to the objects surrounding it in the Byzantine gallery, but its anthropomorphic visceralness nevertheless echoed the stark religiosity and faith in the transubstantiation of the flesh that many of the Byzantine objects on display were originally made to serve.

What Simonds refers to as his "cabinet of curiosities" appropriately occupied a space adjacent to the Rare Book Room (bottom left). This collection of small objects, images, and texts from a wide variety of time periods, some made by the artist and others photocopied from books and magazines, provided a specific set of historical and visual precedents for Simonds's work and, at the same time, demonstrated that his imagery and central concerns are part of a historically and culturally broad yet finite set of visual archetypes or perhaps, to use George Kubler's terminology, part of the replica-mass of a limited set of panhistorical prime objects. Kubler's prime objects consist of the singular, key monuments in the history of art, such as Stonehenge, the Parthenon, and the portal statues at Reims Cathedral. Few remain in completely manifest form, and most are known only through countless copies, what Kubler calls the replica-mass of each prime—"the entire system of replicas, reproductions, copies, reductions, transfers, and derivations floating in the wake of an important work of art."[2] Some replicas in this mass reproduce the prime completely, while others alter it slightly so that, in time, what Kubler refers to as the replica's "drift" from the prime is recognized by a particularly perceptive artist, who then imposes a new scheme on the mass of replicas that more directly corresponds to its current historical moment and circumstances.[3] Simonds engages with his chosen primes and their trailing replica-mass in such a manner by extending their legacy and subsequently shaping it to accommodate new historical circumstances and exhibition contexts.

Throughout his installation, Simonds highlighted the central terms of his art—landscape, body, and dwelling—by calling attention to overarching patterns of shared motifs and ideas through subtle associations and contrasts between his objects and the objects and environments surrounding them. As a result, Simonds's works in this exhibition not only literally represent miniature worlds but also function as dynamic visual, conceptual, and emotional catalysts for imagining many different worlds simultaneously within the preexisting contexts—natural and man-made, historical and geographical—at Dumbarton Oaks.

Imaginative world-making has been central to Simonds's practice from the very beginning, but his dwellings for the Little People, which he began to make in the early 1970s in New York and continues to make whenever he travels to a new city, are emblematic of this process and provide many of the foundational terms for his art and his ongoing approach to exhibition design, as demonstrated at Dumbarton Oaks. Although the urban situations for his early dwellings couldn't be more different than the exhibition spaces at Dumbarton Oaks, a consideration of these dwellings, several films that were made about them, and aspects of the larger historical context for both illuminates the fundamental terms of Simonds's ongoing commitment to creating worlds that are simultaneously imaginary or utopian and real, materially present and yet physically highly unstable, miniature and life size, timeless and timely.

Around 1970, Simonds began making miniature clay dwellings on Greene Street below Houston in New York. At the time, he was sharing a large loft space on Christie Street with Gordon Matta-Clark, not far from Greene Street. His initial motivation was to make a home, to feel at home in a city that was, in fact, his hometown—he was born in Manhattan in 1945—but yet in which he felt like a migratory orphan.[4] He created these dwellings for himself but also for a fantasy community that he called the Little People. At the time, he conceived of these Little People as divided into two groups: the Plains People, the farmers and shepherds who lived at street level in potholes and along curbs (right); and the Cliff-Dwellers, the hunters and nomads who made their homes on the window ledges of the buildings facing the street.[5] For each group, Simonds constructed environments that included dwellings made out of tiny clay bricks loosely modeled on ancient architectural forms, including early Native American cliff dwellings. In all cases, these dwellings appeared to be abandoned or falling into ruin. The two tribes, according to the scenario Simonds developed for them, were culturally polar opposites, and thus constantly at war with one another. But the bigger enemies they both faced were the weather, since the unfired clay bricks out of which their dwellings were made melted in rain or snow, and the passers-by, who either inadvertently destroyed their dwellings, by stepping on them or trying to dislodge them from their surroundings in order to take them home, or willfully destroyed them by throwing stones at them.

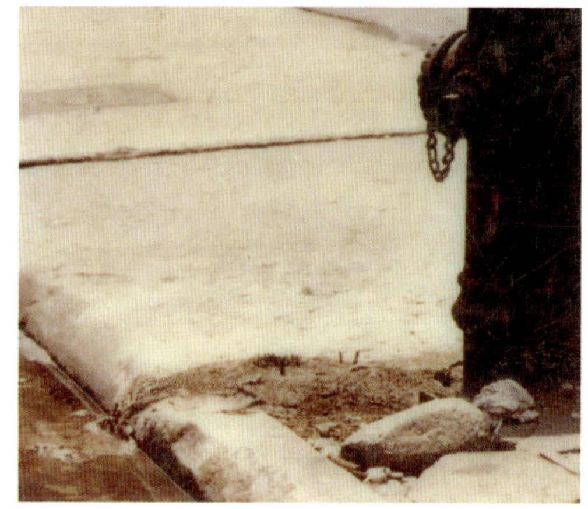

In the early 1970s, artists had already begun to occupy and refurbish portions of the increasing number of empty warehouses and commercial buildings that filled the area between Houston Street and Canal Street west of Broadway. This part of town was not yet the SoHo dominated by commercial art galleries, shops, and restaurants that it came to be by the late 1970s and early 1980s, but it was already an area in transition. Due to its transitory status, the streets were primarily occupied by two distinct groups of people: the increasing numbers of artists who lived there, and the workers and truckers who didn't live there but who were in and out of the area daily, delivering, manufacturing, or picking up goods at the buildings that were still in commercial use. According to Simonds, the artists, his own peers, had little to no interest in what he was doing, and, in some cases, were contemptuous of his activities. But the truckers and workers quickly and enthusiastically engaged him in conversation, took up his stories about the Little People as a matter of course, and began to look for him and his dwellings when they were in the area. This disparity in responses prompted Simonds to look for a neighborhood in which the residents might be more open and willing to engage with him and his Little People. And once he found it in the far East Village, between 14th Street and Houston and Avenues A and D, he traveled there every day on his three-wheeled delivery bicycle filled with supplies, selected sites, and made his dwellings, like an itinerant laborer (left and facing page).

His chosen neighborhood was occupied primarily by Caribbean immigrants and their children. They lived amid thriving drug trafficking and an urban landscape that consisted of twenty to thirty percent vacant lots or buildings. Most of these vacant buildings were in receivership due to deliberate neglect by their landlords and by the city—the hope being that the city could then reclaim entire blocks for urban renewal at some unspecified future date. The early 1970s was a low point financially for New York, and many sections of the city, especially downtown and uptown above 96th Street, looked the way the Lower East Side did. But the community Simonds entered was trying to do something about the gradual ceding of their neighborhood to the ruin the city deemed a necessary preliminary to its own appropriation, even if the neighborhood's efforts to claim small portions of space for parks, community centers, and housing were only temporary footholds. The constant refrain of neighborhood activists, "every time we do something, it gets broke," was emblematic of the situation.[6] It is significant to note that such local groups were often referred to as the "little people" in newspaper accounts concerning proposed urban renewal plans for the city, and that these groups sometimes even referred to themselves in this way, if only in an attempt at subversive irony.

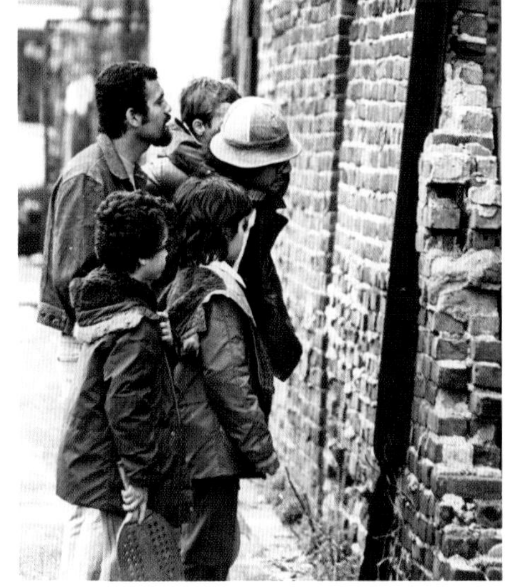

From the late 1960s into the mid-1970s, conversations about the role of public sculpture within urban development had become quite heated, both as a result of several contemporary exhibitions, including *Sculpture in Environment* in New York in 1967, and because of an increasing number of public commissions tied to new building projects in various parts of the city. What is, perhaps, most remarkable about these conversations from the perspective of the present is the fact that no one writing about the sculpture in these exhibitions and/or works commissioned for public spaces assumed that these works should incorporate references to the specific formal, social, or historical circumstances of the sites they occupied into their design. At a moment when the unpredictable dynamics of urban renewal often dictated the terms, an artist's acknowledgment of site meant creating a sculpture that was either physically expendable or could be moved to another site. In her review of *Sculpture in Environment*, the art critic and curator Lucy Lippard described the situation: "Most of New York's neighborhoods are temporary. We could capitalize on the city's impermanent quality instead of sitting back and deploring it. With buildings cavalierly thrown up and mown down, permanent sculpture is often irrelevant. Good sculpture does not automatically become obsolete, but if its setting is changed, it may become unsuitable."[7] Urban renewal created new opportunities for public sculpture, but, at the same time, it could render an individual work unsuitable for its site, allowing it to be removed or even deliberately destroyed. The precarious, eclectic, and ever-changing nature of the urban environment was thus mirrored in public sculpture's presumably tenuous existence. Both were necessarily impermanent and open to transformation.

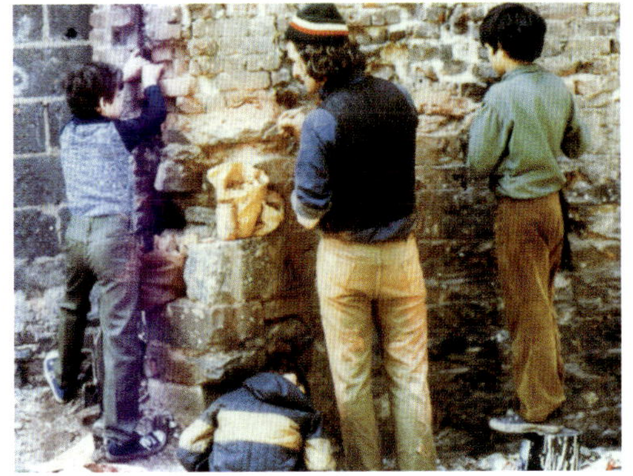

In the face of demands for sculptural impermanence and the concomitant spatially and temporally disorienting urban experiences produced by the fluctuating juxtapositions of old buildings, new buildings, and empty lots, a number of artists made what were referred to at the time as "anti-monuments." Barnett Newman's *Broken Obelisk* and Claes Oldenburg's *Placid Civic Monument*, works completed in 1967 and included in *Sculpture in Environment*, exemplify two general types: an inverted romantic ruin, in the case of *Broken Obelisk*, and a negative and ultimately invisible monument, in the case of *Placid Civic Monument*. For the latter, Oldenburg hired professional grave-diggers to dig and then fill a six-foot-deep rectangular hole behind the Metropolitan Museum of Art. A few photographs of the workers' efforts exist, but the location was not marked and eventually grass grew over the spot, erasing any physical evidence of the work's existence.[8] By calling a highway construction site in Passaic, New Jersey, a "ruin in reverse," Robert Smithson insisted that urban renewal could also be viewed as a form of time-travel: "That zero panorama seemed to contain, that is—all

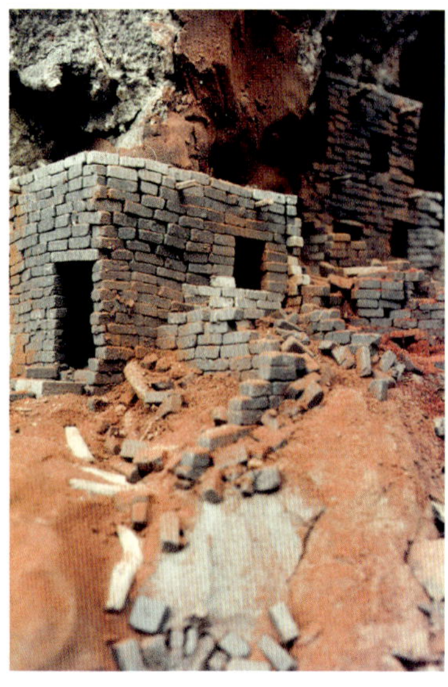

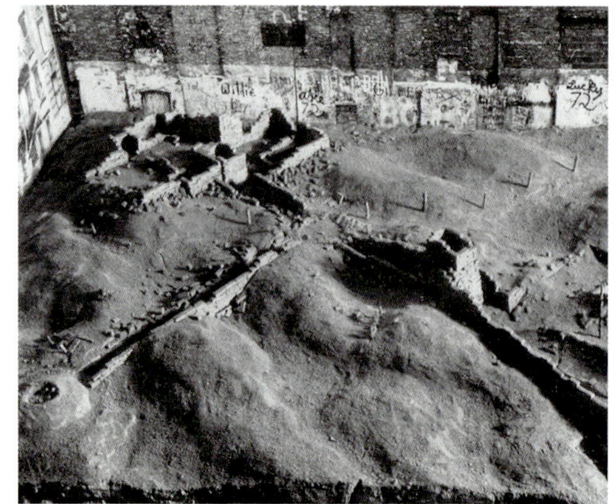

the new construction that would eventually be built. This is the opposite of the 'romantic ruin' because the buildings don't *fall* into ruin *after* they are built but rather rise into ruin *before* they are built. This anti-romantic mise-en-scene suggests the discredited idea of *time* and many other 'out of date' things."[9]

Because of their small scale, precarious locations, and material fragility, Simonds's dwellings for the Little People could be viewed as a type of anti-monument or, because of the way they were constructed, ruins in reverse (top left). And his sculptural interventions were directed at many of the same social, cultural, and material circumstances and effects of urban renewal that Oldenburg, Smithson, and others were engaging. However, Simonds's goal was quite different.[10] In addition to reiterating or commenting on the urban situation on a miniature scale, he offered a life-size alternative that was directed to local communities and not primarily to other members of the art world. In his words, he sought "to make a mythology that existed in real time and space, which members of the community could choose to invest in and make part of their day to day in whatever way they would like."[11] Simonds also invested in the realities of this community by joining their political fights, applying his ideas to more practical built solutions, and inspiring collaboration. Through their gatherings around his dwellings, for example, some residents of one block got the idea to transform a vacant lot adjacent to a Little People dwelling into a playground, which Simonds helped them design and called *La Placita*. As a member of the Lower East Side Coalition for Human Housing, Simonds also helped the community to activate the existing local channels to get permission and some financial support from the city to execute this project. At the same time, he created several fantasy park models for the same space (bottom left).

"Dwelling," a word that can function as a noun and as a verb, reflects Simonds's dual engagement with his chosen community on the Lower East Side. A dwelling can be a physical space in which to live or a description of the temporal experience of dwelling—both can be imagined or real. Simonds describes: "When I'm working I never see Little People. I am not insane. But I do think about them. What are they doing in that corner? It's a place you let your mind relax into . . . I don't think about the Little People. I think about me in there. It's a mental positioning inside. But I also think of them—they're incorporeal, but they're quite alive."[12] And, for Simonds, these modes of spatial and temporal, corporeal and mental dwelling that one can relax into define a particular kind of social interaction and role for him as an artist, one associated with a set of responsibilities rare in twentieth-century urban environments, but quite common in earlier cultures, particularly those possessing vital, communal traditions. Simonds states: "The people on the Lower East Side see me as a kind of folk figure who comes and delivers the Little People. It's not like I'm making things. It's like I'm the carrier, the harbinger. Conceptually, as well as physically, the dwellings fall apart when thought of as objects that can be taken home. They lose all their spatial and temporal expansiveness."[13]

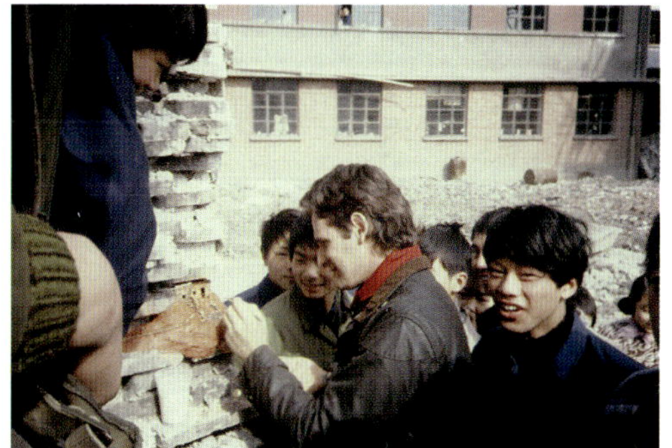

Simonds has also described the dwellings as "the medium through which we talk," and a series of short films made by Simonds and Rudy Burckhardt from 1972–74 elucidates through sound and image how this worked as a form of storytelling.[14] In these films, the people who gather around Simonds while he is making the dwellings express most of the artist's ideas; they become participant-observers in the process by telling the story of the Little People to each other, sometimes becoming the spokespersons for them or for the artist, whereas Simonds is mostly silent or even absent. I think this is a deliberate decision on the part of the filmmaker and the artist, even though, in reality, Simonds directly engaged with his audience while working (right). Because Simonds's voice is absent from the collective conversations in these films, the viewer becomes more aware of the basic ideas and information concerning the Little People as a story that is being told and retold in slightly different ways, even though it is clear that the experience and its perimeters are mutually acknowledged by all of the participants.

In his 1936 essay "The Storyteller," the German cultural critic Walter Benjamin describes the storyteller as a historically situated figure from the past, one who was able, along with the community he served, to exchange experiences and provide social counsel. Whereas increasingly, Benjamin claims, experience itself "has fallen in value" because it is no longer collectively shared:

> Experience which is passed on from mouth to mouth is the source from which all storytellers have drawn . . . there are two groups which, to be sure, overlap in many ways. And the figure of the storyteller gets its full corporeality only for the one who can picture them both. "When someone goes on a trip, he has something to tell about," goes the German saying, and people imagine the storyteller as someone who has come from afar. But they enjoy no less listening to the man who has stayed at home, making an honest living, and who knows the local tales and traditions. If one wants to picture these two groups through their archaic representatives, one is embodied in the resident tiller of the soil, and the other in the trading seaman. Indeed, each sphere of life has, as it were, produced its own tribe of storytellers. Each of these tribes preserves some of its characteristics centuries

later. The actual extension of the realm of storytelling in its full historical breadth
is inconceivable without the most intimate interpenetration of these two archaic
types. Such an interpenetration was achieved particularly in the Middle Ages in
their trade structure. The resident master craftsman and traveling journeymen
worked together in the same rooms; and every master had been a traveling journeyman before he settled down in his home town or somewhere else. If peasants
and seamen were past masters of storytelling, the artisan class was its university.
In it was combined the lore of faraway places, such as a much-traveled man brings
home, with the lore of the past, as it best reveals itself to natives of a place.[15]

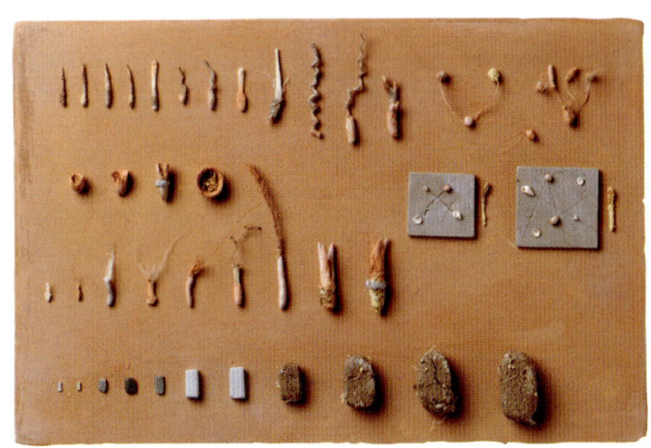

Through the two archaic types of the seaman and the peasant farmer, the resident
craftsman and the traveling journeyman, home and away are combined. This is reflected
in Simonds's sense of himself as a native New Yorker and as an orphan, an itinerant carrier
or harbinger. He comes from somewhere else, but becomes a committed member of the
community through his daily presence and his eventual participation in community groups,
projects, and politics. He is also both a master craftsman, with a finely honed set of skills,
and a journeyman traveling on his bike. What he brings along with his stories of the Little
People, their dwellings, tools, games (left), and temples is an eclectic set of images of built
environments and descriptions of a way of life from an unspecified distant past and an equally
unspecified distant place. The almost mythic timelessness that these environments and
descriptions suggest through their incomplete, abandoned, or ruined conditions and their
lack of historical specificity oddly mirrors and, at the same time, provides a striking and
illuminating contrast to their broader, urban surroundings: a neighborhood struggling to
establish itself, even if temporarily, amid an environment of seemingly immutable ruins,
yet one shaped by the specific political, social, and economic terms of urban renewal in
New York in the early 1970s.

Because of their material ephemerality, Simonds's dwellings also echo an art
historical phenomenon that Lippard described in 1973 as the steady "dematerialization
of the art object."[16] At the time, Lippard was positing a fundamental change in the way
that many artists were making and disseminating their work. Discrete paintings and sculptures had given way to more ephemeral objects, conceptual and installation-based art,
performance, film, and video practices. Lippard characterized this development as a form
of institutional and cultural critique of the seeming self-sufficient art object as commodity
fetish. Since 1973, increasing numbers of critics and art historians have embraced Lippard's

notion of the dematerialized art object to the point that it has become one of the foundational descriptions of artistic practice in the 1960s and 1970s. However, her definition has
posed at least two problems for curators: how to represent dematerialized art and its
legacy in exhibitions, when, for the most part, exhibitions demand objects; and how to
deal with practices, such as Simonds's, that were not initially addressed to art institutions
or even the art world in general. One solution to the first problem has been to revalorize
some of the objects made by artists during the late 1960s and the early 1970s, no matter
how ephemeral or "dematerialized," no matter how slight or secondary to their practice, by
displaying and writing about them as if their discrete physical authenticity and appearance
are central to understanding this crucial period. This solution also addresses the second
problem by sidelining the importance of context to the critique that, according to Lippard
and others writing at the time and since, dematerialized objects were mounting. These
contexts—and they were plural—were physical and well as experiential; dematerialization expressed a desire for integration into contexts other than art institutions as well as
a retreat from the hegemony of these institutions. Negation, as manifested in anti-monuments such as Oldenburg's *Placid Civic Monument* or in Smithson's conception of "ruins in
reverse," was just one approach to the dematerialization that contributed to the object's
relinquishment of a hard and fast materiality.

Once a balance between negation and integration is restored to our sense of
dematerialization as an artistic practice, we can begin to see more clearly how the legacy
for this type of work could include a broader spectrum of contexts and forms of cultural
integration that posit subtle critiques of the formal, cultural, and historical terms of an art
institution. Through exhibition installations like *Landscape Body Dwelling,* one can appreciate
how all of Charles Simonds's individual works, both those made early in his career and those
made since, continue to engage with their contexts because they were not made to function
in relation to singular historical situations, institutional or otherwise. And even though the
early dwellings were fragile and seemingly falling into ruin, they were never truly or exclu-
sively dematerialized in a negative sense. Individually and collectively, they always have the
ability provoke the materialization of new and different stories, new and different worlds.

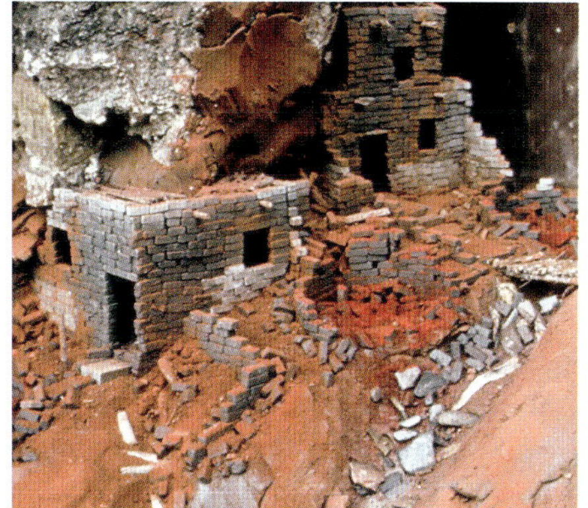

NOTES

1   Ruth Benedict, *Patterns of Culture* (Boston and New York: Houghton Mifflin, 1934), 46.

2   George Kubler, *The Shape of Time: Remarks on the History of Things* (New Haven: Yale University Press, 1962), 39.

3   Kubler, *Shape of Time*, 43. For a more extensive discussion of Simonds's practice in relation to Kubler's text, see Kate Linker, "Charles Simonds' Emblematic Architecture," *Artforum* 17, no. 7 (March 1979): 32–37.

4   Charles Simonds, conversation with author, November 9, 2009.

5   Simonds ultimately conceived of the Little People as consisting of three different groups. See his essay "Three Peoples," in *Charles Simonds* (Valencia: Institut Valencià d'Art Modern, 2003), 122–33.

6   Charles Simonds, conversation with author, November 9, 2009.

7   Lucy Lippard, "Beauty and the Bureaucracy," *Hudson Review* 20, no. 4 (Winter 1967–68): 656. I want to thank my PhD student Amanda Douberley for this citation. Her forthcoming dissertation, "The Corporate Model: Sculpture, Architecture, and the American City, 1946–75," will provide a detailed discussion of the relationship among urban renewal, debates concerning public art, and what she is calling the sculptural landmark.

8   For a contemporary discussion of this work, see Dan Graham, "Oldenburg's Monuments," *Artforum* 6, no. 5 (January 1968): 30–37.

9   Robert Smithson, "The Monuments of Passaic," *Artforum* 6, no. 4 (December 1967): 50.

10 Simonds has frequently noted the importance of both Oldenburg and Smithson to him and to his early development in particular. See, for example, *Charles Simonds*, 146 and 148.

11 Charles Simonds, conversation with author, November 9, 2009.

12 Quoted in Ted Castle, "Charles Simonds: The New Adam," *Art in America* 71, no. 2 (February 1983): 101.

13 Quoted in Herbert Molderings, "Kunst als Gedächtnis/Art as Memory," in *Charles Simonds: Schwebende Städte und andere Architeckturen/Floating Cities and Other Architectures* (Münster: Westfälischer Kunstverein, 1978), 8.

14 Cited in Linker, "Charles Simonds' Emblematic Architecture," 34.

15 Walter Benjamin, "The Storyteller," 1936, in *Illuminations*, ed. Hannah Arendt, trans. Harry Zohn (New York: Schocken Books, 1969), 84–85.

16 Lucy Lippard, *Six Years: The Dematerialization of the Art Object from 1966 to 1972* (New York: Praeger, 1973).

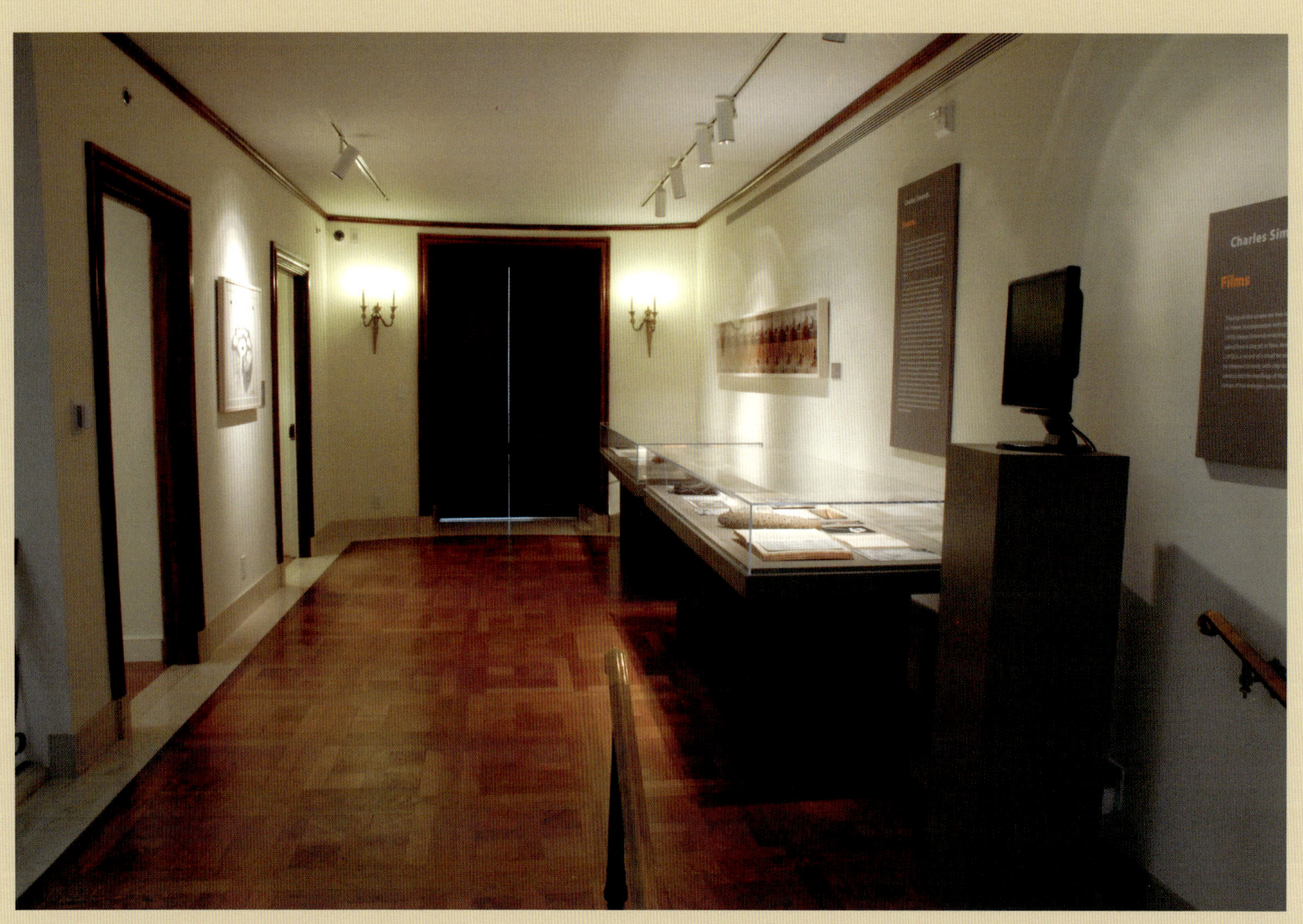

Cabinet of Curiosities
curated by Charles Simonds

with bibliographic information by Linda Lott

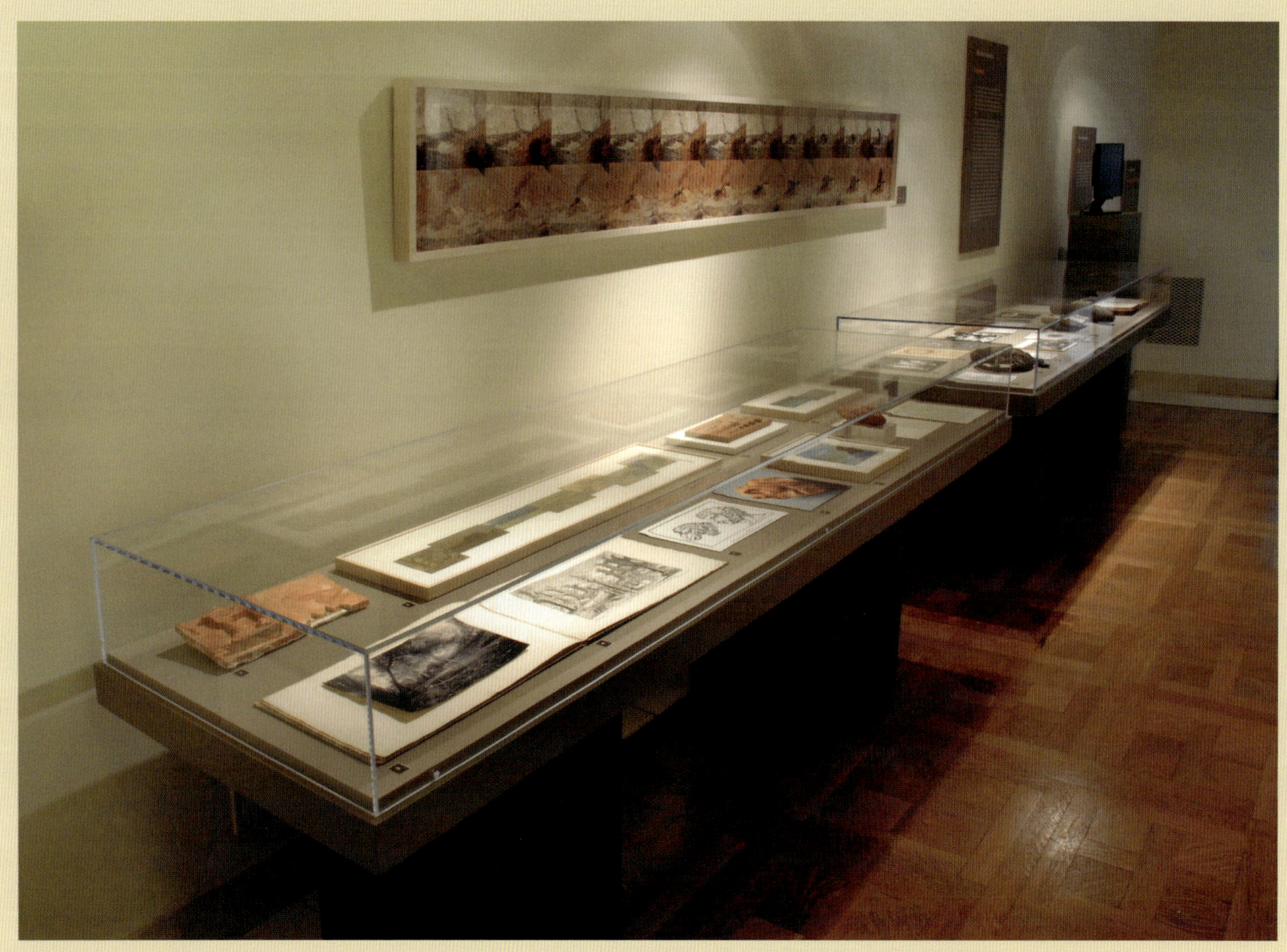

The cabinet of curiosities installed
outside the Rare Book Room,
with a detailed view of the partial
contents of one case (right).

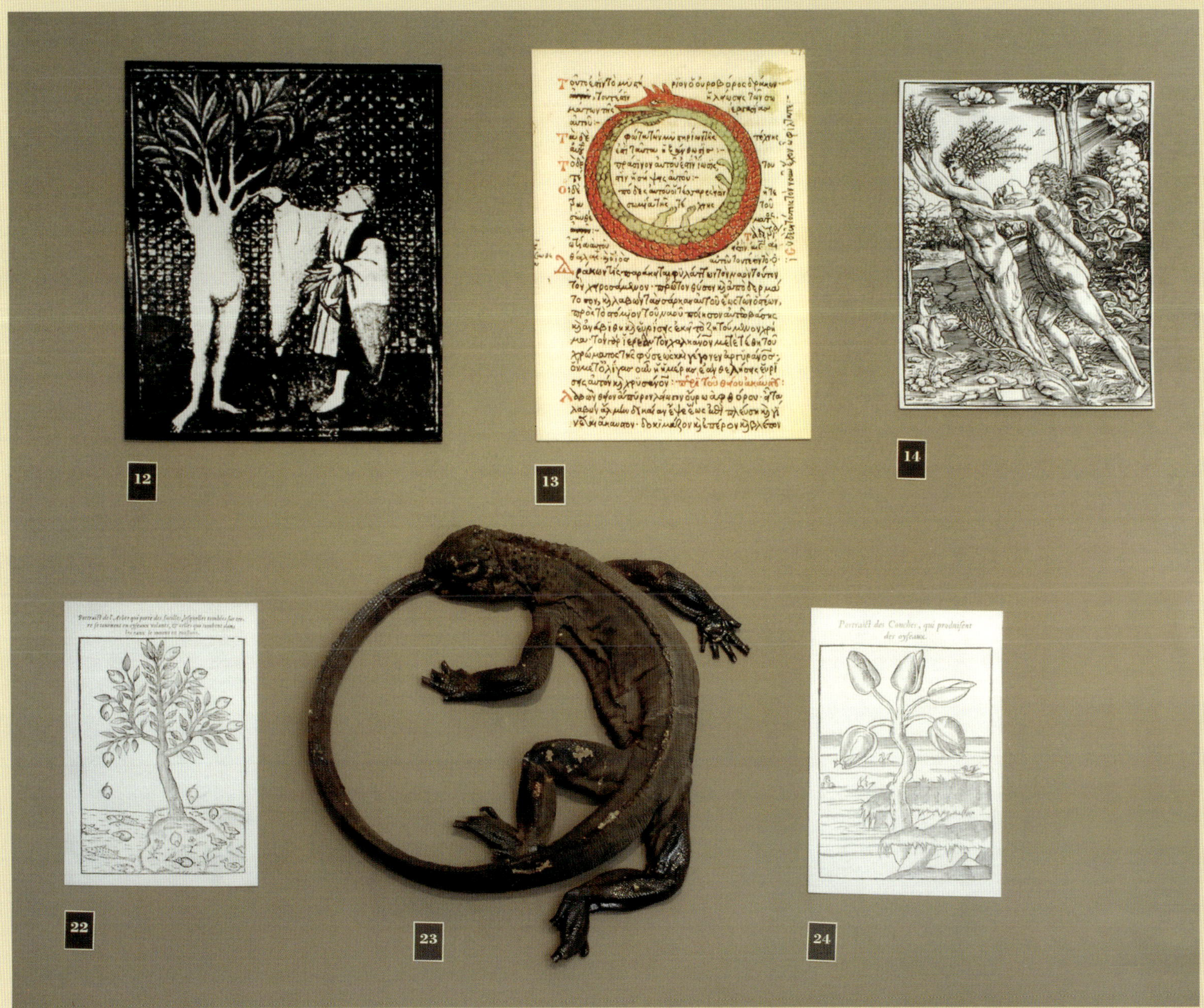

12
13
14
22
23
24

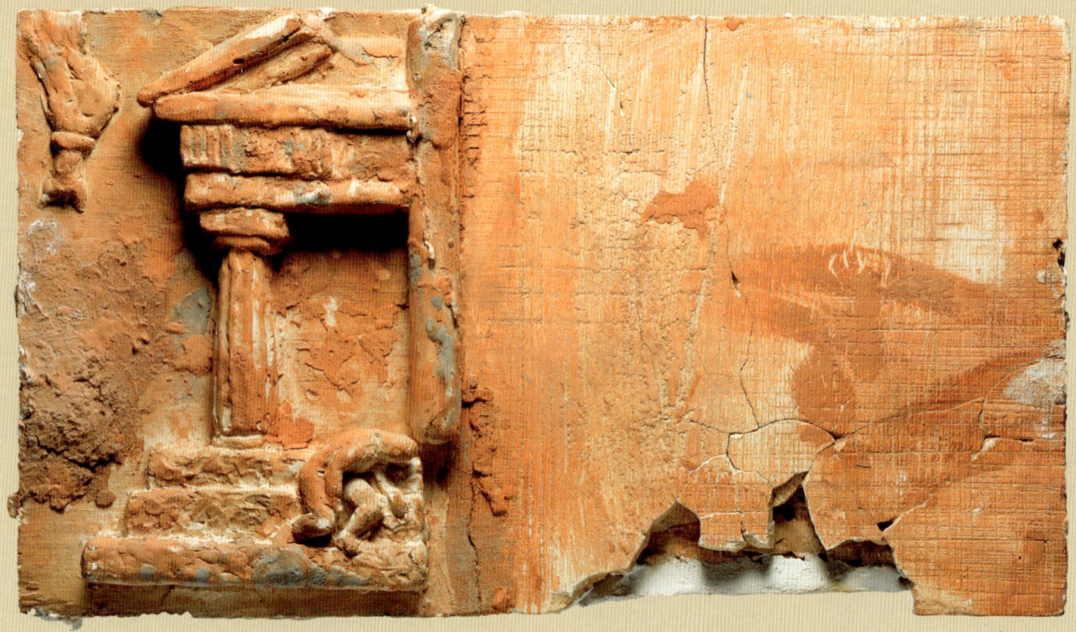

Charles Simonds
Brick Cutting Board, 1969
Plaster, 6½ x 11¾ x 2 inches
Collection of the artist

This plaster cast is of a relief that held a test tube of the artist's blood. When Simonds began making dwellings for his imaginary civilization of Little People, he created the board to provide a "sacred" place on which to cut the bricks used to construct his sculptures.

Charles Simonds, *Three Peoples* (Genoa: Samanedizioni, 1975).

Three Peoples presents the artist's narrative of the three groups in his imaginary civilization; these groups (the Linear, Circular, and Spiral peoples) are known by the geometric forms assumed by their architecture. The book was opened to the title page; a photograph of the cover was displayed next to the book.

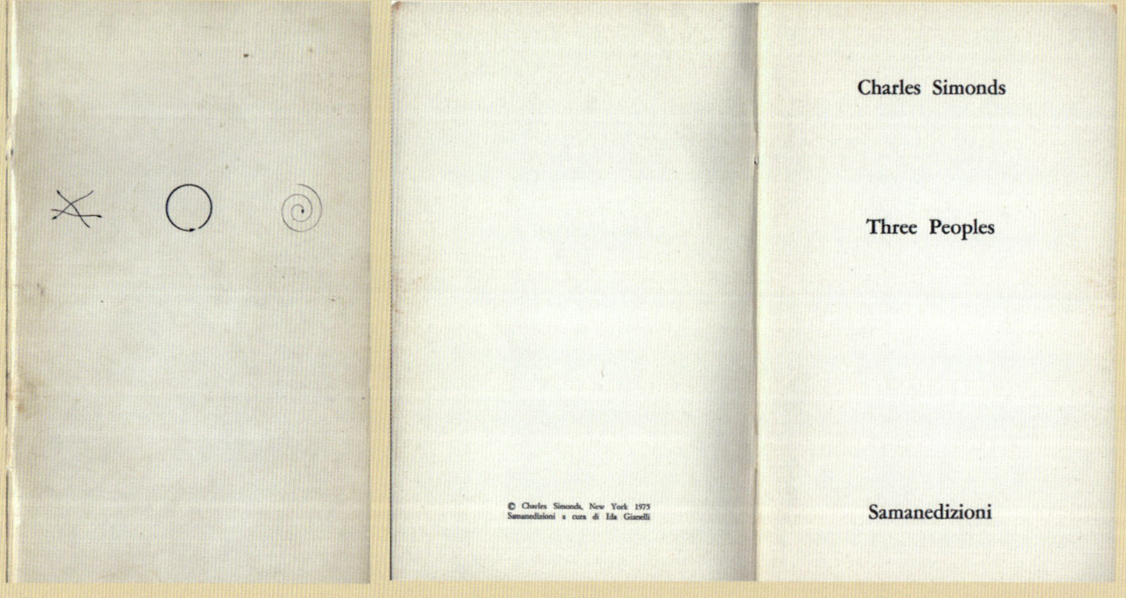

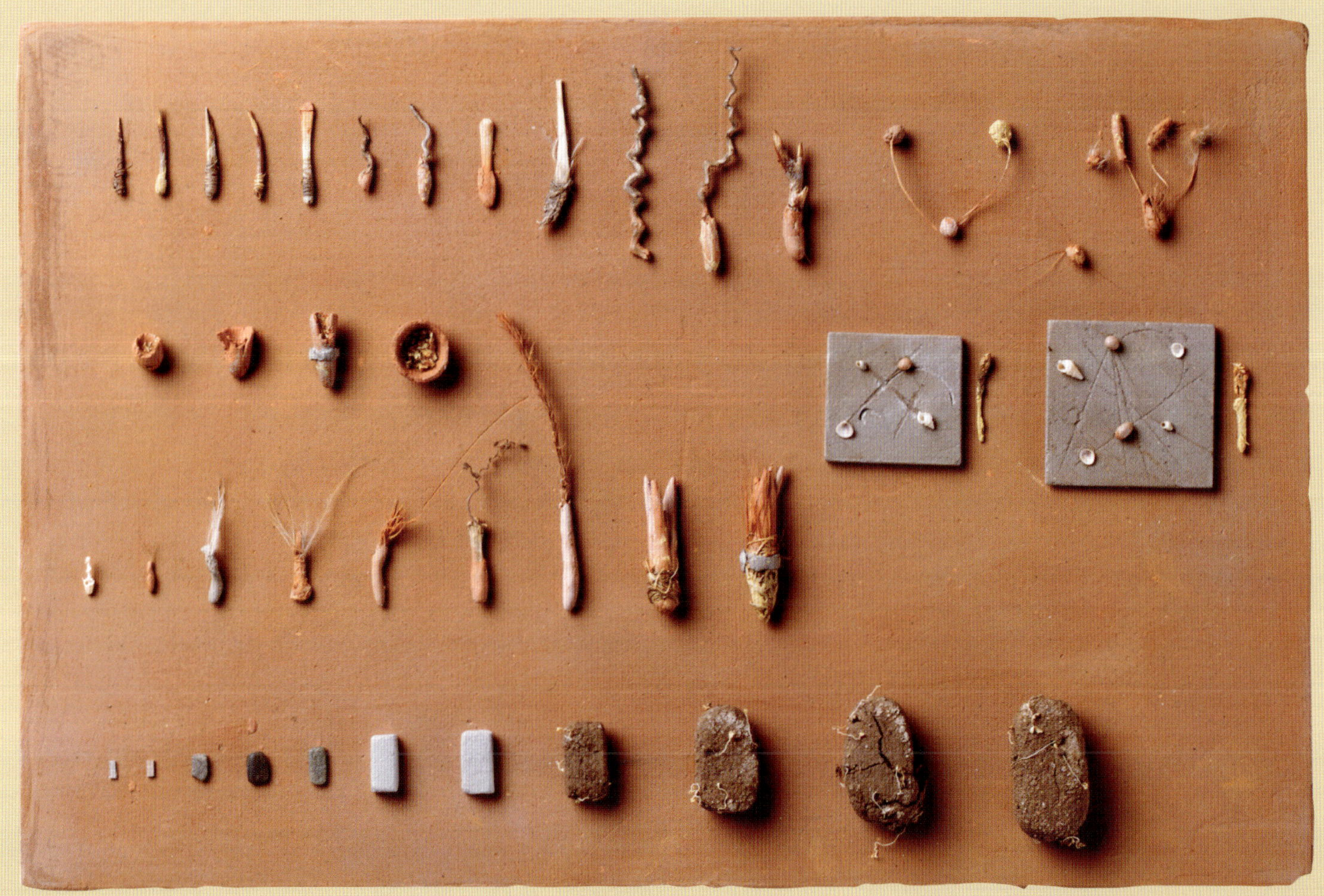

Charles Simonds
Ritual Objects, 1987
Mixed media, 7½ x 9½ x 1 inches
The Lola and Allen Goldring Collection

This collection of ritual objects and artifacts from Simonds's
imaginary civilization includes games, cutting implements,
autoerotic objects, and building materials.

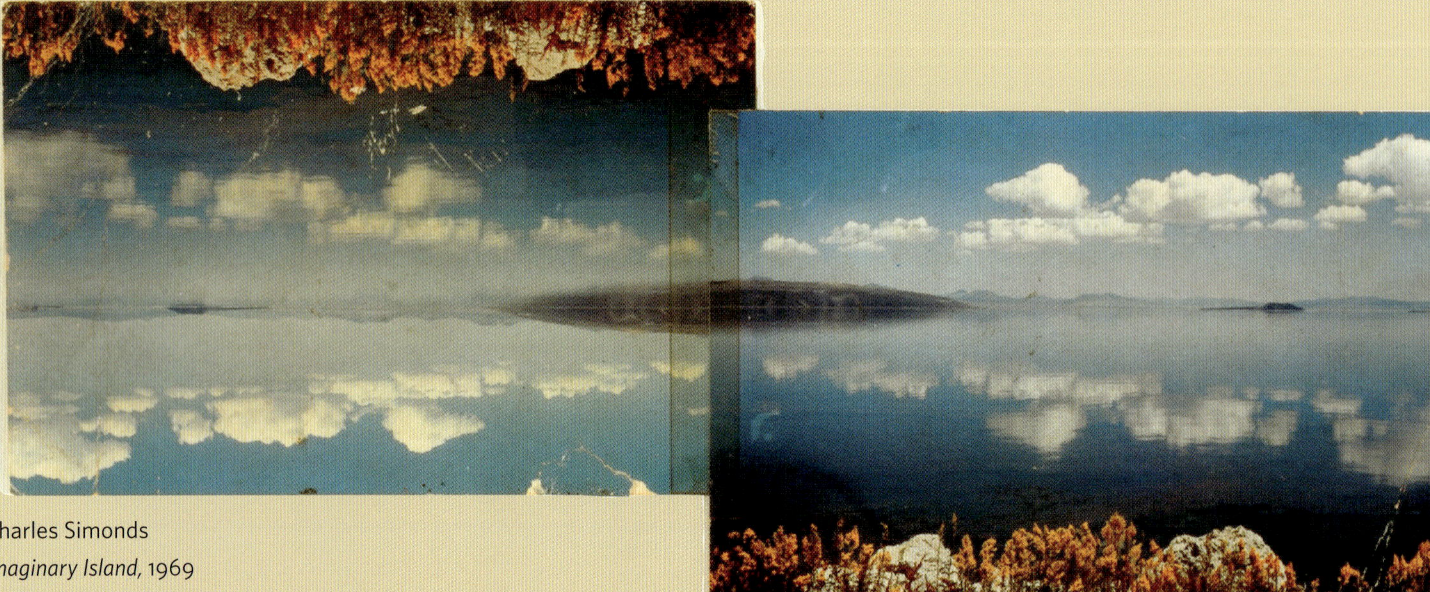

Charles Simonds
Imaginary Island, 1969
Manipulated postcards
Collection of the artist

These are framed postcards
depicting an imaginary landscape.

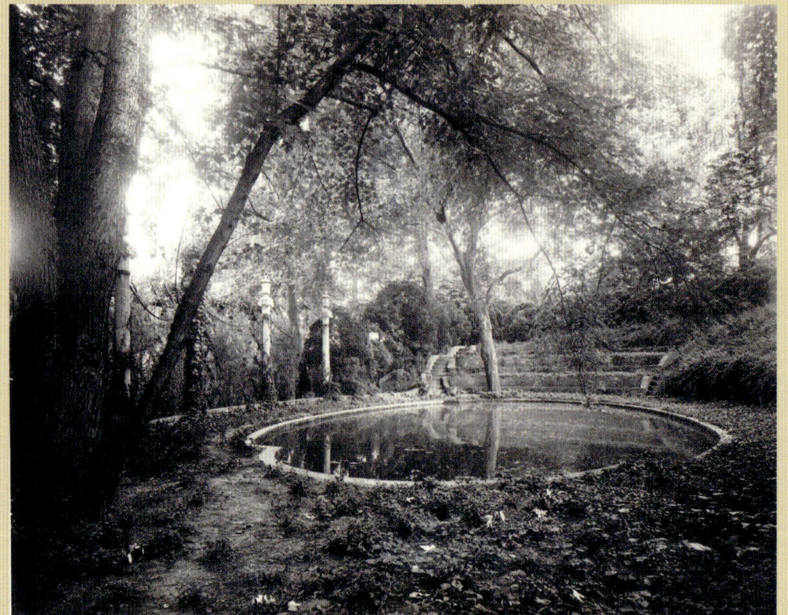

Beatrix Farrand (1872–1959), *Lovers' Lane Pool*,
after 1931, photograph. Rare Book Collection,
Dumbarton Oaks Research Library and Collection.

Lovers' Lane Pool is located on the east side of
the Dumbarton Oaks Gardens, on the boundary
with Montrose Park. The design for the area was
inspired by a Roman garden laid out in 1725 by
Antonio Canerari and situated on the Janiculum
Hill.[1] Farrand wrote a detailed account of
Canerari's design in her *Plant Book* (1980).[2]

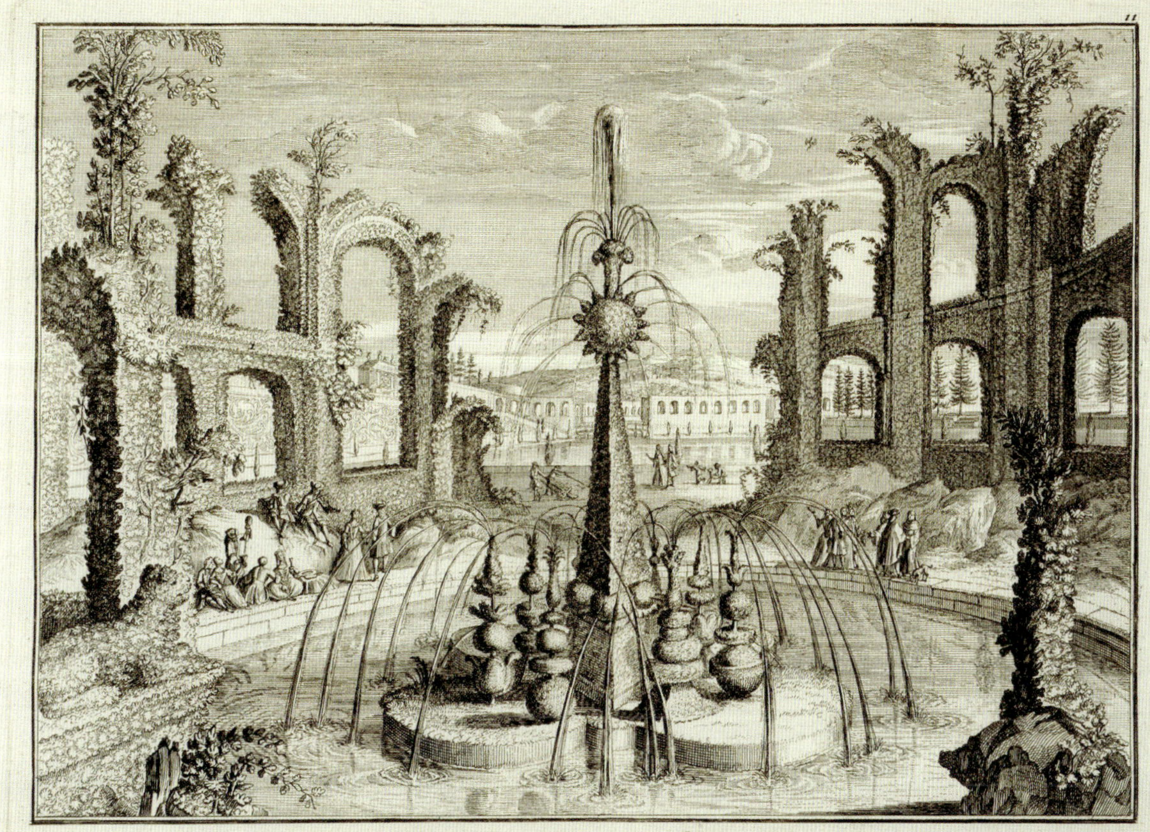

Martin Engelbrecht (1684–1756), *Fonteyn en colise van groente /
Fontaine et colise de verdure [Fountain and Framing Structure of
Greenery]*, from *Diverses rares prospects de belle Jardin d' Anguien*
(Nuremberg: G. W. Gunther, [ca. 1720]).

William Gilpin, in *A Dialogue Upon the Gardens at Stowe* (1749),
wrote that "Water is of as much use in a Landscape, as Blood in a
Body; without these two essentials it is impossible that there can
be Life in either one or the other."[3]

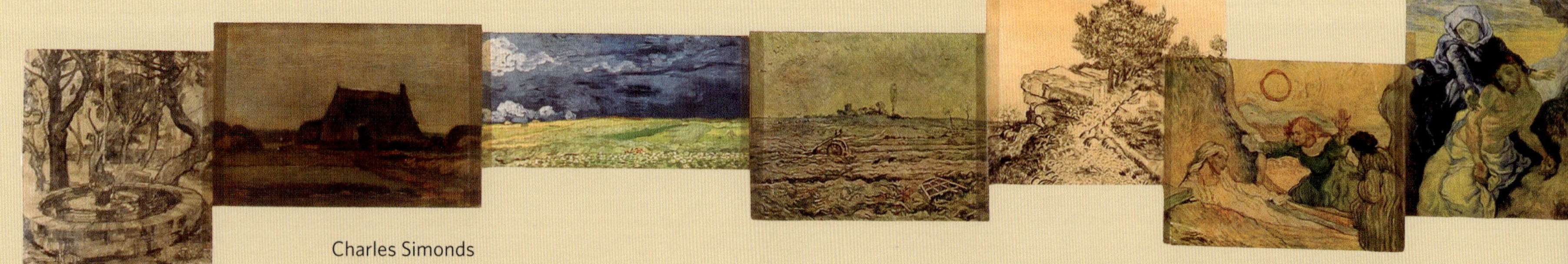

Charles Simonds
Untitled, 1969
Manipulated postcards
Collection of the artist

These framed postcards of Van
Gogh images were arranged
and reformatted by Simonds,
who sees them as a narrative of
birth, death, and resurrection.

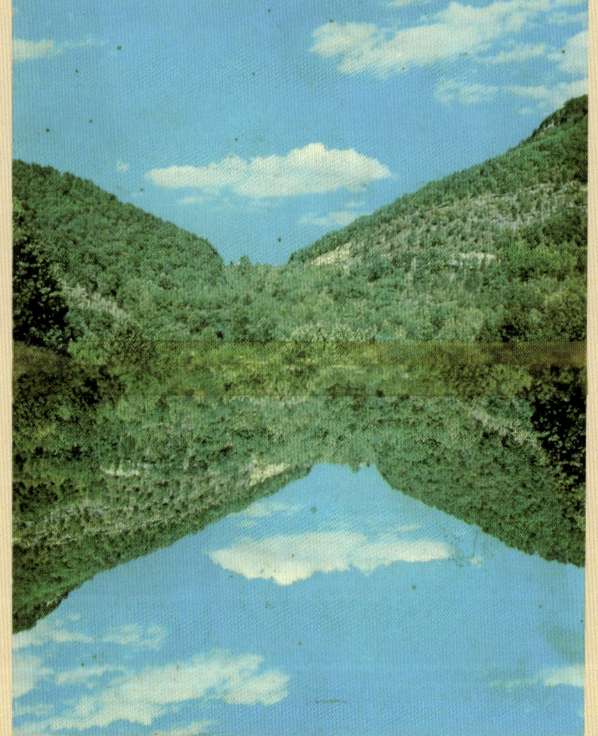

Charles Simonds
Twisted Earth, 1969
Manipulated postcards
Collection of the artist

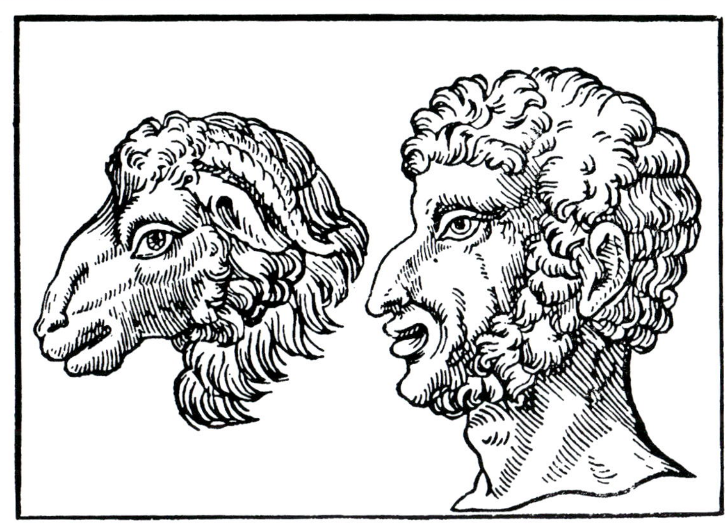

Giambattista della Porta, *The Man and the Ram*,
1588, reproduced in Ernst Kris, *Psychoanalytic
Explorations in Art* (New York: International
Universities Press, 1952), figure 74.

Giambattista della Porta (1535?–1615) was an
Italian scholar, playwright, and polymath who lived
in Naples at the time of the scientific revolution.
Kris presumably took this illustration, which
compares human and animal morphology, from his
publication on human physiognomy (page 91).

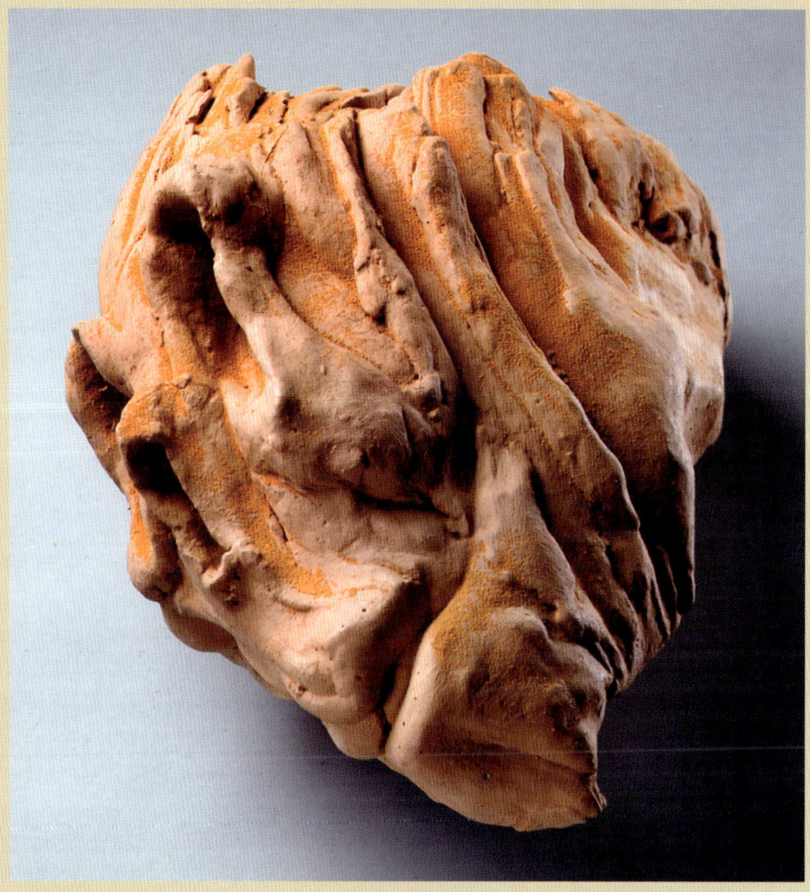

Charles Simonds
Head, 1991
Plaster and clay, 8 x 15 x 11 inches
Collection of the artist

Head, which was inspired in part by
speculation about the relationships
between human and animal physiognomy,
was on view in Pre-Columbian Gallery
One in the Dumbarton Oaks Museum.

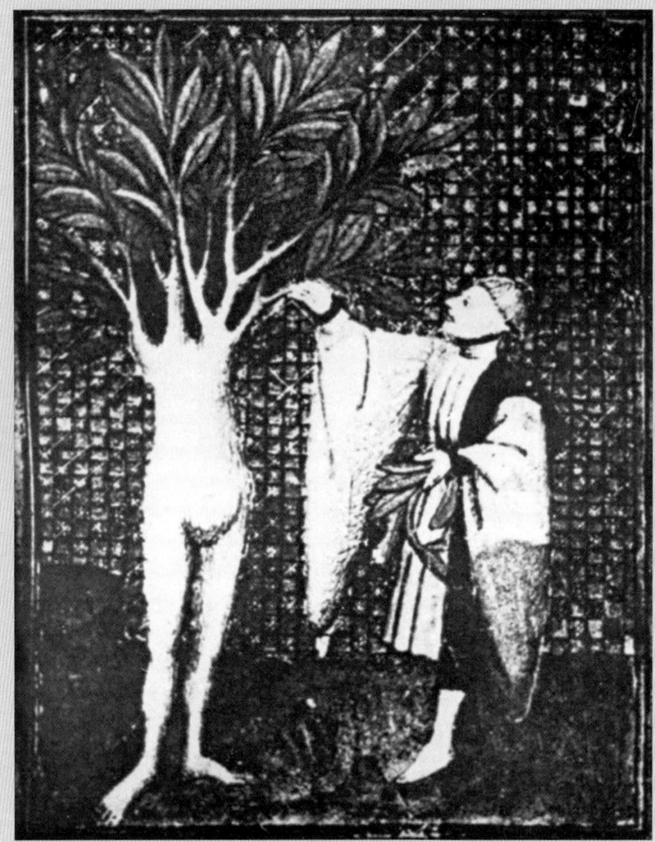

Copy of *Apollo and Daphne*, folio 134 of Christine de Pisan, *L'épître d'Othéa*, ca. 1401. The British Museum, London.

Christine de Pisan (1363–ca. 1434) was an Italian-born writer active in the French court; she wrote entirely in Middle French. In her version of the Apollo and Daphne myth, Daphne is pursued by Apollo, who is smitten with love of her; she calls on Diana to preserve her virginity. Daphne, transformed into a laurel tree, provides Apollo with the means by which to make a chaplet of laurel leaves in the sign of victory. Daphne is shown nude with her head, arms, and shoulders in the process of transforming into branches of the laurel tree, while Apollo is dressed in courtier's robe and hat, plucking laurel branches in order to make himself a crown.

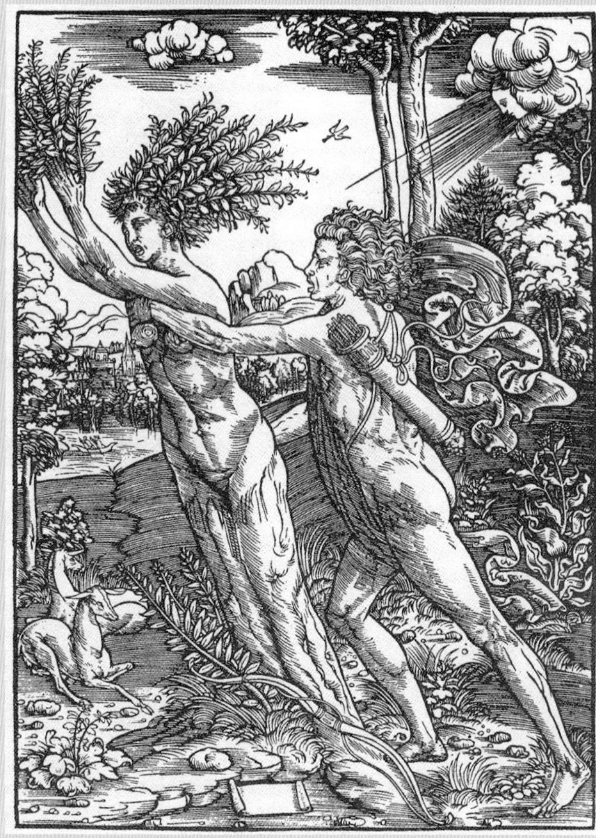

Jacopo Ripanda Bolognese, *Apollo and Daphne*, ca. 1500. Copied by the artist from Ernst and Johanna Lehner, *Folklore and Symbolism of Flowers, Plants, and Trees* (New York: Tudor, 1960), 66.

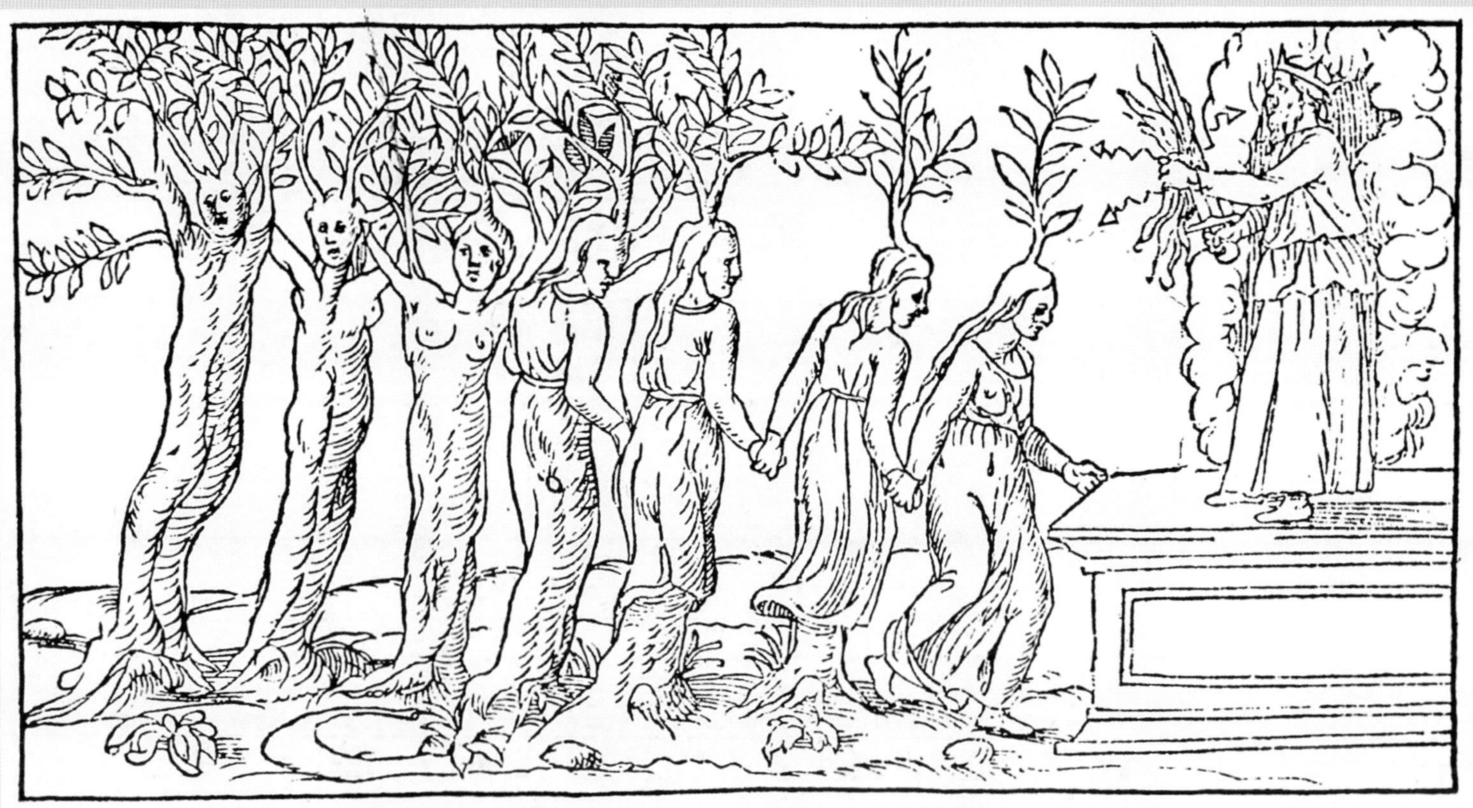

Francesco Colonna (d. 1527), *La Hypnerotomachia di Poliphilo: Cioè pvgna d'amore in sogno, dou'egli mostra, che tutte le cose humane non sono altro che sogno, & doue narra molt'altre cose degne di cognitione* (Venetia: Casa de'Figliovoli di Aldo, 1545).

The *Hypnerotomachia* is probably best known for its woodcuts of the architectural structures and garden settings that serve as a backdrop for Poliphilus's dream. After Poliphilus was rejected by his love, Polia, he wandered into a Dantean wood. He fell asleep and, in his dream, he traveled to the island of Cytherea with Polia. His dreams were comprised of mystical, mythological characters, extraordinary, lush architectural works, and antique garden ornaments. Woven into the story is a blend of erotic allegory, Christian and Middle Eastern symbols, and classical references. The cabinet featured a woodcut, copied from a 1994 reprint of a 1546 French edition of the *Hypnerotomachia*, of a relief on a vase of Ethiopian hyacinth, described by Poliphilus.[4]

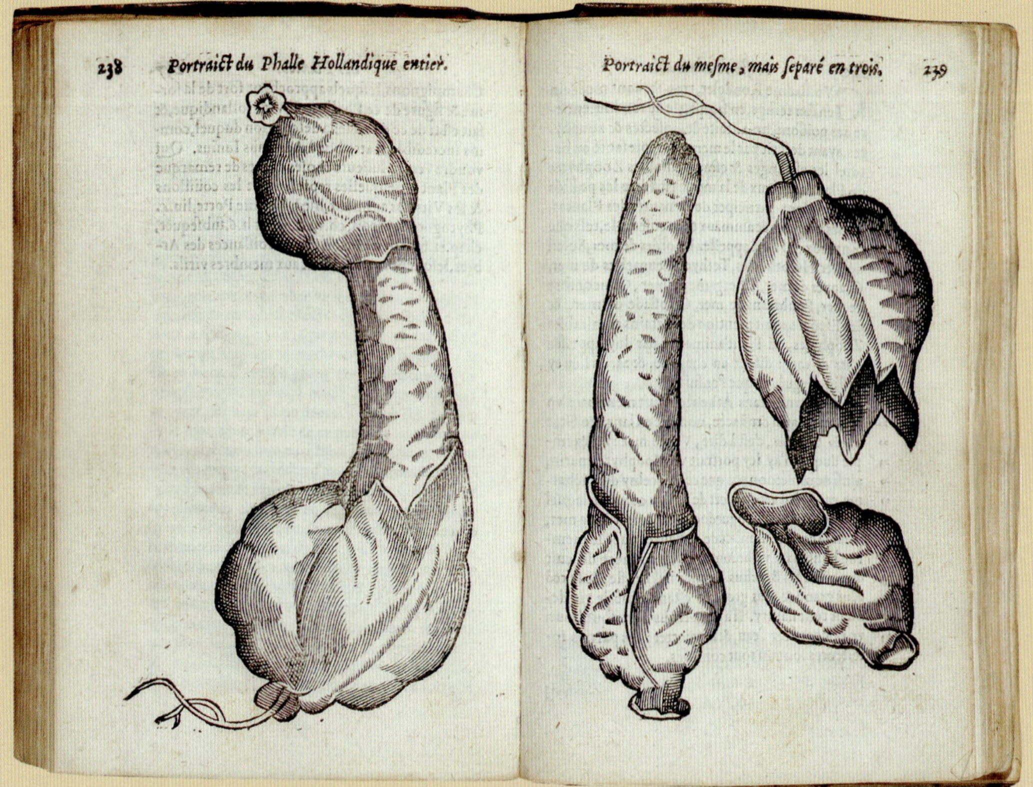

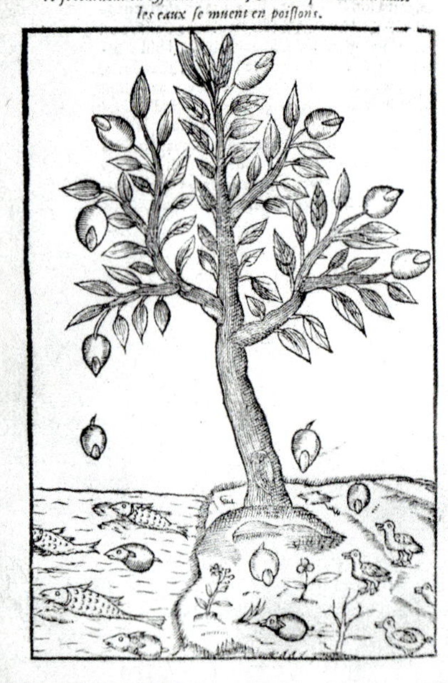

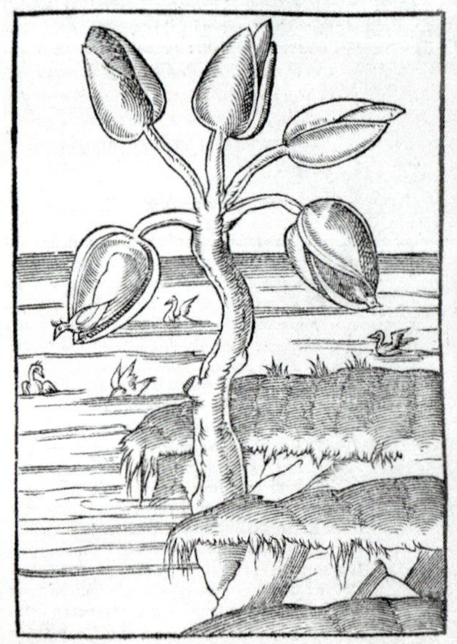

Claude Duret (d. 1611), *Histoire admirable des plantes et herbes esmerueillables & miraculeuses en nature: Mesmes d'aucunes qui sont vrays zoophytes, ou plant-animales, plantes & animaux tout ensemble, pour auoir vie vegetatiue sensitiue & animale; Avec leurs portraicts au anturel, selon les histoires, descriptions, voyages, & navagations des anciens & modernes* (Paris: Chez Nicholas Bvon, 1605).

The cabinet of curiosities featured copies of illustrations from a first edition of the *Histoire admirable des plantes et herbes esmerueillables & miraculeuses en nature*, which compiled accounts of remarkable plants and depicted them with woodcuts. Duret was particularly interested in zoophytes, or plants that have animal properties and transgress the Scholastic distinction between the animal and vegetal. Two examples of zoophytes were exhibited: the Credulity Tree (top right), whose leaves turn into fish or birds depending on whether they fall in water or on the ground; and the Barnacle Goose (bottom right), which was believed to hatch from shells on trees and was said to occur in the northern parts of Scotland and the "Orchades." The book itself was opened to a page showing the "Phalle Hollandique," whole and in three parts (above).

borant, melancholiæ, & perturbationi mentis resistunt , & morbum sacrum curant , ex
R. Mose in aphorismis. Maluę folia Magi lien capræ vocant, ab ea, quæ cum liene simili-
tudinem habet: Sextus torminosis capræ lien bibendum præbet : Plinius maluam vtili-
ter torminibus illini, præterea ad venena, & venenatas puncturas , ad fœminarum pur
gationes , voluptates , conceptus , comitiales , calculosos præstare , vt etiam capra , &
alia promiscuè habere.

PLANTAE ANIMALIVM TESTES REPRAESENTANTES.
Cap. XVIIII.

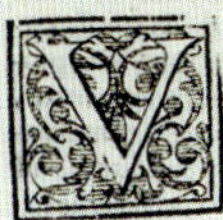

V ARII sunt plantarum bulbi, qui animalium testes mentiuntur, præ-
sertim luxuriosorum, & ita affabrè eos mentiuntur, vt nemo sit, qui
videat, qui se eos cognoscere non fateatur. Natura hominum genera-
tioni satagens, hac testiculorū imagine ad vires venereas, ad concep-
tum, & ad prolem eos valere significauit. Testes pecori , armétoq; ad
crura decidui, subus adnexi, delphino pręlongi vltima conduntur al
uo, elephanto occulti: oua parientium lumbis intus adhærent, qualia ocyssima in Vene
re, buteonibus terni.

ORCHIDVM species denuo sub aspectu m veniunt, contemplator in prima facie
hircinos testes cum sua planta, caninos, & tandem triorchi-
dum, ex accipitrum genere.

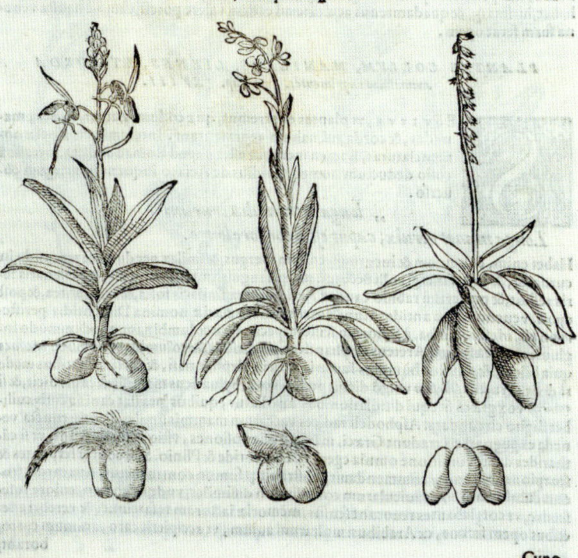

Cyno.

Giambattista della Porta, *Phytognomonica: Octo libris contenta; In qvibvs nova, facillimaqve affertvr methodvs, qua plantarum, animalium, metallorum; rerum denique omnium ex prima eximæ faciei inspectione quiuis abditas vires assequatur . . .* (Naples: Apud Horatium Saluianum, 1588).

Phytognomonica, by the Neapolitan polymath Giambattista della Porta (1535?–1615), was the first work to classify plants according to their natural habitat; as such, it offers an important pre-Linnaean taxonomy. The book applies the medieval belief in the Doctrine of Signatures, which posited that there was a natural correspondence to plants in both the external form and the internal nature of an object. Relationships were also drawn between the appearance of a plant and its potential medicinal properties. Porta's theses were supported by woodcut illustrations; for example, poisonous roots were made to resemble snakes. The concept of resemblance, which goes back to the ancient Greeks, has left its mark in modern plant nomenclature. The plate that was exhibited in the cabinet of curiosities compares orchids with like objects, such as the testicles of a small animal. The name for the Orchidaceae family derives from *Orchis,* a flower whose roots were believed to resemble testicles, which in Greek is ὄρχεις. See also *The Man and the Ram*, page 87.

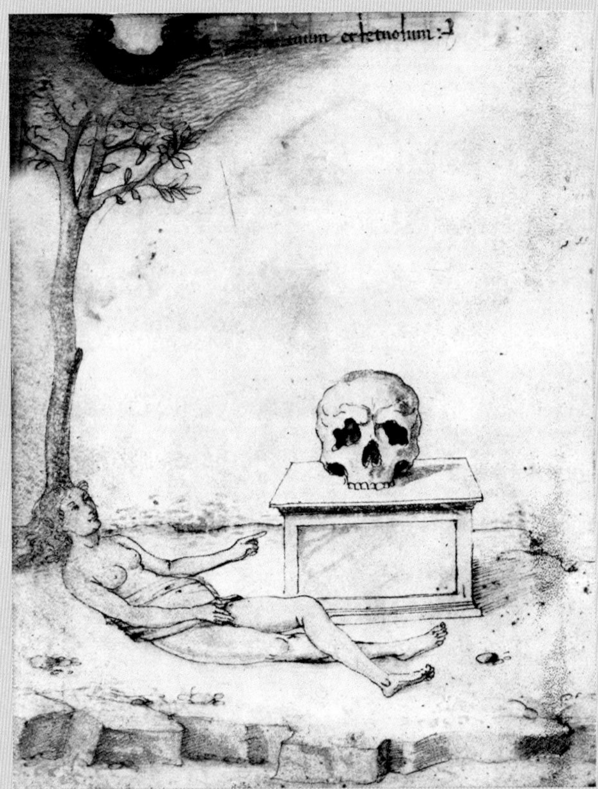

Photograph of *The Skull as the Mortificatio of Eve*, ink drawing from
Miscellanea d'alchimia, fourteenth century. Codex Ashburnham 1166.
Biblioteca Medicea Laurenziana, Florence.

Simonds copied this ink drawing from C. G. Jung, *Psychology and
Alchemy* (New York: Pantheon Books, 1953), where it was reproduced
as figure 135. The illustration depicts the nude figure of Eve reclining
in a natural setting. Beside her, on a tomblike structure, is a larger-
than-life skull lacking its jaw. Eve conceals her nudity modestly with
her right hand and points toward the skull with her left hand. Out
of her head grows a young tree in full foliage. She is thus associated
both with generation and with temptation and death.

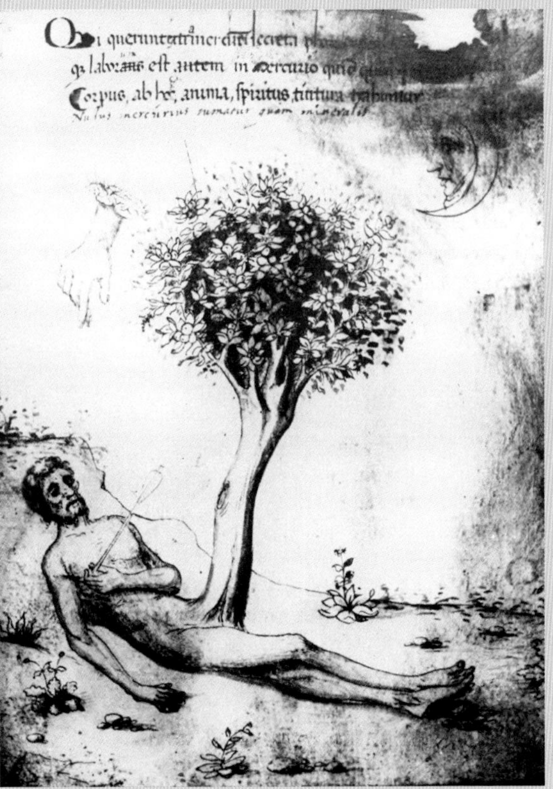

Photograph of *Adam as Prima Materia, Pierced by the Arrow of Mercurius*,
ink drawing from *Miscellanea d'alchimia*, fourteenth century. Codex
Ashburnham 1166. Biblioteca Medicea Laurenziana, Florence.

This reproduction of an ink drawing from the *Miscellanea d'alchimia* depicts
the nude figure of Adam lying in a field. A foliating tree grows from his
loins and an arrow pierces his chest. Above the tree are a crescent moon
and a hand emerging from a celestial cloud. Adam can be interpreted here
as the *prima materia* with the *arbor philosophica* (or tree of life) growing out
of him. As the father of humanity, Adam is the root of the Fall in Christian
belief; he also provides the means of subsequent redemption by furnishing
the tree upon which Christ is crucified. Like Eve, Adam is thus linked to
death and resurrection.

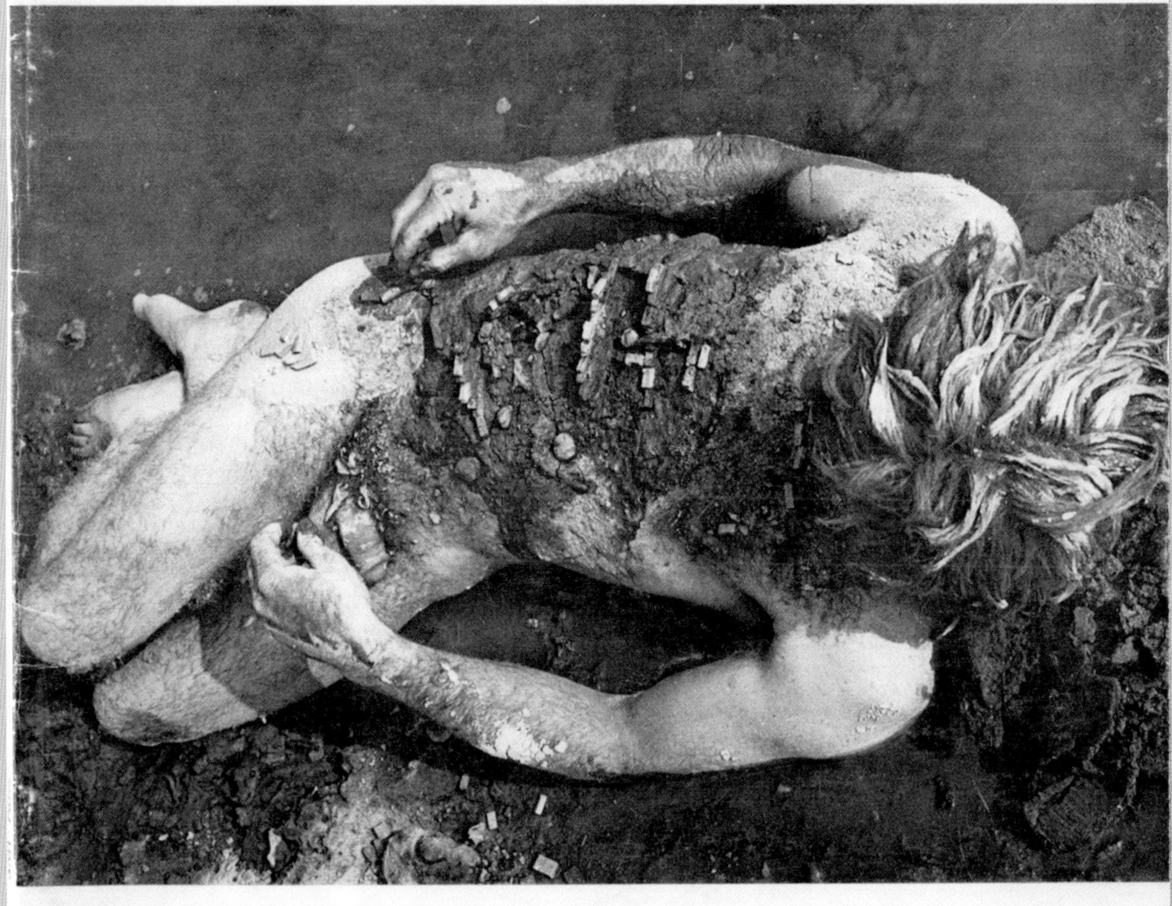

Daniel Abadie, *Charles Simonds* (Paris: SMI, 1975).

The first book on the artist's work features a cover photograph of Simonds enacting one of his *Landscape/Body/Dwelling* rituals.

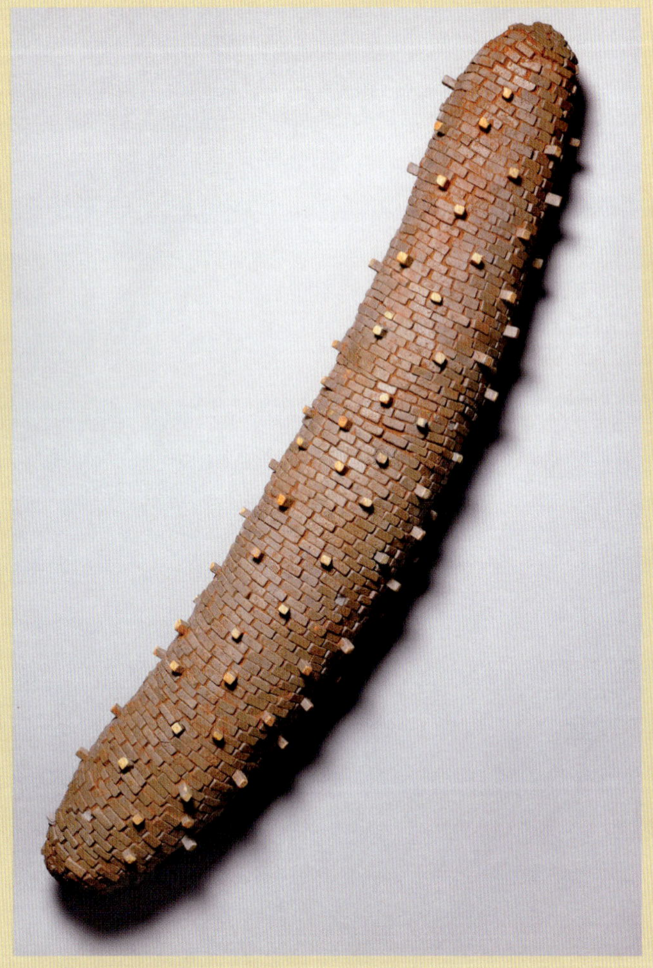

Charles Simonds
It, 1993
Clay and plaster, 3½ x 17 x 3½ inches
Collection of the artist

This dildolike object relates to the
ritual objects on page 83.

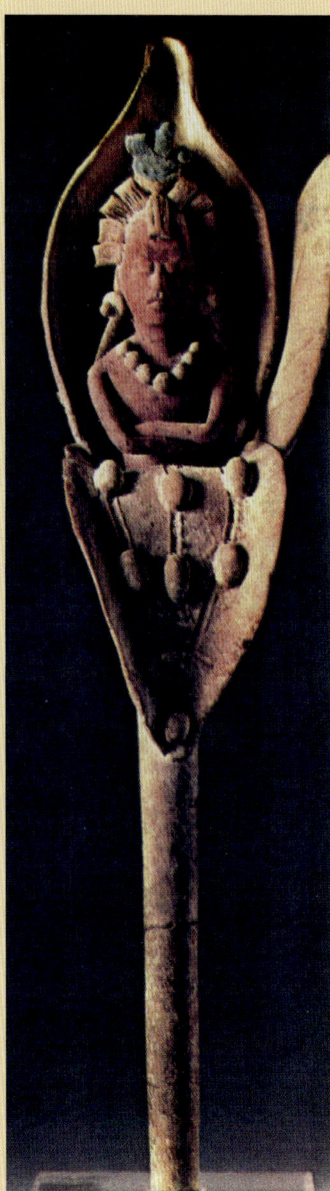

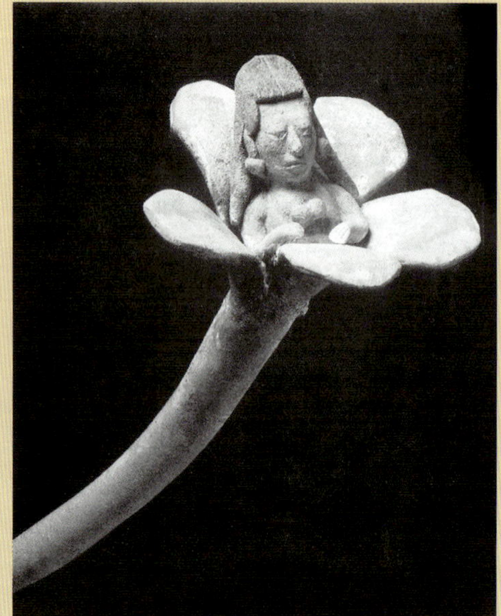

Photographs of Classic Maya Jaina
sculptures representing figures emerging
from flowers, similar to one on view
in Pre-Columbian Gallery Three in the
Dumbarton Oaks Museum.

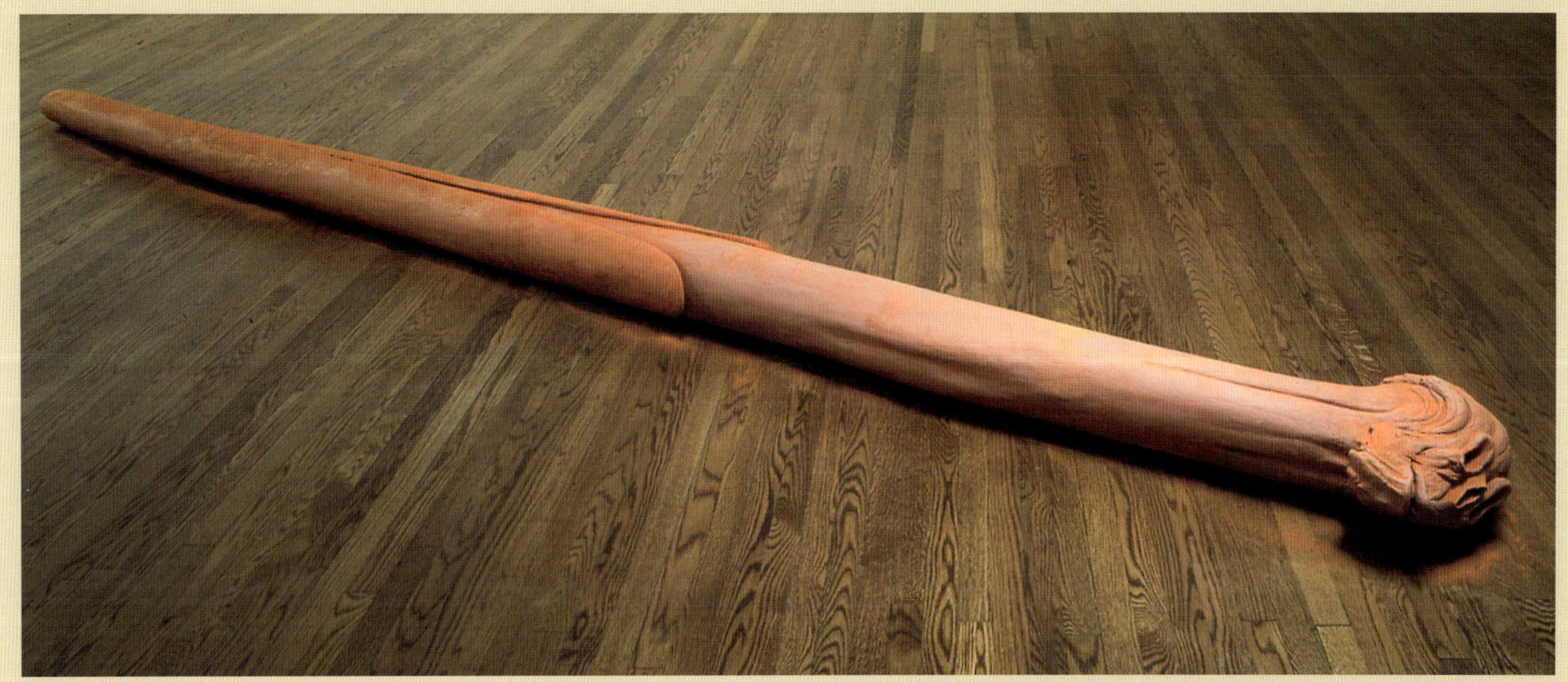

Charles Simonds
Stugg, 1991
Cement, 9 x 177 x 15 inches
Collection of the artist

Stugg, which was on view on the Fountain Terrace in the
garden, begins as a seedpod that sprouts an adolescent
torso and terminates in a visage that is part goat head,
part human face, and part landscape. It evokes both
human-plant transformations and Classic Maya Jaina
sculptures of figures emerging from flowers.

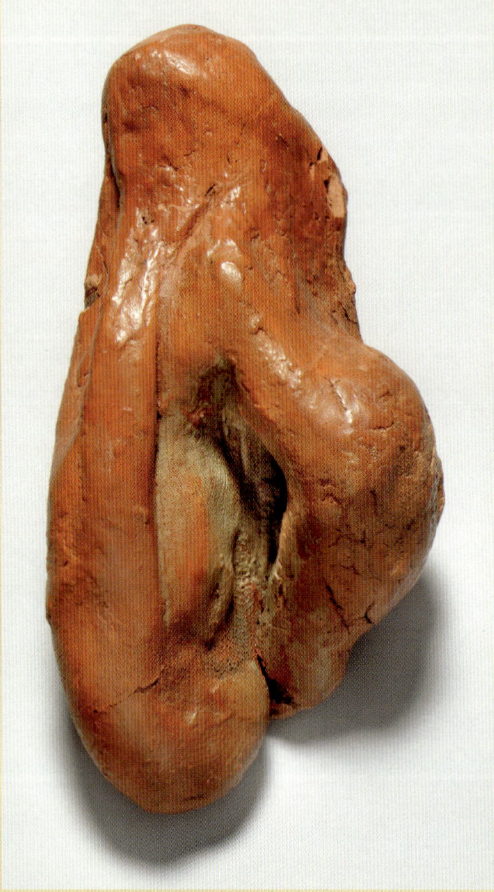

Charles Simonds
Untitled, 1998
Clay and plaster, 6½ x 3¼ x 2 inches
Collection of the artist

Untitled suggests analogies between
body parts and plant tubers, much like
the woodcut illustration seen on page 91.

Reprinted from CLINICAL PEDIATRICS, Vol. 13, No. 10, October 1974
Copyright © 1974 by J. B. Lippincott Company
Printed in U. S. A.

Psychologic Implications of Scrotal Sac and Testes for the Male Child

Anita I. Bell, M.D.*

The uncontrollable retractability of the testes during cold, fear, anger, sexual arousal, and defecation is the basis for castration anxiety and fear of object loss including body parts. The scrotum is associated with the anal area, which is considered "dirty," leading to the concept that sex is "dirty." Because of the fear that a testicle can fall off, boys tend to achieve bowel training later and with more difficulty than girls. Hormonal changes in prepuberty and puberty, which cause increased size and sensitivity, also increase the masturbatory urge. Feeling guilty about masturbation, a boy may think that he has damaged his sac and testes when he perceives that the left testicle hangs lower than the right, a normal state. In cases of cryptorchidism, both sterility and homosexual problems play an important role: physically, if bilateral, sterility and feminizing of the male ensue; psychologically, he develops a depression about his procreative inability and fears homosexual attack. Such attacks are more likely to happen to the cryptorchid boy.

The pediatrician is urged to regularly examine the boy in various positions, particularly before age six. We must caution the pediatrician that his tendency to make a cursory examination may be caused by fears of being accused of making homosexual overtures.

ALTHOUGH THE SCROTAL SAC and the testes have great significance in the psychologic development and continuing mental health of the boy, the average pediatrician gives little attention to these structures aside from their physical and functional status. Indeed, until 1961,[1] even the psychiatric and psychoanalytic journals had virtually neglected the role of the sac and the testes while publishing ample literature on the penis. This neglect of the scrotum and testes has given rise to the unfortunate misconception that the role of these structures is minor in comparison to that of the penis and can thus be treated lightly. When responding to questions about the male genitalia, most adults dealing with children, whether laymen or professionals, refer primarily to the penis, often minimizing or

Clinical Professor of Psychiatry, Georgetown University School of Medicine, Washington, D.C.
Correspondence to Anita I. Bell, M.D., 960 Park Avenue, New York, N.Y. 10028.

CLINICAL PEDIATRICS   October 1974   838

Anita I. Bell (1911–1995), "Psychologic Implications of Scrotal Sac and Testes for the Male Child," *Clinical Pediatrics* 13 (October 1974).

Article by the artist's mother, a renegade Freudian psychoanalyst.

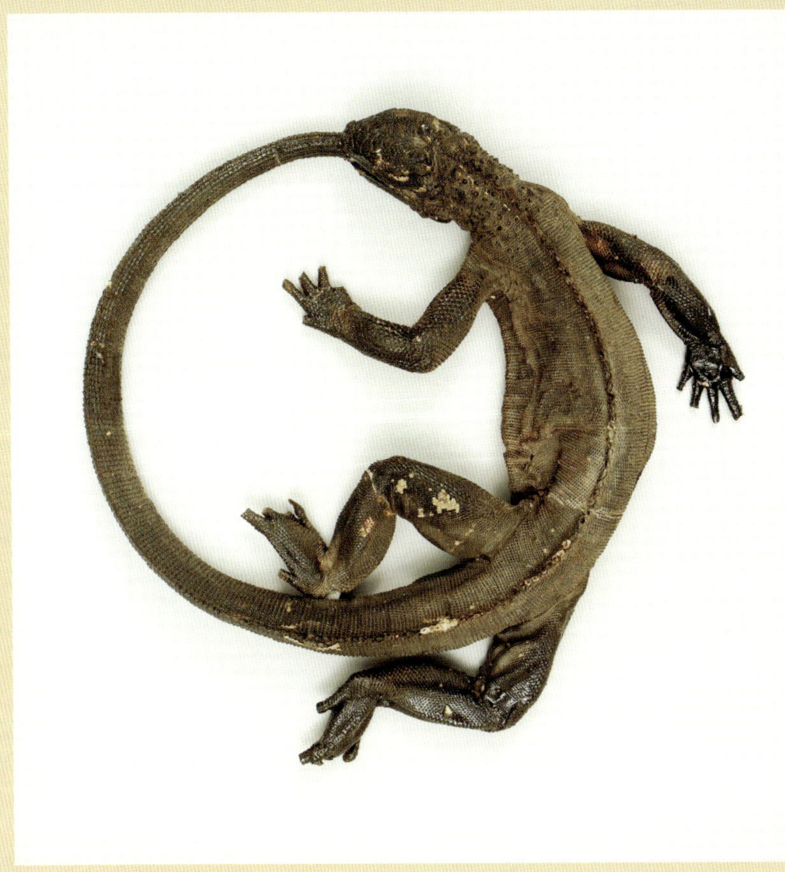

Charles Simonds
Uroboros, 1973
Resin, 12½ x 12½ x 2¾ inches
Collection of the artist

Simonds made a cast of an iguana for the *Uroboros*. He used the circular emblem for eternality in the formulation of the *Growth House* and in his Circular People, one of the three peoples of his imaginary civilization (featured in an installation at the Museum of Modern Art, New York, in 1976). The Circular People devour their past and rebuild it into the present.

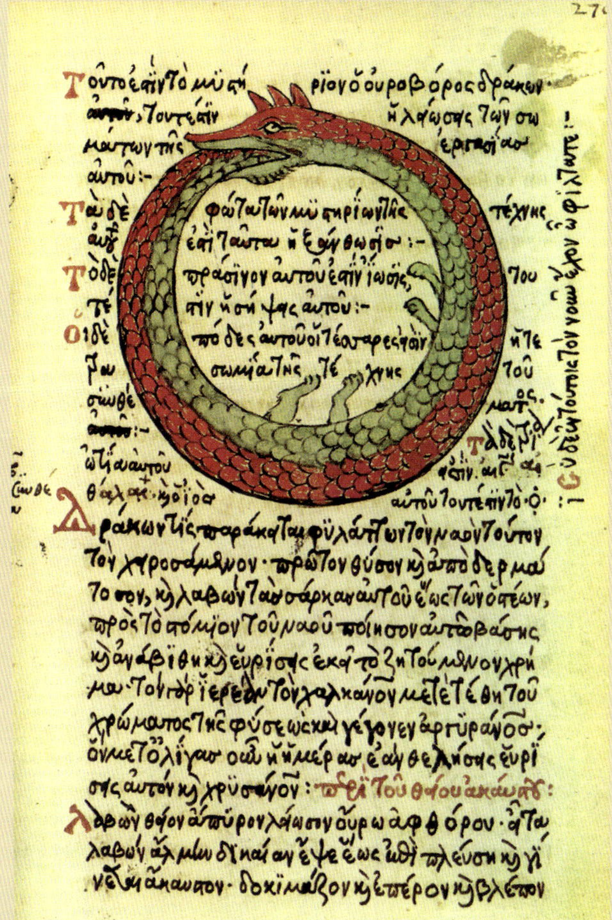

Copy of *Uroboros*, folio 279 of *Livre su l'art de faire de l'or . . .*, 1478. Bibliothèque Nationale de France, Paris.

The uroboros or tail-biting serpent, a symbol of eternity or the universe in ancient Egyptian papyri, is used in the earliest extant alchemical manuscripts. Pictured here with two scaly rings (the inner green and the outer red), three red ears, and four green feet, the uroboros is a hermaphroditic monster, a unity that is also a duality capable of begetting itself upon itself.

1. The Bosco Parrasio was the meeting place of the eighteenth-century Arcadians, who took their name from Jacopo Sannazaro's poem *Arcadia* and whose stated aims were to free Italian poetry from the "barbarism" of the seventeenth century and to return to the simplicity of nature. They adopted the pipes of Pan, along with the pine branch, as their badge. The Arcadians met in the Bosco Parrasio to read their literary compositions. Georgina Masson, *The Companion Guide to Rome* (New York: Harper and Row, 1965), 437–38; and David R. Coffin, *Gardens and Gardening in Papal Rome* (Princeton: Princeton University Press, 1991), 239–43.

2. Farrand wrote in her *Plant Book* (1980): "These seats have been adapted from the well-known open-air theatre on the slope of the Janiculum Hill at the Accademia dell'Arcadia Bosco Parrasio. The shape of the theatre at Dumbarton Oaks was copied from the one in Rome, but the slopes surrounding the Dumbarton Oaks theatre are far steeper than those on the Italian hillside and therefore the seats are considerably raised from one level to another. In order to give seclusion to this little theater, it has been surrounded by cast-stone columns, also baroque in design and taken in their essential ideas from Italian gardens of the baroque period." Beatrix Farrand, *Beatrix Farrand's Plant Book for Dumbarton Oaks*, ed. Diane Kostial McGuire (Washington D.C.: Dumbarton Oaks, Trustees for Harvard University, 1980), 107.

3. William Gilpin, *A Dialogue Upon the Gardens of the Right Honourable the Lord Viscount Cobham at Stow in Buckinghamshire*, 2nd ed. (London: Printed for B. Seeley, 1749), 20.

4. "On the front side of the vase I saw an excellent relief of high-thundering Jupiter, holding in his right hand a sharp golden sword made from a brilliant vein of Ethiopian chrysolite, and in his left a blazing thunderbolt made from a ruby vein. His threatening face was a vein of galactite, crowned with stars sparkling like lightning and standing on a sacred altar of sapphire. His divine and tremendous majesty was being celebrated by a chorus of seven nymphs dressed in white, with indications of solemn singing and reverent applause. They then transformed themselves into green trees of transparent emerald, covered with bright blue flowers, which bowed devoutly to the high god. The last one was entirely turned to a tree, her feet becoming roots; the next all but her feet; the third, all but the part from the waist to the arms; and so on, successively. But the tops of their virginal heads showed that the metamorphosis would happen to each in turn." Francesco Colonna, *Hypnerotomachia Poliphili: The Strife of Love in a Dream*, trans. Joscelyn Godwin (London: Thames and Hudson, 1999), 174.

Selected Bibliography

TEXTS BY CHARLES SIMONDS

"Miniature Dwellings." *On Site* 4 (1973).

"Microcosm to Macrocosm/Fantasy World to Real World" (includes conversation with Lucy R. Lippard). *Artforum* 12, no. 6 (February 1974): 36–39.

Letter to the editor. *Artforum* 12, no. 9 (May 1974): 9.

Charles Simonds. Art/Cahier 2. Paris: SMI, 1975.

"Schwebende Städte/Floating Cities." In *Charles Simonds: Schwebende Städte und andere Architekturen/Floating Cities and Other Architectures*, 46–50. Munster: Wesfälischer Kunstverein, 1978.

Statement. *Artforum* 18, no. 5 (January 1980): 29.

"Working in the Streets of Shanghai and Guilin." *Artforum* 18, no. 10 (Summer 1980): 60–61.

Charles Simonds: House Plants and Rocks, 13 October–10 November 1984. New York: Leo Castelli Gallery, 1984.

"Earth and Sanity." *International Journal of Art Therapy* 1 (1997): 6–9.

Abadie, Daniel. Interview with Charles Simonds. In *Charles Simonds*, 5–14. Art/ Cahier 2. Paris: SMI, 1975. Reprinted in English in *Charles Simonds: An Exhibition at the Albright-Knox Art Gallery, June 11–July 17, 1977* (Buffalo, N.Y.: Buffalo Fine Arts Academy, 1977), 7–14.

———. "Simonds: Life Built to Dream Dimensions." In *Charles Simonds: Museum of Contemporary Art, Chicago, November 17, 1981–January 3, 1982*, 31–34. Chicago: Museum of Contemporary Art, 1981.

———. "El trabajo de Charles Simonds." In *Charles Simonds*, 29–100. Barcelona: Centre Cultural de la Fundació "La Caixa," 1994.

Beardsley, John. "On the Loose with the Little People: A Geography of Simond's Art." In *Charles Simonds: Museum of Contemporary Art, Chicago, November 17, 1981–January 3, 1982*, 26–30. Chicago: Museum of Contemporary Art, 1981.

———. *Spectrum: Charles Simonds*. Washington, D.C.: Corcoran Gallery of Art, 1988.

Celant, Germano. "Charles Simonds' Anthropomorphism." In *Charles Simonds*, 18–28. Paris: Editions du Jeu de Paume, 1994.

Lambert, Jacques. "Las construcciones del espíritu." In *Charles Simonds*, 13–17. Paris: Editions du Jeu de Paume, 1994.

Lippard, Lucy R., with Charles Simonds. *Cracking/Brüchig werden*. Cologne: Verlag der Buchhandlung Walther König, 1979.

Molderings, Herbert. "Kunst als Gedächtnis/Art as Memory." In *Charles Simonds: Schwebende Städte und andere Architekturen/Floating Cities and Other Architectures*, 7–13. Munster: Wesfälischer Kunstverein, 1978.

Neff, John Hallmark. Introduction to *Charles Simonds: Museum of Contemporary Art, Chicago, November 17, 1981–January 3, 1982*, 9–11. Chicago: Museum of Contemporary Art, 1981.

———. "Charles Simonds's Engendered Places: Towards a Biology of Architecture." In *Charles Simonds: Museum of Contemporary Art, Chicago, November 17, 1981–January 3, 1982*, 12–25. Chicago: Museum of Contemporary Art, 1981.

———. "Commentaries." In *Charles Simonds: Museum of Contemporary Art, Chicago, November 17, 1981–January 3, 1982*, 68–73. Chicago: Museum of Contemporary Art, 1981.

Prat, Jean-Louis. "I Remember . . . ." In *Charles Simonds*, 23. Paris: Galerie Enrico
    Navarra, 2001.

Spies, Werner. "World Within World." In *Charles Simonds*, 11–21. Paris: Galerie
    Enrico Navarra, 2001.

Waldman, Diane. "Charles Simonds." In *Age* [exhibition brochure]. New York:
    Solomon R. Guggenheim Museum, 1983.

SELECTED ARTICLES

Apel, Friedmar. "Der Baumeister der Traüme: Wirlichkeit und Gedankenspiel bei
    Charles Simonds." *Sprache im technischen Zeitalter* 6 (July 1978).

———. "Charles Simonds' dynamische Ordnungen/Charles Simonds' Dynamic Order."
    Daidalos 7 (March 1983): 40–43.

Beardsley, John. "Robert Smithson and the Dialectical Landscape." *Arts Magazine* 52,
    no. 9 (May 1978): 132–35.

———. "Charles Simonds: Extending the Metaphor." *Art International* 22, no. 9 (February
    1979): 14–19 and 34.

———. "Charles Simonds: Inhabiting Clay." *American Ceramics* 11, no. 3 (1994): 18–27.

———. "Hybrid Dreams." *Art in America* 83, no. 3 (March 1995): 92–97.

Castle, Ted. "Art in its Place." *Geo* 4, no. 9 (September 1972): 65–75 and 112.

———. "Charles Simonds: The New Adam." *Art in America* 71, no. 2 (February 1983):
    94–103.

Celant, Germano. "Charles Simonds: Little People." *Casabella* 411 (March 1976): 39–41.

Cork, Richard. "Little People Live Here." *The Evening Standard* (London), May 28, 1980.

Deak, Edit. "Vernacular Myth." *Art-Rite* 6 (Summer 1974): 9–11.

Herrera, Hayden. "Manhattan Seven." *Art in America* 65, no. 4 (July–August 1977): 50–63.

Hess, Thomas B. "This and That Side of Paradise." *New York Magazine*, November 22,
    1976.

Hohmeyer, Jürgen. "Für kleine Leute." *Der Spiegel* (Hamburg), November 22, 1977.

Huser, France. "De New York à Ménilmontant." *Le nouvel observateur* (Paris), November 24, 1975.

———. "Charles Simonds, le bâtisseur de rêves." *Le nouvel observateur* (Paris), January, 12–18, 1995.

Jochimsen, Margarethe. "Kunst als soziale Strategie." *Kunstforum International* 27 (March 1978): 72–99.

Jonas, Gerald. The Talk of the Town, "The Little People." *New Yorker,* November 22, 1976.

Kramer, Hilton. "An Artist Emerging From the 60's Counterculture." *New York Times*, December 13, 1981.

Leenhardt, Jacques. "L'urbanisme parallèle de Charles Simonds." *Gazette de Lausanne*, January 31, 1976.

Linker, Kate. "Charles Simonds' Emblematic Architecture." *Artforum* 17, no. 7 (March 1979): 32–37.

Lyon, Christopher. "Charles Simonds: A Profile." *Image and Issues* (Santa Monica) 2, no. 4 (Spring 1982): 56–61.

McConathy, Dale. "Keeping Time: Some Notes on Reinhardt, Smithson, and Simonds." *Artscanada* 32, no. 198–199 (June 1975): 52–57.

Patton, Phil. "The Lost Worlds of the 'Little People.'" *Art News* 82, no. 2 (February 1983): 84–90.

———. "Interview mit Charles Simonds." *Heute Kunst/Flash Art* 24 (January–February 1979): 16–17.

Schneider, Pierre. "Les lilliputiens de Simonds." *L'express* (Paris), December 8–14, 1975.

Schnierle, Barbara. "Traumlöcher und Traditionen." *Tip Magazin* 10 (1979): 36–37.

Semin, Didier. "Entretien avec Charles Simonds." *Beaux-arts* (Paris) 39 (October 1986): 26–31.

Spies, Werner. "Geisterstädte des Unbewußten." *Frankfurter Allgemeine*, February 4, 1995.

GENERAL

Anderson, Maxwell L. *American Visionaries: Selections from the Whitney Museum of American Art*. New York: Whitney Museum of American Art, 2001.

Arnason, H. Harvard. *History of Modern Art. Painting, Sculpture, Architecture, Photography*. 3rd ed. Englewood Cliffs, N.J.: Prentice-Hall, and New York: Harry N. Abrams, 1986.

Beardsley, John. *Art in Public Places: A Survey of Community-Sponsored Projects Supported by the National Endowment for the Arts*. Washington, D.C.: Partners for Livable Places, 1981.

———. *Earthworks and Beyond: Contemporary Art in the Landscape*. New York: Abbeville Press, 1984.

Joachimides, Christos M., and Norman Rosenthal, eds. *American Art in the 20th Century*. Munich: Prestel, 1993.

Lippard, Lucy R. *Overlay: Contemporary Art and the Art of Prehistory*. New York: Pantheon Books, 1983.

Metken, Günter. *Spurensicherung: Kunst als Anthropologie und Selbsterforschung; Fiktive Wissenschaften in der heutigen Kunst*. Cologne: DuMont, 1977.

Meyer, Franz. "Utopie in der Kunst—Kunst als Utopie." In *Utopien: Die Möglichkeit des Unmöglichen*, edited by Jacqueline Baumann, Rosmarie Zimmermann, and Hans-Jürg Braun. Zürcher Hochschulforum 9. Zurich: Verlag der Fachvereine, 1987.

Ruhrberg, Karl. *Kunst im 20. Jahrhundert: Das Museum Ludwig, Köln*. Stuttgart: Klett-Cotta, 1986.

Selz, Peter. *Art in our Times: A Pictorial History, 1890–1980*. New York: H. N. Abrams, 1981.

Sky, Alison, and Michelle Stone. *Unbuilt America: Forgotten Architecture in the United States from Thomas Jefferson to the Space Age; A Site Book*. New York: McGraw-Hill, 1976.

Sondheim, Alan, ed. *Individuals: Post-Movement Art in America*. New York: Dutton, 1977.

Captions and Image Credits

All photographs courtesy of Charles Simonds, unless otherwise noted.

Captions provided for works not fully identified in the text.

page **2** (top). *Dwelling*, Dublin, 1980.

page **2** (bottom). *Dwelling*, Passage Julien Lacroix, Paris, 1975. Photograph by Andre Morain.

pages **3** (bottom) and **17** (bottom). *Landscape/Body/Dwelling*, 1973, still photograph made during the production of the film by the same name. Photograph by Rudy Burckhardt.

page **8** (bottom). Age, 1983, clay, plaster, and wood, 10 feet high, 30 feet diameter. Installed at the Solomon R. Guggenheim Museum, New York.

page **12**. Franz Xaver Messerschmidt, *Character Bust,* from a series of sixty-nine character heads derived from a self-portrait, 1770–83, Musée du Louvre, Paris. Réunion des Musées Nationaux / Art Resource, New York.

page **24** (bottom). Moche architectural maquette, 300–700 CE. Photograph by Juliet Wiersema, with permission of Luis Jaime Castillo.

pages **27** (top) and **32** (top right). Mixteca-Puebla–style necklace with ornaments in the shape of human skulls or monkey heads, 900–1520 CE. Pre-Columbian Collection, PC.B.108, Dumbarton Oaks Research Library and Collection.

pages **27** (bottom) and **32** (center right). Aztec ornament representing Xipe Totec, ca. 1500 CE. Pre-Columbian Collection, PC.B.082, Dumbarton Oaks Research Library and Collection.

page **28** (top, far left). Classic Veracruz *hacha,* 600–900 CE. Pre-Columbian Collection, PC.B.042, Dumbarton Oaks Research Library and Collection.

page **28** (top left). Olmec transformation figure, 900–600 BCE. Pre-Columbian Collection, PC.B.603, Dumbarton Oaks Research Library and Collection.

page **28** (bottom left). Inca maize stalk, fifteenth century. Staatliche Museen zu Berlin, Ethnologisches Museum, VA 64430.

pages **30** (top) and **62** (right). Maya Jaina-style whistle, 600–900 CE. Pre-Columbian Collection, PC.B.559, Dumbarton Oaks Research Library and Collection.

page **32** (bottom right). Mixtec-Aztec necklace with beads in the shape of human skulls, 1200–1520 CE. Pre-Columbian Collection, PC.B.083, Dumbarton Oaks Research Library and Collection.

page **34** (right). Wari mosaic mirror, 650–1000 CE. Pre-Columbian Collection, PC.B.432, Dumbarton Oaks Research Library and Collection.

pages **42**, **43** (top), **70**, **71**, and **72** (top). *Dwelling*, East Houston Street, New York, 1972.

page **43** (bottom). Gordon Matta-Clark, *Splitting* (322 Humphrey Street, Englewood, New Jersey), 1974, color photograph mounted on wood, 40¼ x 60¼ inches. Lambert Collection, Avignon. © 2010 Estate of Gordon Matta-Clark / Artists Rights Society (ARS), New York.

page **44**. Sol LeWitt, installation at Saman Gallery, Genoa, 1975, white crayon lines, black pencil grid, red ceiling. First drawn by Robert Doati, SL; first installation: Saman Gallery, Genoa, May 1975. Photograph by Geoffrey Clements. © 2010 The LeWitt Estate / Artists Rights Society (ARS), New York.

page **45** (top). Daniel Buren, Photo-souvenir *Il sagit de voir: des bandes verticales blanches et vertes qui ne sont que des bandes verticales blanches et vertes et qui reportent à des bandes verticales blanches et vertes qui ne sont que des bandes verticales blanches et vertes,* detail, 1968, Galleria Apollinaire, Milan. © 2010 Artists Rights Society (ARS), New York / DB–ADAGP, Paris.

page **46**. *Dwelling*, PS1, Long Island City, 1975.

page **47**. *Succulent*, 2001, clay and plaster, 59 x 24 x 21 inches, collection of the artist.

page **48** (top). *Singing Monkey*, 1991, clay and cement, 35½ x 32 x 32 inches, collection of the artist. Photograph by Bruce White.

page **48** (bottom). Installation at the Centre d'Étude de l'Expression, Clinique des Maladies Mentales et de l'Encéphale in the Centre Hospitalier Sainte-Anne, Paris, in 1995.

page **49** (top). *Dwelling* (destroyed), installation at the galerie Baudoin Lebon, Paris, 1991, clay and plaster, bricks ½ inch long. Photograph by Andre Morain.

page **51** (bottom). Aby Warburg, "Mnemosyne," plate no. 55. Photograph courtesy of The Warburg Institute, University of London.

page **53** (top). *Head*, 1993, clay and plaster, 26½ x 35½ x 30 inches. Collection Marc and Ilene Steglitz. Photograph by Bruce White.

page **62** (bottom left). Remojadas "Smiling" Figure, 600–800 CE. The Michael C. Rockefeller Memorial Collection, bequest of Nelson A. Rockefeller, 1979. © Metropolitan Museum of Art / Art Resource, New York.

page **69**. *Dwelling*, New York, 1970, clay and wood.

page **72** (bottom). *Park Model/Fantasy*, 1974, clay, wood, and photographs, 6 x 30 x 20 inches. Wallraf-Richartz Museum / Museum Ludwig, Cologne.

page **73**. The artist working in Shanghai, 1980.

ADDITIONAL IMAGE CREDITS

Dumbarton Oaks Research Library and Collection: **cover**, pages **5** (top and bottom), **7** (top and bottom), **13** (top and bottom), **20**, **22**, **24** (top), **25** (top and bottom), **36**, **54**, **55**, **62** (top left), **68** (bottom), **74**, **78**, **80**, **81**, **82** (top and bottom), **83**, **84** (top and bottom), **85**, **86** (top and bottom), **90**, **91**, **96** (left and right), and **97** (left).

Rudy Burckhardt: pages **40** (bottom left) and **45** (bottom).

Erma Estwick: pages **37**, **38**, **39**, **41**, **52**, and **95**.

Eric MacDonald: pages **vi**, **8** (top), **9** (top), **30** (bottom), **50** (bottom), **58** (right), and **65**.

Andre Morain: pages **29** and **35**.

Howard Nathanson: pages **66** and **93**.

Bruce White: pages **21**, **26**, **33**, **87** (right), **89**, and **94** (left).